SHAW on Education

LOUIS SIMON

SHAW
on Education

GREENWOOD PRESS, PUBLISHERS
WESTPORT, CONNECTICUT

LB
775
S6665
S5
1974

Library of Congress Cataloging in Publication Data

Simon, Louis, 1908-
    Shaw on education.

    Reprint of the ed. published by Columbia University
Press, New York.
    Bibliography: p.
    1. Shaw, George Bernard, 1856-1950. 2. Education--
Philosophy. I. Title.
[LB775.S6665S5 1974]   370.1'092'4   73-16953
ISBN 0-8731-7245-4

TO ANN AND CELIA SIMON

Foreword

Throughout most of his long life (1856–1950) George Bernard Shaw was the self-appointed teacher of an intractable class—humanity. A composite Socrates-Voltaire-Rousseau, he enlarged their arena of instruction by means of the press, platform, pamphlet, and play (his chief "battering ram"); and tried to make his fractious students understand that their obsolete theories of life, sham institutions, and traditional morals were cruelly hindering them from becoming what they could become. He trumpeted from the housetops that he had isolated the only path to economic, political, social, cultural, and spiritual welfare. Perhaps his most eloquent objurgations were reserved for what he called capitalist education, which lay the groundwork for all that was spurious to him in society. It was therefore inevitable that Shaw, fully aware that education is the primary factor in that progressive accumulation and refinement of learnings and ideals which make for social advance, should evolve his own system. Almost all of his writings, including the plays, are permeated with educational ideas.

I have neither set up Shaw as a great educator, nor held it legitimate to dismiss most of his ideas as impracticable. These appraisals were largely influenced by the demands of the democratic ideal underlying education, which I have tried to define within limits. There are libertarian as well as totalitarian strands in Shaw's thinking—a complex that can easily be distorted in either direction by prejudices and preconceptions about society and schools. He saw in his special brand of socialism the promise of transforming and elevating society from the plane of chaos and callousness about human growth, to a more civilized one in which social activities and education would be deliberately planned in behalf of desired values. It was clearly impossible, he thought, to exact moral, intellectual, and aesthetic cultivation from people whom societal circumstances—poverty, money-grubbing, war, disease, the vulgarity of mass communications—pervert to a subhuman level. Monstrous institutions, he repeatedly charged, make monsters of quite ordinary men. If Shaw's unteachable class refused to learn his assigned lessons, it was, in one sense, a good thing. Impatient to reach his objective and thus failing to qualify sufficiently his proposed remedies, he frequently resorted to questionable methods—absolute government (with democratic whispers from benevolent, educated rulers), and extermination of the unfit (with humanitarian overtones about painlessness). This state of affairs, despite his violent hatred of cruelty, could easily dominate his schools. One of the purposes of this book is to isolate his recommendations which could be of value to educational authorities in a democratic state.

If challenged to state the main purpose of his educational system, he would have replied promptly: "To make humanity divine." Or, perhaps, he would have written an even longer preface than the one to *Misalliance* in which he had said this. Unfortunately for Shaw the aims he proposed for education have been ignored because they are buried in a mass of discursive polemics. Like all the genuine teachers and prophets of the past, he was convinced that humanity as he found it was not good enough, and that the vital force conducting so noble an experiment with man on earth demanded something better: human nature must be transcended. The chief difficulty, he argued, was that though we always affirm the need to change for the better, we do not sufficiently desire to take the collective trouble to bring it about.

Back to Methuselah is a dramatic parable about human growth in the far distant future; Shaw's program of education is his way of indoctrinating the young to dedicate themselves to similar dreams of perfection. As an evolutionist he was persuaded that since we live in a morally and intellectually expanding world, ideals and methods regarded as sacrosanct in child training must be repudiated. Parental, religious, and school instruction became, for him, vicious indoctrination when it sought to cram a child with man-made dogmas which proclaim that society and the universe are perfected schemes, and that we already know all there is about basic values. Shaw had much in common with the pragmatists in America, who believe that continuous growth—incompatible with closed systems which imprison creative possibilities—is the purpose of all learning. Growth, he believed, was not a haphazard development; it was rather a calculated search for perfection requiring new powers of vision, intelligence, and flexibility of mind so that we could appreciate the way in which the modern world was moving, and adjust our course accordingly. His socialism, evolution, and education constitute a three-pronged assault to clear the way for human development.

Shaw tried to tell us that we could shape the social evolutionary process to our liking. Basic to his vitalist doctrine, presented full dress in the Preface to *Back to Methuselah* and repeated in other works to the end of his life, is his hypothesis of an "evolutionary appetite" as the fundamental progressive force in life. In *Man and Superman* he dramatized the human brain (life's "darling object") as a mechanism, wholly novel in evolution, capable of profound contemplation, of rational choice between alternatives, and of appropriate action—all of which are contingent upon the strength of man's will. Since in the later stages of organic evolution, the struggle for Natural Selection is increasingly replaced in the human area by a struggle between traditions, ideas, and values within man's consciousness, progress for Shaw meant changes in social organization, in transmitted knowledge and ideals, and in processes of learning. Thus education, emanating from a society steeped in vital will and significant purpose, becomes fundamental for the release of human possibilities that are as yet scarcely dreamed of. The rate of evolution in the human sphere, Shaw argued, could thus be speeded up considerably. Whether we find merit in his views or not, they challenge us to exorcise moribund traditions and ideas in life and in education, and to exercise intelligent, purposive choice of values and institutions which will ultimately determine the course of social and human destiny.

Shaw's educational ideas are highly controversial. From the Victorian era to the present, his chief concerns—politics, economics, science, religion—have embroiled his name in lively controversies and civilizational enigmas. In a desperate search for fundamental values Shaw agitated himself and the world with seemingly insoluble problems, which most of the educated give up early in life as hopeless. His polemical and dialectical techniques were deliberately charged to shock the lethargic masses, drugged with what he thought were inert ideas, into joining the intellectual fray and caring intensely about solutions.

The dilemmas raised by democracy, socialism, communism, and religion, with their inevitable impact upon education, will, nevertheless, have to be solved if civilization is to advance or survive. Recognizing that in our fragmented society there was little agreement among educators as to what the goals of learning should be, Shaw attempted to provide principles that would cohere education, religion, economics, and all other problems of human living. The ultimate problem of education, for him as for a free society, was to produce persons for whom freedom and the welfare of the world—even that of future generations—are inextricably rooted in thought and action. This was quite impossible, he claimed, because of the glaring lack of unity regarding basic values; these he wanted hammered out by educated rulers, like the benevolent King Magnus in *The Apple Cart.* The cleavages and conflicts in society between theory and practice, between the arts and the sciences, between education and religion, and between public good and private good, Shaw held, make insuperable difficulties for the educative process. Demanding agreement on essentials—even to the point of embracing a universal religion—Shaw wanted us to decide what it is that we really want and how we are prepared to work for it. This keynote has been sounded frequently in recent years by democratic educators, who, like Shaw, realize that the age of uncontrolled individualism and unplanned pluralism is quite dead. I have suggested elsewhere in this book, in a different context, that a free society must find modes of agreement on basic values, but not in such a way as to produce a totalitarian state. This calls for constructive thinking, social inventiveness, creative planning, and for the application of scientific method to the problems of the times. As an antidote to totalitarian wholeness we need a leadership that can dare to envisage and formulate a great program of democratic wholeness in education for the coming years. Shaw's program of education, despite—or rather because of—the many authoritarian emphases, confronts us with such a task.

It should be stressed that Shaw's educational views are not isolated from the rest of his thought; they form an integral part of his politics, religion, science, and art; they can, in fact, be regarded as more explicit formulations of his basic premises in these areas. Education cannot be talked about in isolation, for the things we say about it will, consciously or unconsciously, involve fundamental convictions about the nature of man, society, and the meaning and purpose of human life—in short, about the basic values of civilization and their worth. In this sense, it can be said that Shaw viewed all of human life in an educational perspective.

His originality as an educator was on a par with his originality as a critic of music and of the theater. The literature about education has frequently failed to interest thoughtful people—particularly disillusioned teachers—because of its tendency to drift into formulized vocabulary and vague moral slogans. This is not true of Shaw's way, for the Shavian touch is evident to an unusual degree. Perhaps it was difficult for a notorious wit and propagandist, armed with invigorating language spiced with epigram, paradox, invective, humorous exaggeration, and the telling aphorism, to inspire confidence as an educator; perhaps the fifteen other reputations he claimed have obscured his attempts in this role. Saturated in the fine arts, in vitalist philosophy, and in social controversy, all of which enter into his doctrine, Shaw wrote uniquely about teachers, schools, learning, and culture. The multiplicity of his ideas includes programs of instruction for such diverse persons as political leaders, criminals, doctors, and actors. To disagree categorically with his views about secondary education, religion, sex, or child training is to discover that he is intensely interesting and compelling, always ready with strange twists and turns away from the traditional and conventional. This is especially evident in the criticisms of his own early education in Dublin and in London. There is, behind his writings on education, a great deal of memory and bitter experience to which can be attributed his deeply personal views; yet these are frequently profounder and more subtly concrete than the generalizations and abstractions of the professional educator. Shaw dared to probe where few modern educators ever venture; and what he says often sharpens awareness of our own concerns. Perhaps we need to appraise and use, in the formulation of our educational theory, the insights and intuitions of artists and writers who have communicated configurations of life in novel and revealing ways. Shaw's education is not of the text book.

Acknowledgments

I AM DEEPLY INDEBTED in more ways than could be detailed here to Professor Louise M. Rosenblatt of the School of Education in New York University, who read and criticized two different versions of the manuscript; her unceasing interest, advice, and encouragement made the completion of the work possible. For valuable assistance with a longer version, I owe a debt of gratitude to Professor William P. Sears and to Professor Fred C. Blanchard of the School of Education in New York University. I am under exceptional obligations to these officials and editors of Columbia University Press— Mr. Henry H. Wiggins, Dr. William Bridgwater, Miss Anita Lila Weiner—who contributed far beyond what was required in guiding the work to its final form.

I wish to thank the Public Trustee and the Society of Authors, by whose permission as copyright owners I have been able to quote extensively from the many works of Shaw. Many thanks are due to these publishers for permission to quote from the following works:

Appleton-Century-Crofts, Inc., for *George Bernard Shaw: His Life and Works*, and *Bernard Shaw: Playboy and Prophet*, by Archibald Henderson; and *Education and Morals*, by John

L. Childs; Oxford University Press for *A Study of History*, by Arnold J. Toynbee (Abridgment of vols. I–VI by D. C. Somervell); George Allen & Unwin, Ltd., for *Letters and Selected Writings*, by Sydney Olivier; Methuen & Co., Ltd., for *English Thought in the Nineteenth Century*, by D. C. Somervell; Victor Gollancz, Ltd., for *Shaw*, by C. E. M. Joad; Theatre Arts Books for *Ellen Terry and Bernard Shaw: A Correspondence*, edited by Christopher St. John; Alfred A. Knopf for *Bernard Shaw and Mrs. Patrick Campbell: Their Correspondence*, edited by Alan Dent; and *The English People*, by D. W. Brogan; Dodd, Mead & Company for *G.B.S. 90*, edited by S. Winsten; Harper & Brothers for *G.B.S.: A Full Length Portrait*, and *G.B.S.: A Postscript*, by Hesketh Pearson; and *Evolution: The Modern Synthesis*, by Julian Huxley; Roy Publishers for *Bernard Shaw: A Chronicle*, by R. F. Rattray; New Directions for *Bernard Shaw*, by Eric Bentley; Charles Scribner's Sons for *George Bernard Shaw: Critic of Western Morale*, by Edmund Fuller; McGraw-Hill Book Company, Inc., for *The Universe of G.B.S.*, by William Irvine; University of London Press for *A Short History of English Education from 1760–1944*, by H. C. Barnard; Longmans, Green & Co. for *British History in the Nineteenth Century*, and *English Social History*, by G. M. Trevelyan; The Macmillan Company for *The Idea of Progress*, by J. B. Bury, and *Democracy and Education*, by John Dewey; Ernest Benn, Ltd. for *Edwardian England 1901–1910*, by F. J. C. Hearnshaw; Simon & Schuster for *A History of Western Philosophy*, by Bertrand Russell; Philosophical Library for *The World As I See It*, by Albert Einstein; William Morrow & Company for *The Victorian Sunset*, by Esme Wingfield–Stratford.

Contents

SHAW on Education

THE PRIEST. What freaks these pinks are! Belonging neither to the west, like you, nor to the east, like me.

THE NATIVE. [swinging the censer] Neither to the north nor south; but in that they resemble us. They have much to teach us.

THE PRIEST. Yes; but they are themselves unteachable, not understanding what they teach.

THE NATIVE. True: they can teach; but they cannot learn.

THE PRIEST. Freaks. Dangerous freaks. The future is with the learners.

Buoyant Billions, ACT III

1 Doctrines and aspirations

Wₕₑₙ a channel steamer carried George Bernard
Shaw to the London of the later seventies, he was thrown into
an age of transition unparalleled in the history of man. Darwinism, socialism, and universal education were just beginning
to exert their profound impact. The singularly distilled product
of this age, Shaw, in shaping his socialist-evolutionist creed,
began, like the great Victorians before him—Owen, Carlyle,
Ruskin, Butler, Mill, Morris—to question the processes of democracy, material progress, and traditional concepts of human
nature. Since socialism was for Shaw a method of organizing
society whereby an individual could achieve aesthetic and

Guide to Footnotes: In the footnotes the sources of quotations from
Shaw's prefaces and plays have been indicated without page citations.
The reader can easily check the context by scanning the sectional head-
ings usually found in the prefaces—particularly the one to *Misalliance*
which is frequently quoted. The source of any unplaced quotations, both
from and about Shaw, can be ascertained by referring to the immediately
preceding source cited in the footnotes or in the text. Since such quotations derived from the same page or pages just cited, it was thought
best to omit numbering them in the interests of a smoother text. For
specific editions of works by and about Shaw used in this book the
reader should consult the appended bibliography.

The eccentricities and inconsistencies of Shaw's spelling and punctua-
tion—particularly in the dialogue from the plays—have been kept intact.

mental growth, it was inevitable that because of the heritage left him and the intellectual climate in which he wrote, Shaw should challenge the processes and ends of education in a society which to him denied such growth.

The great upsurge of democracy and industrialism brought forth the humanitarians, who attacked a hierarchical social order and sought a leveling of classes through a more equitable distribution of wealth and through education. The spokesmen of the privileged classes took the position that education for the poor "would be prejudicial to their morals and happiness: it would teach them to despise their lot in life . . . and would render them factious and refractory . . . and insolent to their superiors." [1]

Earlier in the century Saint-Simon and Fourier in France, and Robert Owen in England, appalled by the social conditions that stunted the mental growth of people, believed in varying degrees that man is entirely the creature of circumstance and that environment controls development. "By judicious training," wrote Owen in his *First Essay on the Formation of Character*, "the infants of any one class in the world may be readily transformed into men of any other class." The later Utilitarians, Bentham and the two Mills, urged the benefits of abundance, equality, security, and emphasized the education of the masses. In 1859, John Stuart Mill had asked: "Is it not almost a self-evident maxim that the State should require and compel the education up to a certain standard, of every human being who is born its citizen?" [2] As a professor of Fine Art at Oxford, Ruskin was a destructive critic of the existing social and educational system. Viewing art as an essential instrument of educa-

[1] Quoted in Hamilton, *England, A History of the Homeland*, p. 272. (These are the words of Giddy, the President of the Royal Society, spoken in the House of Commons.)

[2] *On Liberty*, p. 157.

tion, Ruskin, like Shaw, saw education linked with craftsman-
ship, nature, and religion as an aid in breaking down class
distinctions. In *Unto This Last* (1860) there is an appeal for a
new social order based on justice and a recognition of the
brotherhood of man. These ideals, Ruskin thought, could be
realized only through adequate education of the masses. In
1854 the Christian Socialists, Maurice and Kingsley, founded
the Working Men's College [3] where poor people could gain
not merely technical equipment, but a higher, more liberal
education in the humanities, and where they might share a
social life and intercourse which characterized the older universities. Modern developments such as the Workers' Educational Association [4] and the University Extension movement
owe much to the work of F. D. Maurice. Matthew Arnold,
who embodied the results of his observations as a school in-
spector in *Popular Education in France* (1861), *A French
Eton* (1864), and *Schools and Universities on the Continent*
(1868), outlined an elaborate scheme for the reconstruction of
English education, especially above the popular level.[5] Many
of his recommendations which would have given England a
national system of secondary education were set aside by
Parliament when the Endowed Schools Act of 1869 was
passed. Arnold held that a state system of education was what

[3] Thomas Hughes, author of *Tom Brown's School Days*, and F. J.
Furnivall, who organized the New Shakespeare Society, the Shelley
Society, the Browning Society—all of which Shaw joined as a young
man—also helped found the College.

[4] See Shaw's Preface to the Workers' Educational Association *Year
Book* for 1918, one of his most concentrated attacks on schools and
teachers, in *Doctors' Delusions*.

[5] See Trevelyan, *British History in the Nineteenth Century*, p. 353:
"It was characteristic of the two nations that whereas the German people
already enjoyed good schools, but not self-government, the rulers of
England only felt compelled to 'educate their masters' when the working
men were in full possession of the franchise."

was most needed to remedy the greatest of wants in English civilization, the want of mind. If belief in education is the essence of the human ideal, it would be difficult to find a more eloquent plea for culture and education than Arnold's.[6] Herbert Spencer's *Education: Intellectual, Moral and Physical* (1861) argued for the need of developing man's potential through education; and Thomas Huxley, who popularized the aesthetic pleasure and spirit of adventure provided by the study of science, wanted an educational ladder set up by the state. The Fabian Society, appearing in 1884 with such members as the Webbs, Olivier, Wallas, and Shaw, propagandized extensively for social and educational reform. No sooner had Shaw joined the Fabians than he provided them with a "Manifesto" which begins with "Wealth cannot be enjoyed without dishonor" and stresses "That the State should secure a liberal education and an equal share in the National Industry to each of its units."[7] According to Edward Pease it was the Fabian Society with Sidney Webb as chief catalyst that brought about the London University Act of 1898 and the Education Acts of 1902 and 1903.[8]

Despite these and numerous other voices it was not until 1870 that England took the first steps toward a national system of education. Even then no provision was made for secondary education. It did not abolish the voluntary system—the private, religious, and charitable schools—but allowed it to remain with the help of government grants alongside the schools erected by the School Boards. These "board schools"

---

[6] See Schilling's interesting essay on Arnold in *Human Dignity and the Great Victorians,* and Lippincott's in *Victorian Critics of Democracy.*

[7] The entire tract is quoted in Pease, *The History of the Fabian Society,* pp. 41–43.

[8] *Ibid.,* pp. 139–62. Webb was Chairman of the Technical Education Board from 1893 almost continuously until the Board came to an end in 1904.

were to give non-sectarian religious instruction of a character
which would not offend the susceptibilities of parents. W. E.
Forster, who piloted the Education Act of 1870 through the
House of Commons, said: "Our object is to complete the present voluntary system, to fill up gaps . . . not to destroy the
existing system in introducing a new one." [9] Since churchmen
hostile to this undenominational education hastened to set
up additional voluntary schools, a controversy arose in which
Shaw was later actively concerned.[10] Though the Act of 1870
had not made education compulsory, it had empowered the
local school boards to apply compulsion if they chose. It was
not until the Act of 1876 that compulsory education up to
the age of twelve was introduced. Elementary education thus
became general, but not free. Tuition fees were actually re-
tained as late as 1891. The Act of 1902, sponsored by Arthur
Balfour and Robert Morant, reorganized education on a
municipal basis and swept away the voluntary system of
school boards.[11] These were replaced by county councils responsible for both secondary and elementary education. Although England now had a coordinated national system of
education, there still remained the dual system of "provided"
and "non-provided" or denominational schools. When the
question of government grants to all kinds of schools came up,
Shaw, as the Progressive candidate for the Borough of St.
Pancras in the London County Council, supported equal

[9] Quoted in Gregg, *A Social and Economic History of Britain 1760–
1950*, p. 510.

[10] See Cole and Postgate, *The British Common People 1746–1938*,
p. 325. The authors stress that "the principal obstacle to the development of any general system of public education was the religious quarrel."

[11] See Brogan, *The English People*, p. 32. "It is revealing that although
school boards have been abolished since 1902 a large part of the English
middle and upper classes still talk [even Shaw as late as 1944] of
'board-school' boys."

funds for all schools and was consequently defeated in the election of 1904.[12]

It is significant that war dramatized the need for educational reform. The Act of 1902 came after the Boer War, the Act of 1918 after World War I, and the Act of 1944 during World War II. In 1918 the Fisher Act brought the secondary schools into the national system, and the Hadow Report of 1926 widened the conception of what secondary education should mean. From this time on, the public schools (such as Eton and Harrow), although they assumed superiority over the State secondary schools, nevertheless were subjected to a gradual breaking-down of their exclusiveness. In 1942 a committee was appointed "to consider means whereby the association between the Public Schools . . . and the general educational system of the country could be developed and extended." [13] The Fleming Committee recommended that the opportunities of education in public schools "should be made available to boys and girls capable of profiting thereby, irrespective of the income of their parents." The report, however, did little to satisfy those who were antagonistic to the social divisions exemplified by the public schools, since only 25 percent of state school students were to be admitted.[14] The Act of 1944 finally embraced a coordinated system of national education. Before 1944 the great majority of children did not go to a secondary school, but received their education from eleven to fourteen years of age in a "senior" division of the elementary school. A secondary education is now seen to be the privilege of all, not just of a few. However, the Act of 1944 left intact the public and private schools on the grounds

---

[12] For Shaw's reasons see Chapter 8, "Religious Education," in this book.

[13] Quoted in Barnard, *A Short History of English Education from 1760–1944*, p. 284.

[14] *Everybody's Political What's What* attacks such a scheme.

that it was desirable to retain variety in educational provision.[15] "But it may conceivably be argued," Barnard suggests, "that the new scheme was devised so as not to interfere too drastically with the existing class structure of the community."[16] Sir Fred Clarke in his *Education and Social Change* (1940) had warned that England's "habit of thinking about education in terms of class . . . has made our educational categories and terminology the chaotic things they are." Although the last war has shaken the citadel of privilege, the controversy concerning the expensive public schools continues.

The state entered the picture when the voluntary schools found themselves unable to cope with the rising demand of the lower social and economic classes. Arnold, Mill, Kingsley, Ruskin, Morris, and Shaw attacked the dual tradition of schools for the masses as separate and distinct from a system of schools for the elite—a tradition which has been, and still is, a tenacious one in British education. Contemporary authorities, aware of the perils of uniformity and conformity that extreme coordination and centralization can bring about, have stressed the decentralization of administration, the prominent part played by private agencies, and the avoidance of official directions concerning curriculums and methods of teaching.

While Forster's great Act of 1870 contributed to eliminating universal illiteracy within a generation, the negative aspects of universal education were evidenced as early as the eighties. Viewing mass education as mass degeneration, Toynbee states:

The bread of universal education is no sooner cast upon the waters than a shoal of sharks arises from the depths and devours the chil-

[15] Curtis, *History of Education in Great Britain*, p. 397.
[16] *A Short History of English Education*, p. 371.

dren's bread under the educator's very eyes. The edifice of universal elementary education was, roughly speaking, completed by Forster's Act of 1870; and the Yellow Press was invented some twenty years later . . . by a stroke of irresponsible genius which had divined that the educational philanthropist's labour of love could be made to yield a royal profit to a press-lord.[17]

"The achievement of compulsory literacy," writes Wingfield-Stratford, "had created an enormously increased opportunity for the arts of mass suggestion." [18] And Trevelyan, viewing the age of transition from aristocracy to democracy, from authority to mass judgment, deplores those middle years of the century when "industrial change was already creating the mass vulgarity which was destined to swamp that high standard of literary culture with the advent of the new journalism." [19] The good intentions of democratic education, Toynbee suggests, provided a number of stumbling blocks. Not only were the masses exploited by the forces of mass suggestion and at the same time divorced from their traditional culture, but they have also unwittingly become the victims of a "utilitarian spirit in which the fruits of education are apt to be turned to account when they are brought within everybody's reach." [20] Somewhat cynically, Toynbee sums up mass education as "an instrument of worldly ambition or of frivolous amusement." He considers the rise of dictatorship in the twentieth century the direct result of the "elaborate and ingenious machinery for the mass-enslavement of semi-educated minds."

While such views may be rejected on various grounds, they

[17] A. J. Toynbee (D. C. Somervell, editor), *A Study of History*, p. 292.
[18] Wingfield-Stratford, *The Victorian Sunset*, p. 204. See the following for a similar point of view: Ensor, *England 1870–1914*, pp. 143–44; Hamilton, *England*, pp. 362–63.
[19] Trevelyan, *English Social History*, p. 521.
[20] Toynbee, *A Study of History*, p. 292.

are essential to an understanding of Shaw's denunciations of education in what he called the democratic-capitalist nations. A consideration of the modern mass media of communications was always uppermost in Shaw's mind when he discussed education. He would agree with Toynbee's statement that "if the people's souls are to be saved, the only way is to raise the standard of mass-education to a degree at which its recipients will be rendered immune against the grosser forms of exploitation and propaganda." This constituted a major educational aim for Shaw.

The impact of *Das Kapital* and *Progress and Poverty* on nineteenth-century thought—particularly on Shaw—was profound and far-reaching. Socialist thought was based on the premise that if inequalities of wealth and class distinctions persist, no educational system will help matters much. This concept was basic to Shaw's thinking about education and explains his life-long vituperation of capitalistic education. Somervell sums up aptly the socialist concept of education with this metaphor:

The Liberal individualist of the first half of the century had been content that there was a natural "ladder" whereby the enterprising could climb into the upper regions of the industrial and social system. He was prepared to demand that this natural "ladder" should be broadened by the introduction of free State-supplied elementary education. But this artificial broadening of the ladder was of somewhat illusory benefit if those who climbed it found all the seats at the top already occupied. The Socialists rejected the philosophy of the ladder altogether. To them it seemed by no means desirable that the most gifted members of the working class should climb out of the working class. . . . The aim of the Socialists was to "level up" a whole society. The ladder . . . ought to be broad enough for all to proceed up it abreast.[21]

[21] Somervell, *English Thought in the Nineteenth Century*, p. 206.

While Marx and Engels looked forward to such a leveling off by revolutionary means, Shaw and the Fabians accepted a program of socialism by installments. They have been content to promote such reforms as are necessary to the establishment of a socialist state, the final result of a long series of measures. For them socialism meant a new organization of society in which the means of production would be owned by the state. Shaw, deviating from Marx as well as from the Fabians, demanded absolute equality of income for all. The assumption was that if economic security were automatically assured, the development of one's higher faculties could more effectively be realized. This is a basic theme in all the contributions to the *Fabian Essays* (1889), which Shaw edited. Sydney Olivier's essay, like Shaw's, sounds this theme: "But when society has insured for man the opportunity for satisfying his primary needs . . . his advance in the refinements of social morality . . . is solely and entirely a matter of education." In this period when schools were not yet free, Olivier added: "The schools of the adult are the journal and the library, social intercourse, fresh air, clean and beautiful cities . . . the museum, the art gallery, the lecture hall, the drama, and the opera; and only when these schools are free and accessible to all will the reproach of proletarian coarseness be done away with." [22] Graham Wallas' contribution to *Fabian Essays* describes the schools of the future with "associated meals on tables spread with flowers, in halls surrounded with beautiful pictures or even, as John Milton proposed, filled with the sound of music." [23] That the human potential could be realized by socialist organization was a premise basic to

[22] Shaw preferred this "self-education" of the adult to formal schooling. See Chapter 8, "Secondary Education" in this book.
[23] See the utopian picture of education in William Morris' *News from Nowhere* (1891) which Shaw admired.

all Fabian concepts and to Shaw's ideas about education. Yet such visions of human growth have been blurred by the twentieth-century phenomena of global war, fascism, and communism. Disillusioned by the advent of war, the success of revolutionary socialism in Russia, and the crushing of evolutionary socialism in Italy and Germany, Shaw frequently departed from Fabian doctrine and flirted, particularly during the thirties, with the promised benevolent efficiency of dictatorship, both right and left. This, too, colored his views about education. Aware of the gap between theory and practice, Shaw eloquently asked Victorian and twentieth-century man to take a good look at our society and our methods of educating people and to do something about it. It was this intense desire—to communicate his creed of a vital concept of the community to which all individuals must dedicate their lives—which caused him to resort to the questionable means of benevolent dictatorship in order to realize the ends he sought. That is, while he never deviated from his socialist ideals, he frequently toyed with dictatorship as an accelerated means of achieving them. As a result of his insistence on an all-powerful state, his views about education are at times of questionable value to a democratic society.

The two pillars of Shaw's thought about education, man, and society are socialism and evolution.[24] If socialism is a way of organizing society, then Creative Evolution for Shaw is his mystic, philosophic-religious creed by which growth is to be achieved. Marx's *Das Kapital* and Darwin's *Origin of Species* had laid the groundwork in the middle of the last century for newer conceptions of man and society. "The appearance of

[24] See Pettet's doctoral dissertation, Shavian Socialism and the Shavian Life Force, which attempts to establish the close relationship between Shaw's socialism and evolution.

Origin of Species," writes Bury, "changed the situation by disproving definitely the dogma of fixity of species and assigning real causes for transformism." [25] The great difficulty was that numerous distinguished thinkers of the nineteenth and twentieth centuries offered conflicting hypotheses as to the essential causes for transformism. There was also the further complication that the history of the doctrine of evolution falls into two supplementary but quite different lines of development. One is the general philosophical conception of evolution as the master key to the understanding of the development of the cosmos, our universe, the earth, organic life, man, social institutions, and human culture. The other is the specific biological interpretation of the laws of heredity which explains how organic life has developed on this particular planet. Why Shaw condemned the concept of the "survival of the fittest" in economic areas will be dealt with later. Although Shaw courted briefly the biological breeding of the Superman, "The Just Man Made Perfect," he is primarily concerned in most of his work with evolution as it relates to social institutions, human culture, man and the educative process.

Since Darwin's account of evolution postulated the intervention of no spiritual force, no mind, no god, there raged—it is still going on—a great controversy concerning the origin of variations in species. Jean Baptiste Lamarck had before Darwin enunciated a definite doctrine of organic evolution in which the theory of mutability was based on the notion of the inheritance of acquired characters. Weismann offered the hypothesis of the continuity of the germ plasm and his disproof of the doctrine of transmission of characters. At the

---

[25] Bury, *The Idea of Progress,* p. 335. See Somervell, *English Thought in the Nineteenth Century,* p. 124: "The history of the theory of evolution is itself an example of 'evolution' in the looser sense of the word."

turn of the century many biologists were following the lead of DeVries who held that new species arise through sudden mutations or sports, rather than as the result of slowly accumulated changes. That changes occurred "as the result of living things' desire to adapt themselves better to dead things and possibly to use dead things for their own purposes"[26] had been suggested by Samuel Butler, to whom Shaw was much indebted for his own doctrine of Creative Evolution. Butler thus rediscovered the path to vitalism, which predicated an elastic faculty or an intuitive perception which can will change or growth in all living things.[27] In his preface to *Back to Methuselah,* which is an eloquent attack on Darwinism, he draws chiefly from *Life and Habit* and argues for Butler's version of Lamarck.

It was inevitable that theories of evolution should leave their mark upon sociology, ethics, philosophy, and education. The notion that change appears to be one of the most universal processes tended to undermine the spirit of the romantic and idealistic philosophers. Progress, many thinkers suggested, might become a consciously controlled phenomenon, bearing mankind to higher levels beyond mere materialist goals. Earlier in the century Spencer held in his *Synthetic Philosophy* that evolution proceeded from simple to complex with individualism as its goal. Extending the principle of evolution to sociology and education, he was optimistic in his contention that "always towards perfection is the mighty

[26] C. E. M. Joad, "Shaw's Philosophy," S. Winsten, editor, *G.B.S. 90,* p. 73.
[27] See Julian Huxley, *Evolution: The Modern Synthesis,* p. 458: "The lamarckian views of literary men such as Butler and Shaw are based not on scientific fact and method, but upon wish-fulfilment. . . . One of the main achievements of science has been to reveal that the facts of nature frequently fail to accord either with the wishes or with the apparently logical preconceptions of human beings."

movement towards a complete development and a more un-
mixed good." [28] Huxley, Darwin's disciple, although believing
that man could in our day control the evolutionary process
to his advantage, qualified this with: "I know of no study
which is so saddening as that of the evolution of humanity as
it is set forth in the annals of history. Even the best of modern
civilization appears to me to exhibit a condition of mankind
which neither embodies any worthy ideal nor even possesses
the merit of stability." [29] Protesting against the fatal confusion between evolution and progress, Huxley in his *Evolution
and Ethics* (1853) had declared that "the progress of society
depends not on imitating the cosmic process, still less in running away from it, but in combating it." [30] That progress
would not come through the "survival of the fittest" but
through social reform and education was Huxley's belief. Despite Huxley, the phrase "survival of the fittest" had become
increasingly popular in common speech and was somehow
held to justify either imperialism, war, or unrestrained competition. One of the first of such "social" Darwinists was
Walter Bagehot who in his *Physics and Politics* (1869) saw
such conflict, with war as the primary instrument of social
evolution. F. W. Headley's *Darwinism and Modern Socialism*
(1910) argued for healthy competition as preferable to col-
lectivism, which paralyzes initiative; and Karl Pearson's *National Life from the Standpoint of Science* (1901), a much
more influential book, held on "scientific grounds" that "history shows one way and one way only, in which a high state

[28] Quoted in Bury, *The Idea of Progress*, p. 340.
[29] *Ibid.*, p. 344.
[30] Quoted in Somervell, *English Thought in the Nineteenth Century*,
p. 140. Somervell explains that this confusion was due to misapplications,
rather than applications of Darwinism—that is a confusion between "fittest and best."

of civilization has been produced, namely, the struggle of race with race and the survival of the physically and mentally fitter race." [31] On the other hand, Hobhouse, assuming in his trilogy [32] that public affairs must be interpreted from the standpoint of moral and social evolution, denied a "pseudo-philosophy of struggle taken over uncritically from biology," [33] thus precursing to some extent Shaw's views in the Preface to *Back to Methuselah* (1921). Further, Hobhouse's *Mind in Evolution* had attempted to present a picture of the linear sequence of mental evolution, a theme dramatized in *Man and Superman* and extended in *Back to Methuselah*. While Shaw may neither have read Hobhouse nor have been influenced by him, it should be noted that such concepts of evolutionary growth were in the air at the turn of the century. Nietzsche, whose Superman may be confused with Shaw's, preached that if we take evolution seriously as furnishing a moral standard for life we must develop a whole new set of specific ideals and values. Seeking an intuitive rather than a mechanical explanation of evolution, Bergson in his *Creative Evolution* (1901) recognized that there is an interpenetration of the present and future which provides the conditions out of which new forms can arise. The essence of conduct for Bergson must be directed towards goals, ends which, while not yet actual, are operative in the determination of the directions which conduct shall take. [34] And it should be recalled that ideals of

[31] Quoted in Hearnshaw, editor, *Edwardian England 1901–1910*, p. 245.

[32] *Mind in Evolution* (1901), *Morals in Evolution* (1906), *Development and Purpose* (1913).

[33] Hearnshaw, *Edwardian England*, p. 249.

[34] See Mead, *Movements of Thought in the Nineteenth Century*, for an interesting analysis of Bergson's thought. See also Russell, *A History of Western Philosophy*, p. 791: "Bergson's irrationalism made a wide appeal . . . for instance to Shaw whose *Back to Methuselah* is pure Bergsonism."

growth, adopted by John Dewey and the instrumentalists in America, were affecting views about education. In *Democracy and Education* (1916) Dewey had stated: "Growth is regarded as *having* an end instead of *being* an end. . . . In reality there is nothing to which growth is relative save more growth." [35] Shaw probably never read Dewey—he does not seem to refer to him anywhere in his writings—but it is interesting to note that Lilith's mystical speech, which brings down the curtain in *Back to Methuselah*, reflects in poetic-dramatic terms Dewey's idea of growth. The great concepts of socialism and evolution may be considered the two great problems which the twentieth century has yet to resolve.

To Shaw the theater was a means of educating people— particularly the "educated"—into a better understanding of whatever was grist for his mill: the evils of capitalism, war, selfishness, money-getters, the future, the family, marriage, sex, the will to grow. Shaw frequently admitted that he was a teacher whose aim was the making of better men and women. Deliberately pedagogic and propagandistic, Shaw believed that art, particularly dramatic art, must improve morals and behavior by destroying stereotyped concepts of life.

The Shavian theater had to struggle for its existence during the nineties. Victorian authors had concentrated on the novel at the expense of the drama, which as Shaw claimed, was also eclipsed by the great reputation of Shakespeare, who "is for an afternoon, not for all time." [36] What Shaw meant was only that "bardolatry" impeded the growth of the modern drama, and he carried on a personal war with Sir Henry Irving and his theatrical projections of Shakespeare cut to his

[35] *Democracy and Education,* p. 60 (Dewey's italics).
[36] *Dramatic Opinions and Essays,* I, 406.

own patterns. While Shaw respected Wilde's paradoxes, he was critical of his lack of realism and serious purpose. Pinero and Jones were seen in many of Shaw's reviews in *Our Theatres in the Nineties* as being only superficially in revolt. The appearance of Ibsen's *A Doll's House* (1889) and *Ghosts* (1891) aroused such a storm that Shaw defended the Norwegian dramatist in *The Quintessence of Ibsenism* (1891). Shaw admired Ibsen for his method of injecting ideas and discussions in a realistic plot. Victorian drama had been glaringly devoid of any such intellectual content. To Shaw the theater was a cathedral where thought must flourish. In the Preface to *The Shewing-Up of Blanco Posnet*, he demanded that the theater must be "a most powerful instrument for teaching the nation how and what to think and feel." And in the Preface to *Three Plays by Brieux*, he deplored the childishness of the current London theater, which "is occupied with the elementary education of the masses instead of with the higher education of the classes." Viewing the theater and the cinema as part of the complex of the mass media of communications, which, in the hands of greedy merchants, can vitiate whatever good the schools do, Shaw asserted that "bad theaters are as mischievous as bad schools." [37] It is not surprising that in practically all of Shaw's major plays there is much dialogue about education, formal and informal. The theater, for Shaw, was a major constituent of the educative process.

[37] Preface to *Plays: Pleasant and Unpleasant*, II.

2 *Prisoner of the school*

Whether it is a preface, a letter, a political or economic tract by Shaw, or even a piece of early musical or theatrical criticism, invariably one comes across a comment, criticism, or reminiscence about his own education. What he read, the music he picked up in his musical ménage, the pictures he enjoyed in art galleries, stimulating friendships—all that contributed to his emotional, artistic, and intellectual growth, as well as that which did not, has been recorded. Although Shaw has not given the world a documented account of himself in an autobiography, over a span of sixty years or more he left much material with which one can reconstruct a fairly clear picture of his own education. In a letter to Archibald Henderson he wrote: "It is quite true that the best authority on Shaw is Shaw. My activities have been in so many watertight compartments that nobody has yet given anything but a sectional and inaccurate account of me except when they have tried to piece me out of my own confessions." [1] The Henderson and Pearson biographies of Shaw do attempt, to some extent, to describe his education, pieced out of his

---

[1] Quoted in Henderson, *Bernard Shaw: Playboy and Prophet,* p. 8.

own confessions.[2] But there are far too many lacunae. There is no pretension in this section to having completely filled them in—a whole volume might be needed to do the job adequately. This presentation is primarily designed as a sort of backdrop for as complete a formulation as is possible of Shaw's theories about education.

That all autobiographies are lies is Shaw's contention. "I do not mean unconscious, unintentional lies: I mean deliberate lies. No man is bad enough to tell the truth about himself during his lifetime, involving, as it must, the truth about his family and friends and colleagues."[3] Whether Shaw's pronunciamentos about his family, his friends, or the schools he attended, or about his reading as a youth may or may not be "deliberate lies," a presentation of these judgments, criticisms, and evaluations could be considered important in a number of ways. Shaw's comments about his own education constitute a valuable facet of autobiographic writings. This presentation may be of value in providing clues to the origin of Shaw's theories in many areas of education, although it would be precarious to draw any hard and fast conclusions. It might be interesting to compare what Shaw has said about the theory and practice in the schools of his day with statements to be found in other authoritative sources.

In his correspondence with Mrs. Patrick Campbell, Shaw emphasized that what was done to him in his childhood was "nothing at all of an intentional kind."[4]

---

[2] In 1956 Henderson's *George Bernard Shaw: Man of the Century* and St. John Ervine's *Bernard Shaw: His Life, Work and Friends* appeared. Both books present a more detailed account of Shaw's youth and schooling than any of the earlier biographies.

[3] *Sixteen Self Sketches*, p. 71.

[4] *Bernard Shaw and Mrs. Patrick Campbell: Their Correspondence*, p. 52.

I wasn't spoiled; and I wasn't helped. No direct ill treatment was added by anybody to the horrors of the world. Nobody forbade me to discover what I could of its wonders. I was taken—and took myself—for what I was: a disagreeable little beast. Nobody concerned himself or herself as to what I was capable of becoming, nor did I.

In his *Everybody's Political What's What* (1944) Shaw, discussing the onerous conditions attached to parentage and child life (irrelevant and unnecessary in a well-regulated society), says of his bringing up:

I am myself the fruit of an unsuitable marriage between two quite amiable people who finally separated in the friendliest fashion. . . . They and their three children never quarrelled: though not an emotional household it was not an unkindly one. Its atmosphere of good music and free thought was healthy; but as an example of parental competence to guide, educate, and develop children it was so laughably absurd that I have been trying ever since to get something done about it.[5]

As Archibald Henderson puts it: "He was uncontrolled and unquestioned and uncounselled and uninstructed to a very unusual extent."[6] And Shaw: "We met life's difficulties by breaking our shins over them, gaining such wisdom as was inevitable by making fools of ourselves."[7] However, despite this anarchical upbringing, Shaw has paid tribute to his mother who, although herself subjected to "the constraints and tyrannies, the scoldings and browbeatings she had suffered in her childhood as the method of her education,"[8] avoided exposing her children to what she had known.

Though she had been severely educated up to the highest standard for Irish "carriage ladies" of her time, she was much more like a Trobriand islander as described by Mr. Malinowski than like a modern Cambridge lady graduate in respect of accepting all the

[5] *What's What*, p. 75.
[6] *Playboy and Prophet*, p. 9.
[7] *Self Sketches*, p. 29.
[8] Preface to *London Music*.

habits, good or bad, of the Irish society in which she was brought up as part of an uncontrollable order of nature.

In the Preface to *London Music*, Shaw has elaborated on his mother's education. She had been "tyrannously taught French enough to recite one or two of Lafontaine's fables; to play the piano the wrong way; to harmonize by rule from Logier's Thoroughbass." Of the value of money, of housekeeping, of hygiene, she knew nothing, for she had been simply but rigorously trained "to sit up straight and speak and dress and behave like a lady, and an Irish lady at that."

Shaw's mother was the daughter of a country gentleman, and was brought up by a grandaunt, a puritanical martinet whom she detested. All that had been taught her as religion and discipline Mrs. Shaw regarded as "tyranny and slavery." In reaction against this oppression, she "abandoned her own children to the most complete anarchy." [9] Henderson believes that Mrs. Shaw "allowed her own children every opportunity to develop naturally and freely," [10] and associates this with Shaw's statement that there is no greater crime than to mold the plastic mind and temperament of a child. However, Henderson's idea of a natural and free upbringing does not concur with Shaw's oft-repeated assertion that he would not want "any human child to be brought up as I was brought up, nor as any child I have known was brought up."

Of his father, Shaw wrote:

My father was an Irish Protestant gentleman of the downstart race of younger sons. He had no inheritance, no manual skill, no qualifications of any sort for any definite social function. He must have had some elementary education; for he could read and write and keep accounts more or less inaccurately, and he spoke and dressed like an Irish educated gentleman and not like a railway porter. But

[9] *Self Sketches*, p. 25.   [10] *Playboy and Prophet*, p. 11.

he certainly had not a university degree; and I never heard him speak of any school or college of which he could claim to be an alumnus.[11]

George Carr Shaw was a member of a large family which spoke of itself as "the Shaws" and had access, on the strength of a second cousinship, to Bushy Park, the seat of the bachelor Sir Robert Shaw. Apparently Shaw's relatives on the distaff side forgot that Lucinda Elizabeth Gurley, "having never been taught what marriage really means, nor experienced impecuniosity,"[12] might marry an adventurer. "She married him and her disappointed and infuriated aunt disinherited her, not forseeing that the consequences of the marriage would include so remarkable a phenomenon as myself."[13] Although George Carr Shaw assured his bride that he was a life-long teetotaler (he had been denounced as a drunkard by her relatives), it turned out that he was a dipsomaniac, who during the honeymoon in Liverpool had been discovered with a wardrobe full of empty bottles. In principle, Shaw states, his father was an ardent teetotaler. "Nobody ever felt the disgrace and misery and endless mischief of drunkenness as he did: he impressed it so deeply on me in my earliest years that I have been a teetotaller ever since." In a later work Shaw writes of his early reverence for his father's omniscience:

When I was a child tormenting my elders with endless whats and wheres and whens and hows and whos, the nursemaids said, "Ask no questions and you will be told no lies," which was true, but not edifying. My father, who was to me omniscient and infallible, was my chief victim; and one of the miracles which still puzzles me is the extent to which, under this pressure, he imparted to me so much information on matters in which he must have been as ignorant as myself.[14]

---

[11] *Self Sketches*, p. 74.
[13] Preface to *London Music*.
[12] *Ibid.*, p. 25.
[14] *What's What*, p. 70.

Shaw believed that the early realization of his father's "drink neurosis" had a profound effect on him. "The wrench from my childish faith in my father as perfect and omniscient to the discovery that he was a hypocrite and a dipsomaniac was so sudden and violent that it must have left its mark on me." [15] And with regard to his mother: "I can only imagine the hell into which my mother descended when she found out what shabby-genteel poverty with a drunken husband is like."

"A devil of a childhood," Shaw once wrote to Ellen Terry, "rich only in dreams, frightful and loveless in realities." [16] And in an earlier letter: "The fact that nobody cared for me particularly gave me a frightful self-sufficiency, or rather a power of starving on imaginary feasts, that may have delayed my development a good deal, and leaves me to this hour a treacherous brute in matters of pure affection." [17]

The father tippled, joked, or raged, and the mother, disillusioned early, devoted herself completely to her only salvation, music. The children, two daughters and Bernard, were handed over to nurses, governesses, and apothecaries. Shaw has observed that he would have been much more decently brought up if his parents had been too poor to afford servants. "We children were abandoned entirely to the servants, who, with the exception of Nurse Williams, who was a good and honest woman, were utterly unfit to be trusted with the charge of three cats, much less three children." [18] He hated the servants, who thumped him on the head when he was troublesome, and liked his mother because "her almost complete neglect of me had the advantage that I could idolize her to the utmost pitch of my imagination and had no sordid or disillusioning contacts with her." The servants who were sup-

[15] *Self Sketches,* p. 28.
[16] *Ellen Terry and Bernard Shaw: A Correspondence,* p. 157.
[17] *Ibid.,* p. 86.   [18] Preface to *London Music.*

posed to watch him play on the banks of the canal or round the fashionable squares where the "atmosphere was esteemed salubrious and the surroundings gentlemanly" actually took him into the slums to visit their friends who lived in squalid tenements. Frequently a male acquaintance treated them in public house bars to lemonade and ginger beer. "Thus was laid the foundations of my lifelong hatred of poverty, and the devotion of all my public life to the task of exterminating the poor and rendering their resurrection forever impossible."

Shaw liked to declare that he was born able to read without effort. A governess, Miss Hill, apparently puzzled him with her attempts to teach him to read. "I can remember," Shaw asserts, "no time at which a page of print was not intelligible to me and can only suppose that I was born literate." Miss Hill also failed to communicate to him a taste for poetry when she recited "Stop; for thy tread is on an empire's dust." She only succeeded, "poor lady, in awakening our sense of derisive humor." The governess also taught the children subtraction and multiplication, but failed with division because "she kept saying two into four, three into six, and so forth without ever explaining what the word 'into' meant in this connection." This, however, was explained to him on his first day at school, but he adds dramatically: ". . . I solemnly declare that it was the only thing I ever learnt at school. However, I must not complain, for my immurement in that damnable boy prison effected its real purpose of preventing my being a nuisance to my mother for at least half a day." It was a favorite contention of Shaw's that one of the primary purposes of public schools is to relieve parents of the responsibility of caring for their children for some part of each day.

In discussing the children of "Bohemian Anarchists" (his

parents), Shaw states that "the problem of how much and when children can be kindly and safely left to their own devices, and how much guided and ordered, is the most difficult part of parental policy." [19] The line between tutelage and free thought varies from individual to individual.

No child can be governed so completely as to have no will of its own: the task would be too much for any parent. But a child left to do anything it likes at all ages and on all occasions will swallow matches or set the house on fire with them, and refuse to learn the alphabet and multiplication table. On the whole it is safer to delegate the child's education to a conventional school, as Voltaire's was to the Jesuits, leaving it to react by its own strength, than to risk its having to learn with difficulty in its sixteenth year what it could have been taught early in its sixth.

Very frequently with Shaw, there are violent premises and tame conclusions about schools. "The damnable boy prisons" are better than no schools at all. His glorification of the self-educated—he cites himself as an example—does not prevent him from ignoring the value of even the poor schools of the day.

His clerical uncle, William George Carroll, taught him so well that he knew more Latin grammar than any other boy in the First Latin Junior of the Wesleyan Connexional School. "Snobbishly preparatory for the university, this school took no subjects seriously except Latin and Greek, with a pretence of mathematics (Euclidean), of English history (mostly false and scurrilous), and some nominal geography of which I have no recollection." [20] Despite emphasis on the classics Shaw explains that he forgot what Latin he had learned primarily because he was kept in a class where the master never called on him to recite "because he knew I could, and therefore devoted himself to trapping the boys who could

[19] *Self Sketches,* p. 34.　　　　[20] *Ibid.,* p. 40.

not." [21] Another reason was that the teaching techniques consisted mainly "of asking a boy once a day in an overcrowded class the Latin for a man or a horse or what not." [22] Shaw's *Political What's What* contains a vivid account of the teaching methods:

My school was conducted on the assumption that knowledge of Latin is still the be-all and the end-all of education. . . . I was given no reason why I should learn Latin instead of some living language. There was, in fact, no reason, as there were plenty of translations of all the classics that have any survival value. The method of teaching was barbarous: I was ordered to learn the declensions and conjugations and instalments of the vocabulary by rote on pain of being caned or "kept in" after school hours if I failed to reel off my paradigms without prompting. When I could do this . . . Caeser's commentaries and Virgil's famous epic were thrust into my hands, and without a word of explanation as to what these old commentaries had to do with me. . . . Why, if I was to have a dead language forced on me, they should not have begun with Greek instead of the culturally inferior Roman I was not told, perhaps because the reason was too silly, being that the school had not yet advanced from the Norman conquest to the Renascence. [23]

Above all Shaw denounces not so much the punishments as the imprisonment for half the day, "condemned to sit still, silent and attentive all the time, except for half an hour of relaxation in the playground, during which I yelled and ran about like a mad creature in a reaction against prolonged unnatural restraint." [24]

Shaw relates that he escaped from this classical school "just

[21] Preface to *Misalliance*.   [22] Preface to *London Music*.

[23] *What's What*, p. 159. See also *Self Sketches*, p. 41: "If the pupil could not give the book answer, he received a bad mark and at the end of the week expiated it by suffering not more than six 'tips' (slaps across the palm with a cane) which did not hurt sufficiently to do more than convince me that corporal punishment, to be effective, must be cruel."

[24] *What's What*, p. 160.

as Homer was threatening, but not before I was confronted with algebra without a word of the explanation that would have made it interesting to me." [25] Although Euclid gave him no trouble, he failed in the examinations because "the questions stated, not the problems, but their numbers in the book, of which I knew nothing, having picked up all the solutions in class." [26] He never forgave his teachers for their failure to explain the practical value algebra and geometry might have in later life.

Not a word was said to us about the meaning or utility of mathematics: we were simply asked to explain how an equilateral triangle could be constructed by the intersection of two circles, and to do sums in a, b, and x instead of in pence and shillings, leaving me so ignorant that I concluded that a and b must mean eggs and cheese and x nothing, with the result that I rejected algebra as nonsense, and never changed that opinion until in my advanced twenties Graham Wallace and Karl Pearson convinced me that instead of being taught mathematics I had been made a fool of.[27]

Only in literature could the school establish a claim to have foreseen his future success. Once when the class was set to write essays, he received a first class "for a very florid description of the Liffey pool below bridges." [28] However, no serious importance was attached to this subject since it was not Latin.

[25] As to Homer's *Iliad*, he says: "I had already devoured for myself the stately English of Lord Derby which I preferred to Pope's pretty rhymes."
[26] *Self Sketches*, p. 41.
[27] *Ibid.*, p. 40. See *What's What*, p. 182: "J. L. Joynes, amazed at my ignorance told me that a and b meant neither bacon and eggs nor brandy and Bibles. But, being the son of a famous Eton master and educated accordingly, he failed to explain what they did mean; and not until I had in the course of my literary work to take the matter into serious consideration did I find out for myself."
[28] *Self Sketches*, p. 41.

Shaw boasted in the Preface to *Misalliance* that he was a confirmed idler, and consequently failed disgracefully in examinations. "None of my schoolmasters really cared a rap whether I learnt my lessons or not, provided my father paid my schooling bill, the collection of which was the real object of the school." Examinations and lessons were never a source of anxiety to him, and Shaw stated that he could not understand the boys who prepared their lessons and studied for examinations. Comparing his experiences with those of Dr. Johnson, Shaw asserted that Sam's schoolmasters did care whether he learned anything by beating him savagely enough to force him "to lame his mind—for Johnson's great mind was lamed—by learning his lessons. . . . I did not learn my school lessons, having much more important ones in hand, with the result that I have not wasted my life trifling with literary fools in taverns as Johnson did when he should have been shaking England with the thunder of his spirit." Although this analogy between taverns and lessons may be questionable, it does illustrate Shaw's profound antipathy to forced learning in the schools. Again and again he insists that "my schooling did me a great deal of harm and no good whatever: it was simply dragging a child's soul through the dirt."

After some years of imprisonment at the Wesleyan School, Shaw's Uncle William examined him, and finding that he was learning nothing, sent him to a very private school in Glasthule, near Dalkey. Young Shaw left the school soon after, when the family moved to Dublin. George John Vandaleur Lee, music teacher and family friend, being concerned about the boy's education or lack of it, proposed the Central Model Boys School on Marlborough Street. The Model School was in theory undenominational, but everyone was aware that most of the students were the sons of Roman Catholic shopkeepers.

In *Sixteen Self Sketches,* Shaw reveals his "snob tragedy" after, he confesses, a silence of eighty years.

I am not sure that if Marlborough Street had been explained to me as an experimental model school for pupils, not of the laboring "common people" but for the children of persons of modest means engaged in retail instead of wholesale trade, Catholic or Protestant, I might have been spared all my shame; for I was already in revolt against the Shaw snobbery, and observant of the fact that my father's tailor had a country house in Dalkey, a yacht in Dalkey Sound, and could afford to send his sons, much better dressed and equipped than I, to expensive preparatory schools and to college.[29]

Shaw relates that he became a boy who had lost caste outside the school and with whom no Protestant young gentleman would speak or play. "Not so within the railings. There I was a superior being, and in play hour did not play, but walked up and down with the teachers in their reserved promenade." When he was thirteen, after a half year of the Model School, he flatly refused to go back. Shaw's father, as much ashamed of it as the boy himself, entered him in a day school of the Incorporated Society For Promoting Protestant Schools in Ireland. It was called the Dublin English Scientific and Commercial Day School. "This was my last school prison."

This school did not prepare for the university and excluded classics from its curriculum. Apparently it was, as Shaw says, a school for pupils whose fathers, like his own, could not afford to send them to Trinity College. It trained for business, not for scholarship. The headmaster, who was preparing himself for ordination in the Established Protestant Episcopal Church of Ireland, had little contact with the students except when they were to be caned. "The teaching method was the Wesleyan all over again." [30]

[29] *Ibid.,* p. 42.   [30] *Ibid.,* p. 50.

At the Wesleyan School, Shaw had neglected his lessons
and had been given to lying, particularly to the schoolmasters.
At the Model School he experienced the birth of a new
moral passion, and at this new school "lying was beneath my
new moral dignity as a head boy." But he was still recalcitrant
during the reading lessons in history which ignored Ireland
and glorified England. "I always substituted Ireland for England in such dithyrambs." The teachers only smiled for they
were Fenians too.

Once, Shaw reveals, the classroom was left for more than
an hour without the supervision of a teacher who had ordered
the students not to make a noise. "We kept quiet for perhaps
a minute. Then we 'went Fantee,' roaring, and wrecking
everything wreckable in the room. I did as the rest did." This
experience stimulates Shaw to some of his favorite conclusions
about democratic society:

Many years later I was to see the same thing happen twice among
adults, once to a company of first class passengers on a liner, and
once at a Fabian Society spree. It did not surprise me to see it de-
picted in a Russian educational film. It taught me how thin is the
veneer of bourgeois civilization, and why I, no more than Shakespeare or Dickens, can be persuaded that, without natural leaders
and rulers, democratic civilization can be achieved under the pre-
text of Liberty by Unlimited Suffrage for unqualified nobodies
elected by politically uneducated everybodies. . . .

The Preface to *London Music* tells of another unfortunate
experience with schools. Since it was Shaw's early ambition to
be a great painter like Michelangelo, he attempted to obtain
instruction in art at the School of Design presided over by the
South Kensington Department of Science and Art. But he felt
that he wasted his time "by filling up ridiculous examination

papers in practical geometry and what they called freehand drawing."

With competent instruction I daresay I could have become a painter and draughtsman of sorts; but the School of Design convinced me that I was a hopeless failure in that direction on no better ground than that I found I could not draw like Michael Angelo or paint like Titian at the first attempt without knowing how. But teaching, of art and everything else, was and still is so little understood by our professional instructors (mostly themselves failures) that only the readymade geniuses make good; and even they are as often as not the worse for their academic contacts.

In general Shaw recalled with horror and indignation the evil things he picked up in the schools he attended in Ireland.

I was taught lying, dishonorable submission to tyranny, dirty stories, a blasphemous habit of treating love and maternity as obscene jokes, hopelessness, evasion, derision, cowardice, and all the blackguard's shifts by which the coward intimidates other cowards. And if I had been a boarder at an English public school instead of a day boy at an Irish one, I might have had to add to these deeper shames still.[31]

By imprisoning him for half the day, these schools, Shaw declared, kept him "from the books, the great public picture gallery, the music, and the intercourse with Nature which really educated me." [32]

Of his teachers Shaw admitted that he could recollect a few whose classes interested him and whom he certainly would have pestered for information and instruction if he could have got into any decent human relationship with them. "But these rare cases of the good teacher," Shaw argues in the Preface to

[31] Preface to *Misalliance*.
[32] Preface to Workers' Educational Association *Year Book* for 1918, in *Doctors' Delusions*.

Misalliance, "actually do more harm than good; for they encourage us to pretend that all schoolmasters are like that."
And he adds bitterly: "Of what use is it to us that there are
always somewhere two or three teachers of children whose
specific genius for their occupation triumphs over our tyran-
nous system and even finds in it its opportunity?"

The advent of George John Vandaleur Lee, "mesmeric con-
ductor and daringly original teacher of singing," must have had
a great influence on Shaw's education. He has written much
about this man, who not only initiated him into eating brown
bread and sleeping with open windows, but into a saturation
with music which always remained with him. Mrs. Shaw had
gone to Lee for singing lessons and "he trained her voice to
such purpose that she became indispensable to him as an amateur prima donna." [33] Lee was an unorthodox teacher of singing who dissected birds and, with the connivance of medical
friends, human subjects, in his search for the secret of bel
canto. The famous ménage à trois came about when Lee came
to live with the family. He was an indefatigable organizer of
concerts and opera, with Mrs. Shaw as his prima donna and
chorus leader. Rehearsals were held in the front parlor. "I was
acquiring during this time an equipment which enabled me
not only to pose as Corno di Bassetto when the chance arrived,
but to add the criticism of pictures to the various strings I had
to my bow as a feuilletonist."

The family also shared a cottage in Dalkey, "high up on
Torca Hill, with all Dublin Bay from Dalkey Island to Howth
visible from the garden, and all Killiney Bay with the Wicklow
mountains in the background from the hall door." Lee bought
this cottage and presented it to Mrs. Shaw. These Dalkey days
Shaw recalls as the happiest of his life.

[33] Preface to *London Music.*

Great as is my debt to famous books, great pictures, and noble
music for my education I should be even more ignorant than I am
but for my removal at the age of ten from the street in which I was
born . . . to Torca Cottage, high on Dalkey Hill. . . . I had only
to open my eyes there to see such pictures as no painter could make
for me.[34]

Henderson quotes Shaw speaking of his youth: "My university
had three colleges: "Lee's Musical Society, the National Gallery, and Dalkey Hill." [35]

As a boy he was permitted to prowl in the Dublin National
Gallery which contained "one of the finest collections of its
size in Europe." [36] Whenever he had any money he bought
volumes of the Bohn translation of Vasari and read them with
great interest. At fifteen, Shaw states, he knew enough about
quite a few Italian and Flemish painters to recognize their
works at sight.

In a letter to Archibald Henderson in 1905, Shaw declares
that he has always been "more consciously susceptible to music
and painting than to literature so that Mozart and Michelangelo count for a great deal in the making of my mind." [37]
The musical activities of his family provided many opportunities for listening to the great composers, particularly Mozart,
whose opera *Don Giovanni* he loved.

In my small-boyhood I, by good luck, had an opportunity of learning the Don thoroughly, and if it were only for the sense of the
value of fine workmanship which I gained from it, I should still
esteem that lesson the most important part of my education. Indeed

[34] *Self Sketches,* p. 117.   [35] *Playboy and Prophet,* p. 50.
[36] Of Lee he writes in the Preface to *London Music:* "There were
holes in his culture which I had to fill up for myself. His richer pupils
sometimes presented him with expensive illustrated books. He never
opened them; but I did. . . . He never visited the Dublin National
Gallery."
[37] *Playboy and Prophet,* p. 31.

it educated me artistically in all sorts of ways, and disqualified me only in one—that of criticizing Mozart fairly.[38]

The young Shaw was naturally taken to the opera. In his mother's album he had seen the photographs of all the great opera singers in evening dress. In the Preface to *Heartbreak House* he relates:

In the theater I found myself before a gilded balcony filled with persons in evening dress whom I took to be the opera singers. I picked out one massive dark lady as Alboni, and wondered how soon she would stand up and sing. I was puzzled by the fact that I was made to sit with my back to the singers instead of facing them. When the curtain went up, my astonishment and delight were unbounded.

He had also been delighted by the theater where on his first visit he saw a Christmas pantomime and a play by Tom Taylor. Barry Sullivan, the greatest actor of the day, made a deep impression on him. "His stage fights in *Richard III* and *Macbeth* appealed irresistibly to a boy spectator like myself." [39]

Derogations of universities, university graduates, and academics in general abound in Shaw's writings. He has always been fond of comparing his education with that of a university graduate. "I cannot too often repeat," he begins his essay "Am I an Educated Person?" in *Self Sketches,* "that though I have no academic qualifications I am in fact much more highly educated than most university scholars." He cites as an example his musical education which had not ceased even in his ninety-second year.

It has gone on from Rossini, Meyerbeer, and Verdi to Wagner, from Beethoven to Sibelius, from British dilutions of Handel and Mendelssohn to the genuine English music of Elgar and Vaughan

---

[38] *Music in London 1890–1894,* I, 296.
[39] Preface to *Ellen Terry and Bernard Shaw: A Correspondence.*

Williams and from whole-tone mode of Debussy and the chromatic mode of Schonberg to the experiments of Cyril Scott in the technical chaos which ensued when the forbidden consecutives and unprepared unresolved discords and "false relations" of the old textbooks became the latest fashion. . . .

How is this for textbook jargon? Can any university graduate who has had Virgil and Homer, Horace and Juvenal, rubbed mercilessly into him at Eton, Harrow, Winchester, or Rugby, beat it?

Habitually belittling university musicians such as the Doctors of Music, Shaw maintained that the effect of such degrees was the imitation of outmoded composers. To support his contention he cited Bach and Elgar who never had a lesson in thoroughbass. "Personal experience of contemporary developments in art is far more instructive than any study of ancient documents can be."

No memorizing examinee can feel the development from Aeschylus to Euripides and its dégringolade to Menander as I felt the development from Donizetti to Wagner, from Bouguereau to Gauguin, from Leader to Wilson Steer and Monet, from Canova to Rodin, from Scribe and Sardou to Ibsen, from Barry Sullivan to Irving, from Colenso to Inge, from Tennyson to Browning, from Macaulay to Marx, from Max Weismann to Herbert Dingle, from Tyndall to Clerk-Maxwell, Planck, and Einstein . . . in short, from adoring rehearings of the masterpieces of the dead to the pressures on my living self of startling departures that were new to me.

That no person is educated without living experiences was Shaw's conviction. The vital difference between reading and experience is not measurable by examination marks. On the strength of this difference Shaw claimed to be one of the best educated men in the world and dismissed "95 percent of the academic celebrities as . . . nitwits."

In many of his works, Shaw has attacked that "Pontifex Maximus" of the conditioned reflex, Ivan Pavlov, who prac-

ticed vivisection, which to Shaw was an abomination of the
scientific method. It is interesting to note in the Preface to
London Music how in his disparagement of this "academician"
he brings in his own education. Shaw points out that Pavlov,
although he butchered dogs, was not by nature a bad man;
he was well meaning, intelligent, and devoted to science. "He
even bore a strong resemblance to myself. It was his academic
environment that corrupted, stultified, and sterilized him. If
only he had been taught to sing by my mother no dog need
ever have collapsed in terror at his approach; and he might
have shared the laurels of Alexander." Although this evaluation
of Pavlov may seem somewhat facetious, it is understandable
in view of Shaw's approach to science and to the scientific
method.

Although he was brought up in a home in which musical
activities were dominant, he had to achieve a technical orientation in music largely through his own efforts. When George
Vandaleur Lee sold the cottage in Dalkey and concluded his
tenancy in the Hatch Street home in Dublin, Shaw's mother
decided to renounce her amateur status and to go to London to
teach singing for a living. Mrs. Shaw settled her husband and
young Shaw in comfortable lodgings and simply left with her
two daughters. "Meanwhile nobody ever dreamt of teaching
me anything. At fifteen when the family broke up, I could neither play nor read a note of music. . . . When the house
became musicless I was forced to teach myself how to play
written music on the piano with a diagram of the keyboard in
it or else be starved of music." [40]

[40] Preface to *London Music*. See also "The Religion of the Pianoforte,"
Fortnightly Review, 61 (February, 1894), 255–66, where Shaw describes a fingering technique, all his own. "My reward was that I gained
penetrating experiences of Victor Hugo and Schiller from Donizetti,
Verdi, and Beethoven; of the Bible from Handel; of Goethe from Schu-

He purchased one of Weale's Handbooks which contained a diagram of the keyboard and an explanation of musical notation, and began his self-tuition, not with Czerny's five-finger exercises, but with the overture to *Don Giovanni*. Although Shaw admits he never acquired any real technical skill as a pianist, he acquired what he wanted, namely, the power to read a musical score and learn its contents as if he had heard it rehearsed by his mother and her musical friends. Eventually he bought Wagnerian scores and Beethoven symphonies, thus discovering the musical regions that lie outside opera and oratorio. He studied academic texts and actually worked out exercises in harmony and counterpoint with the aid of an organist friend named Crament. "I read Mozart's Succinct Thoroughbass, and this, many years later Edward Elgar told me, was the only document in existence of the smallest use to a student composer." [41] It all ended, Shaw boasts, in his knowing much more about music than any of the great composers, "an easy achievement for any critic, however barren. . . . For awhile I must have become a little pedantic; for I remember being shocked, on looking up Lee's old vocal score of *Don Giovanni*, to find that he had cut out all the repetitions which Mozart had perpetrated as a matter of sonata form."

When he eventually rejoined his mother in London, Mrs. Shaw discovered that he could play accompaniments but was misusing his voice; she taught him, on his insistence, how to sing properly. "I developed an uninteresting baritone voice of no exceptional range which I have ever since used for my private satisfaction and exercise."

---

mann; of Beaumarchais and Molière from Mozart; and of Merimée from Bizet besides finding in Berlioz an unconscious interpreter of Edgar Allan Poe."
[41] Preface to *London Music*.

Shaw felt that his early saturation with music profoundly influenced everything he ever wrote. At the Malvern Festival of 1939 he said:

My method, my system, my tradition, is founded upon music. It is not founded upon literature at all. I was brought up on music. I did not read plays very much because I could not get hold of them, except, of course, Shakespeare, who was mother's milk to me. . . . If you study operas and symphonies, you will find a useful clue to my particular type of writing.[42]

Despite the fact that school made little impression on him, Shaw claimed he was a highly educated boy all the same. He repeatedly asserted that he loved to read everything except "unreadable schooltexts" which were, to him, insults to the soul of a child. Exhilarating was the discovery of such books as *The Pilgrim's Progress* and *The Arabian Nights.* Annoyed by the superior airs of a schoolfellow who boasted of having read Locke's *Essay On Human Understanding,* Shaw states in the Preface to *Misalliance* that he "attempted to read the Bible straight through and actually got to the Pauline Epistles before I broke down in disgust at what seemed to me their inveterate crookedness of mind." Although nothing could induce him to read a textbook of history at school, he read Robertson's *Charles V* and his *History of England* from end to end. French and English history were not school subjects, but by reading with great entertainment the historical novels of Dumas père he "had a vivid conspectus of France from the sixteenth to the eighteenth century." [43] The Waverley novels of Scott provided a "taste for history and an acquaintance with its personages and events which made the philosophy of history real for me when I was fully grown." [44]

[42] Quoted in Rattray, *Bernard Shaw: A Chronicle,* p. 20.
[43] *What's What,* p. 180.
[44] *Ibid.,* p. 181. See also *Self Sketches,* p. 165: "But he [Shaw's father]

With respect to the manner in which he was taught history, Shaw tells of a class of about fifty boys seated in alphabetical order. Each day a chapter in "The Student's Hume" was assigned, and the teacher would go through the chapter and through the alphabet asking questions about facts and dates. "As my name began with the letter S, I could calculate within ten lines or so what question would fall to me." [45] However, when he was at home reading *Quentin Durward, A Tale of Two Cities*, or *The Three Musketeers* he "was learning it [history] very agreeably." Shaw emphasizes here "the impossibility of learning history from a collection of bare facts in the order in which they actually occurred," and that it is only through the medium of works of art that history can best be understood. Citing his play *In Good King Charles's Golden Days*, Shaw states:

For the actual occurrence of the incidents in it I cannot produce a scrap of evidence, being quite convinced that they never occurred; yet anyone reading this play or witnessing a performance of it will not only be pleasantly amused, but will come out with a knowledge of the dynamics of Charles's reign . . . that ten years of digging up mere facts in the British museum or the Record Office could not give.

In his teens, Shaw says in the Preface to *London Music*, he was already "saturated with English literature, from Shakespeare and Bunyan to Byron and Dickens." As a child one of the books he delighted in was an illustrated Shakespeare "with a picture and two or three lines of text underneath it on every third or fourth page. Ever since Shakespearean blank verse has been to me as natural a form of literary expression as the Au-

---

must have done some reading in his youth; for he knew Scott's novels and encouraged me to read. I read The Pilgrim's Progress to him and remember his telling me not to pronounce grievous as grievious."
[45] *What's What*, p. 183.

gustan English to which I was brought up in Dublin, or the latest London fashion in dialogue." [46] Shaw attributes his literary ability to his "having been as a child steeped in the Bible, The Pilgrim's Progress, and Cassell's Illustrated Shakespeare." [47]

He disliked all children's books. When most children are just mastering their alphabet, he was absorbed in Charles Lever's *A Day's Ride*. The novels of Dickens impressed him deeply.

When I first read *Great Expectations*, I was not much older than Pip was . . . and I also struggled with *Little Dorrit* at this time. The books impressed my imagination most fearfully, so real they were to me. Now it is pretty clear that Dickens, having caught me young . . . must have left his mark on me very deeply. [48]

Although Shaw insists he was a freethinker before he could think, he went to church as a youth because it was genteel to go to church and believe in hell. As a child, he was sent every Sunday to a Sunday school, where "genteel little children repeated texts, and were rewarded with cards inscribed on them." [49] After an hour of this they would be marched into an adjoining church to sit around the altar rails and fidget. "I suffered this, not for my salvation, but because my father's respectability demanded it." He hated "the unnaturally motionless figures of the congregation, and their set faces, pale with malignant rigidity produced by the suppression of all expression." [50]

Taught to hold the Bible in reverence, he was shocked as he was buying a pennyworth of sweets to see a shopkeeper tear a leaf out of a dismembered Bible to wrap them in. "I was hor-

[46] Foreword to *Cymbeline Refinished*.   [47] *What's What*, p. 181.
[48] *Music in London 1890–1894*, II, 316. See also Henderson, *Playboy and Prophet*, p. 43 where the author quotes Shaw: "I think my treatment as an adult at home (like the Micawber's treatment of David Copperfield) made school very difficult for me."
[49] *Self Sketches*, p. 76.   [50] *On Going to Church*, p. 44.

rified, and half expected to see him struck by lightning." [51] He
ate the sweets, believing with his Protestant mind that the
shopkeeper as a Roman Catholic would go to hell, Bible or no
Bible. Shaw said he grew out of this idea that all Roman
Catholics go to hell when they die, and all Protestants to
heaven if they are good children "when I was promoted from
petticoats to knickerbockers." [52]

"If a child is told any story, however absurd or impossible,
by someone whom it regards as infallible (mostly a parent), it
will accept it as gospel truth and hold it thoughtlessly until it
is driven to reason about it, which may possibly never happen." [53] As a child he had asked his father what a Unitarian
was, and was told "that Unitarians believed that Jesus was not
crucified, but was seen running away down the other side of
the Hill of Calvary." Shaw said he believed this for nearly
thirty years.

The family atmosphere was really one of "derisive freethinking," [54] for by the time he was ten the family had given
up even the pretense of churchgoing, and Sonny Shaw of saying his prayers.

. . . the rest of my development was in a family atmosphere so
sceptical, so Bohemian, anarchic, and on its educational side aesthetic, that in my teens I was a professed atheist, with no reverence
whatever for the Trinity but a profound and lasting respect for
Michael Angelo and Raphael, for Handel, Mozart, and Beethoven.[55]

His maternal Uncle Walter, a ship's surgeon who always visited them between voyages, contributed vastly to this free-

[51] *What's What*, p. 181.
[52] *Ibid.*, p. 326. See also *Self Sketches*, p. 76: "Imagine being taught
that there is one God, a Protestant and a perfect gentleman, keeping
Heaven select for the gentry against an idolatrous impostor called the
Pope."
[53] *Self Sketches*, p. 47.   [54] *Ibid.*, p. 130.
[55] *What's What*, p. 326.

thinking family scepticism. A most exhilarating person "whose profanity and obscenity in conversation were of Rabelaisian exuberance," [56] he taught the boy "a stock of unprintable limericks that constituted almost an education in geography." Full of the Bible, he quoted the sayings of Jesus as models of "facetious repartee." Shaw's Preface to *Immaturity* tells of Uncle Walter teaching him an elaborate conversation of Daniel in the lion's den and King Darius, in which each strove to outdo the other in Rabelaisian repartee.[57] Shaw's father apparently also contributed to this comedic aura of freethinking, for "he was in the grip of a humorous sense of anticlimax," particularly where sacred ideas or conventions were concerned.

Thus when I scoffed at the Bible he would instantly and quite sincerely rebuke me, telling me, with what little sternness was in his nature, that I should not speak so; that no educated man would make such a display of ignorance; that the Bible was universally recognized as a literary and historical masterpiece. . . . But when he had reached the point of feeling really impressive, a convulsion of internal chuckling would wrinkle up his eyes; and . . . would cap his eulogy by assuring me, with an air of perfect fairness, that even the worst enemy of religion could say no worse of the Bible than that it was the damndest parcel of lies ever written.

Although he loathed learning Bible verses by heart, he did enjoy reading the Bible. Shaw explains that he was too infantile then to realize his more mature conclusion that the reason he could read and remember Bible stories and not read school books was that the Bible was a work of art. ". . . the Bible stories were translated when English literary art was at the summit of its majesty, the translators having believed that

---

[56] *Self Sketches,* p. 32.
[57] Shaw has compared his training with that of Mark Twain. "His training as a Mississippi pilot must have been, as to religion, very like my training as the nephew of a Transatlantic surgeon."

they were Englishing the very words of God himself." [58] As
one might suppose, the Bible plays an important role in Shaw's
theories about religious education.

Owing to his grandmother's and father's financial difficulties,
Shaw was made a clerk in a prominent firm of Dublin estate
agents. He would not have gone to a university even if the opportunity had been given him, for he did not believe in
school and knew that he would never distinguish himself aca-
demically. The Protestant University of Dublin had become
associated in his mind with rowdiness, dissipation, and drunkenness. What particularly annoyed him was not the lack of an
opportunity to study a profession at a university, but the snobbish pretensions of his family, his class. "I have illustrated the
wretched lot in our society of the Downstart, as I call the boy-
gentleman descended through younger sons from the plutoc-
racy, for whom a university education is beyond his father's
income, leaving him by family tradition a gentleman without
a gentleman's means or education, and so only a penniless
snob." [59] At the turn of the century he had written in the essay
"Who I Am, and What I Think" that the class which has the
pretensions and prejudices and habits of the rich without its
money is about the "worst-off of all." [60] What he abominated
was being a poor relation of the rich, for then one is educated
"neither at the proletarian school and the Polytechnic nor at
the University, but at some cheap private adventure academy
for the sons of gentlemen."

The financial reasons were not the main reasons. Shaw has
explained carefully in his Preface to *Immaturity* his reasons for
repudiating attendance at a university. For one thing he lacked

[58] *What's What*, p. 181.
[59] *Self Sketches*, p. 20. See Preface to *Immaturity* for a more detailed
discussion of primogeniture and its relation to education.
[60] *Self Sketches*, p. 85.

the competitive instinct for prizes, distinctions, and examinations; and he insists he could not learn anything that failed to interest him, particularly since his preferences were not academic. He was by this time disillusioned with schools in general, with forced learning, and with callous teachers. "I am firmly persuaded that every unnatural activity of the brain is as mischievous as any unnatural activity of the body, and that pressing people to learn things they do not want to know is as unwholesome and disastrous as feeding them on sawdust." In his teens and in later life, Shaw states he was "entirely untouched by university idealism." He adds:

When it reached me later on, I recognized how ignorantly I had spoken in my boyhood; but when I went still further and learnt that this idealism is never realized in our schools and universities, and operates only as a mask and a decoy for our system of impressing and enslaving children and stultifying adults, I concluded that my ignorance had been inspired. . . . I have not since changed my mind.

This is a battery of some of Shaw's basic assumptions, charged with a Marxian social and economic slant which lays the groundwork for a Shavian system of education. If with Marx the opium of the people is religion, with Shaw it is education.

Of his job in the estate agency he says in "My Office-Boyhood" (*Self Sketches*): "No more than at school was anything explained to me. If some odd job puzzled me I was told to 'see what was done last time.'" Shaw insisted that he had that rare faculty for learning and generalizing from experience, and that consequently this apprenticeship became useful to him when Henry George explained land in its political significance to him. He also acquired a fair knowledge of business routine in this office, developed a very neat handwriting when he was promoted to cashier, as well as a familiarity with legal contracts, and established habits of industrious work. When later he was writing his five novels in London, his daily routine of filling five quarto pages a day, wet or fine, whether he felt like it or not, was made easier by his office training. "I had so much of the schoolboy and the clerk still in me," he explained in the Preface to *Immaturity*, "that if my five pages ended in the middle of a sentence I did not finish it until the next day. On the other hand, if I missed a day, I made up for it by doing a double task on the morrow."

The land agency clerkship secured for him the society of "gentlemen apprentices" from the university who had paid big premiums to be taught a genteel profession. "They learnt little for their money except the scraps of opera I taught them." [61] Shaw confesses that in intellectual discussion with these university men he "got severely battered." When informed that he did not know what a syllogism was, he went to the dictionary and found out "like Molière's bourgeois hero that I had been syllogizing all my life without knowing it." When another gentleman apprentice happened to remark that every boy thinks he is going to be a great man, Shaw admits that this hit home. "The shock that this gave me made me suddenly aware that this was my own predicament, though I could do nothing that gave me the smallest ground for classing myself as born to the hierarchy of Shakespeare, Shelley, Mozart, Praxiteles, and Michael Angelo." His youthful diffidence and cowardice told him he was only "an ignorant duffer." All this served to make him realize that he was not doing what he really wanted to do, that he hated his position, and that he would have to leave it. This he did when he was twenty.

Although Shaw admits he was worsted at times in intellectual discussion with his fellow employees, R. J. MacManus,

[61] *Self Sketches*, p. 55.

who has contributed a chapter, "Shaw's Irish Boyhood," to the volume *G.B.S. 90,* has a different version. This boy atheist created a sensation among his fellow clerks when he "calmly dissected the Thirty-Nine Articles and threw them in their faces with smiling audacity. . . . He quoted Shelley and Tom Paine and Mary Wollstonecraft at them, and there was no reply." Shaw, however, has refuted MacManus's statements in the piece, "Biographers' Blunders Corrected":

I had never read the 39 Articles, and did not know of their existence. As to Mary Wollstonecraft, I had never heard of her. Paine had been held up to me as a drunken staymaker without a redeeming trait. . . . It was then part of the education of a gentleman to convince him that the three most religious men in Europe [Voltaire and Rousseau as well] had been impious villains. . . . Shelley cured me of all that. I read him, prose and verse, from beginning to end. This took place at the end of my teens.[62]

This discrepancy in fact is mentioned here in order to shed light on Shaw's account of his reading. However, it should be noted that Pearson in his two books about Shaw cites many instances to show that Shaw's memory frequently lapsed.

Though he did not count it as such, his literary activity began at the time when he was still a clerk. He had struck up a friendship with Edward McNulty, later the author of three novels of Irish life, and had kept up a correspondence, "writing immense letters to one another illustrated with crude drawings and enlivened by burlesque dramas."[63] On several occasions he had sent reams of manuscript to various journals. There were other fruitful friendships. Chichester Bell, a cousin of Alexander Graham Bell, and consequently a nephew of Melville Bell, the inventor of the phonetic script known as "visible speech," was a physician who had studied chemistry and physics in the school of Helmholtz. Shaw learned much from

[62] *Ibid.,* p. 169. [63] *Ibid.,* p. 58.

him. "We studied Italian together; and though I did not learn
Italian I learned a good deal else, mostly about physics and
pathology. I read Tyndall and Trousseau's Clinical Lectures.
And it was Bell who made me take Wagner seriously." His
literary activity began in earnest when he wrote a letter in 1875
to the editor of *Public Opinion* in which he attacked the influence of the noted evangelists of his day, Moody and Sankey.[64]
Convinced by this time that he lacked a marketable technical
skill in music and painting, and that, as a potentially great
man, he could not continue clerking or cashiering at the land
agency, he decided that there was nothing left but writing.
Within a year he left for London to join his mother and sister.

Shaw's Preface to *The Irrational Knot* contains a valuable
presentation of attitudes with which he entered the world of
London. "I was familiar with the greatest in that world [of
art]: mighty poets, painters, and musicians were my intimates.
I found the world of artificial greatness founded on convention
and money so repugnant and contemptible by comparison that
I had no sympathetic understanding of it." Here also one finds
the famous confession of how, though his family needed his
financial help urgently, he chose deliberately to be a burden
to them. "Well, without a blush I embraced the monstrosity.
I did not throw myself into the struggle for life: I threw my
mother into it." Mrs. Shaw, as teacher of music, worked for his
living "instead of preaching that it was my duty to work for
hers; therefore take off your hat to her and blush." Again he is
preoccupied with the kind of education he possessed, comparing it with that of university graduates:

Behold me, then, in London in an impossible position. I was a
foreigner—an Irishman—the most foreign of all foreigners when
he has not gone through the British university mill. I was not, as I
shall presently show, uneducated; but what I knew was what the

[64] The letter is quoted in Henderson, *Playboy and Prophet*, p. 38.

English university graduates did not know; and what they knew I either did not know or did not believe.[65]

The late nineteenth century was an age which talked about a world of problems; it was therefore an age in which debating societies flourished. The autobiography of John Stuart Mill and the novels of Disraeli testify to this popularity of meetings and discussions. Shaw's activities in London debating societies during the years 1876–1885, the lean years when he was writing the five novels, constituted an education not available in Dublin, on politics, economics, manners and public speaking.

His impecuniosity and shabbiness were such that he walked the streets of London in torn shoes and in trousers worn in the seat. "I remember once buying a book entitled *How To Live on Sixpence a Day* . . . I carried out its instructions faithfully for a whole afternoon; and if ever I have an official biography issued I shall certainly have it stated . . . that I lived for some time on sixpence a day." [66] Shaw complained that at school he "was not taught manners nor loyalties, nor held to any standards of dress or care of my person . . . I was undertrained civically and socially." [67] Thus in London he realized acutely the need "of educating, disciplining, and forming myself which should have been done for me when I was a child." He relates how he improved his table manners and company manners by reading a volume called *The Manners and Tone of Good Society* which he calls "an admirable textbook." Pearson states that Shaw's one remembered lesson in good manners had been administered by an aunt; and when he found himself poor and shabby in London, he devoured books on polite behavior in the British Museum.[68] This freed him from the fear

[65] *Self Sketches*, p. 65.   [66] *Dramatic Opinions and Essays*, I, 83.
[67] *What's What*, p. 81.
[68] *G.B.S.: A Full Length Portrait*, p. 46.

of behaving incorrectly which haunts the socially untrained. He was untutored in manners, Shaw points out, because of his father's dipsomania, which cut the family off from the social drill that puts one at one's ease in private society, and because of his mother's belief that correct behavior is inborn and need not be taught.[69]

When George Vandaleur Lee obtained a post as music critic on *The Hornet*, he turned the duties and financial rewards over to Shaw. The young critic was so unorthodox as to call Wagner a great composer, and Lee was discharged. In 1879, Shaw in desperation obtained work with the Edison Telephone Company. His job was to persuade London shopkeepers to allow telephone wires to be attached to their premises. "My shyness made the business of calling on strangers frightfully uncongenial; and my sensitiveness . . . made the impatient rebuffs I had to endure . . . ridiculously painful to me." Having read Tyndall and Helmholtz, Shaw declares he was "the only person in the entire establishment who knew the current scientific explanation of telephony." [70] This was Shaw's last commercial job, which he deliberately left "in order to recover my destitute freedom." [71]

His friendship with James Lecky was both profitable and important in his life. Lecky was a musical scholar and the author of the article on "temperament," (systems of tuning keyed instruments) in the first edition of Grove's *Dictionary of Music and Musicians*. It was Lecky who stimulated Shaw to study "temperament," shorthand, phonetics, and Gaelic, and it was through him that he got to know the scholar, Alexander Ellis and the Oxford phoneticist, Henry Sweet. Shaw's lifelong preoccupation with a new phonetic alphabet is undoubtedly due

[69] Preface to *Immaturity*.   [70] Preface to *The Irrational Knot*.
[71] Preface to *Immaturity*.

to his association with these men. In the winter of 1879, Lecky "dragged me to a meeting of the Zetetical Society." [72] This was a junior copy of the famous Dialectical Society founded to discuss Mill's essay *On Liberty*. The members—women were admitted on equal terms with men—freely discussed politics, religion, and sex. The Zetetical was completely dedicated to the worship of Mill, Malthus, Darwin, Spencer, and Ingersoll; its tone was atheistic and revolutionary.

It was at this first meeting of the Zetetical that Shaw, feeling that he had made a fool of himself when he joined in a discussion, resolved he would become an effective public speaker or "perish in the attempt." He "persevered doggedly," frequented all the meetings in London where debates followed lectures, spoke in the streets and in the parks. "I infested public meetings like an officer afflicted with cowardice, who takes every opportunity of going under fire to get over it and learn his business." [73] As Winsten remarks, he was now "ready to enter his University, the street corner." [74]

His skill as a speaker was not acquired by practice alone, "for practice only cured my nervousness, and accustomed me to speak to multitudes as well as to private persons." [75] Richard Deck, "a superannuated Alsatian basso profundo opera singer," taught Shaw how to articulate and emphasize his consonants for public delivery. "He taught me that to be intelligible in public the speaker must relearn the alphabet with every consonant separately and explosively articulated, and foreign vowels distinguished from British diphthongs." In accordance with Deck's teaching he practiced the alphabet as a singer practices scales. Lessons in elocution, Shaw advised, should

[72] *Self Sketches,* p. 93.
[73] *Ibid.,* p. 96. See also *What's What,* p. 226: "My own education has been gained from discussion."
[74] "Introduction," *G.B.S. 90.*   [75] *Self Sketches,* p. 104.

always be taken by public speakers. "But art must conceal its artificiality." In a letter to Henderson he once wrote:

I believe my career as a public speaker was also an important part of my training. There was a period of twelve years during which I delivered three harangues every fortnight, many of them in the open air, at the street corners and before audiences of all sorts, from university dons and British Association Committees to demonstrations of London washerwomen, always followed by questions and discussion.[76]

There were literary evenings in University College with such groups as F. J. Furnivall's New Shakespeare Society and his Browning Society, which was "reputedly an assembly of long-haired esthetes but really a conventicle where evangelistic ladies discussed their religion." [77] When Furnivall founded a Shelley Society, Shaw joined that too and promptly proclaimed himself "like Shelley, a Socialist, Atheist, and Vegetarian." He also joined a debating society called the Bedford, founded by Stopford Brooke. One night at a public meeting at the Non-conformist Hall in 1884, Shaw heard Henry George, the author of *Progress and Poverty.* "He struck me dumb and shunted me from barren agnostic controversy to economics."

It flashed on me then for the first time that the conflict between Religion and Science . . . the overthrow of the Bible, the higher education of women, Mill on Liberty, and all the rest of the storm that raged round Darwin, Tyndall, Huxley, Spencer, and the rest, on which I had brought myself up intellectually was a mere middle-class business. . . . The importance of the economic basis dawned on me.[78]

He immediately bought a copy of *Progress and Poverty* and joined a Georgite society called the Land Reform Union.

[76] *Playboy and Prophet,* p. 7. [77] *Self Sketches,* p. 96.
[78] Quoted in Henderson, *His Life and Works,* p. 96.

When Shaw went to a meeting of Hyndman's Social Democratic Federation, prepared to defend George, he was "contemptuously dismissed as a novice who had not read the great
first volume of Marx's Capital." [79] Shaw promptly went to the
British Museum, his daily resort, and read Marx in Deville's
French translation. He returned to Hyndman's disciples to an-
nounce his complete conversion by it. "Immediately contempt
changed to awe for they had not read the book themselves, it
being then accessible only in Deville's French version. . . .
From that hour I was a speaker with a gospel, no longer an
apprentice trying to master the art of public speaking."

Although he applied for membership in the Social Democratic Federation, he withdrew his application on hearing of
the newly born Fabian Society in which he recognized "a more
appropriate milieu as a body of educated middleclass intelligentsia: my own class in fact." Shaw's observation with respect
to the Fabian Society and his own education is interesting: "I
joined the Fabian Society and so provided myself with abler
colleagues who filled up the gaps left in my culture by my
exclusively aesthetic education, which nevertheless qualified
me to impose on them histrionically as a capable platform
leader and literary spokesman." [80]

These able colleagues "knocked much nonsense, ignorance,
and vulgar provinciality out of me; for we were on quite ruthless critical terms with one another." [81] One of them was Sidney Webb whom he had first met at the Zetetical Society. Webb
was "greatly my superior in political knowledge, administrative
experience, and that miraculous power of quick assimilation
and unfailingly memorized mind storage . . . in which I was
and am wretchedly deficient." [82] Shaw believed that the wisest

[79] *Self Sketches*, p. 97.   [80] *What's What*, p. 261.
[81] *Self Sketches*, p. 111.   [82] *What's What*, p. 261.

thing he ever did was to force his friendship on Webb—and to keep the relationship.

In his autobiographical essays Shaw frequently cites "fruitful friendships" [83] which contributed to his growth. Besides Webb at this time, there was James Leigh Joynes, an Eton master who was a vegetarian, a humanitarian, and a Shelleyan. He lost his Eton post because he had toured Ireland with Henry George. There was Henry Salt, who was married to Joynes' sister and who was also dedicated to Shelley, vegetarianism, and humanitarianism. An Eton house master, Salt eventually "shook the dust of Eton from his feet," went to live in a laborer's cottage, and founded a Humanitarian League. Salt published several monographs on Shelley, De Quincey, and Thompson, a translation of Virgil, and an autobiography entitled *Seventy Years Among Savages*. Intimate in the Salt home, which Shaw frequently visited, was Edward Carpenter whom they called the "Noble Savage," and who fed more on Whitman and Thoreau than on George or Marx. Through his association with this coterie, it is not difficult to understand the origin and growth of Shaw's humanitarian and vegetarian principles.

At the Land Reform Union in the eighties he had also met Sydney Olivier who later became a peer. Shaw has described him in a contribution to his biography. "He . . . and Sidney Webb had passed into the upper division of the Civil Service, Olivier heading the competition list, apparently so easily that I never heard either of them speak of it, though to me it was a wonder, as the passing of even an elementary school examination has always been for me an impossible feat." [84] In a letter

[83] *Self Sketches,* pp. 107–12.
[84] "Some Impressions," in Sydney Olivier, *Letters and Selected Writings.*

to Henderson in 1931, Olivier commented on Shaw's education
during this early Fabian period.

> Webb and I were university graduates, I from Oxford, and we often
> judged Shaw's education and his appreciation of academically and
> socially established humanities to be sadly defective. . . . On the
> face of his conversation I thought his apprehension and sympathies
> in regard to a good deal of the springs of human conduct perversely
> shallow and limited, and his controversial arguments often cheap
> and uncritical . . . But two things impressed me to a contrary
> estimation of his critical make-up: the extraordinary ability and
> acuteness, within their scope, of his early novels and his under-
> standing and extensive knowledge of music.[85]

Olivier was a friend of Graham Wallas, who also joined the
Fabians. "For some years the leaders in the Politbureau or
Thinking Cabinet of the Fabian policy were Webb, Olivier,
Wallas, Shaw, and the Tory Democrat Hubert Bland." [86] These
colleagues, Shaw comments, stimulated his own literary performance. "Thus the reputedly brilliant extraordinary Shaw
was in fact brilliant and extraordinary because he had in the
Fabian Politbureau an incomparable threshing machine for
his ideas." These were the "friendships that went to the making
of G.B.S. the brilliant."

In his earlier biography of Shaw, Archibald Henderson
quotes Shaw as saying that the economic training at these
societies, particularly The Economic Club "to which university
professors like Edgeworth and Foxwell stuck to us pretty constantly," [87] corresponded to the highest form of university
instruction. Rattray writes that a group of the most scholarly
Fabians, formed for the study of Marx and Proudhon, constituted itself into a class in which each student took his turn at
being professor.[88] Called the "Hampstead Historic," the group

---

[85] *Playboy and Prophet*, p. 145.   [86] *Self Sketches*, p. 111.
[87] *His Life and Works*, p. 158.
[88] *Bernard Shaw: A Chronicle*, p. 51.

met in private houses, and finally in the Hampstead Public Library.

Two other fruitful friendships which contributed to Shaw's growth should be mentioned—those of William Morris and William Archer. Shaw had a great admiration for Morris and shared his fundamental conception of socialism, and of art as work-pleasure. Although there were doctrinal differences between them, they appreciated each other. Shaw once said: "No man was more liberal in his attempts to improve Morris's mind than I was; but I always found that, in so far as I was not making a most horrible idiot of myself out of misknowledge (I could forgive myself for pure ignorance), he could afford to listen to me with the patience of a man who had taught my teachers." [89]

What Morris taught me was in the main technical—printing for example. And I soon came to realize that his most characteristic trait was integrity in the artistic sense. By watching Morris, I first learned that Ruskin wasn't strong as a critic of works of art . . . I learned a great deal from Morris because Morris and I worked together in Socialism.[90]

In 1885 William Archer found Shaw in the British Museum, poring over Deville's French version of Marx and the orchestral score of *Tristan and Isolde*. Archer got him a job as book reviewer with the *Pall Mall Gazette* and later the appointment of art critic to *The World*. "Archer, a Scot with family connexions which brought him a knowledge of the Norwegian language, was deeply under the spell of Ibsen; and he communicated the magic to me verbally. This and our anti-clerical views made a strong bond between us." [91] Some time later when Archer pro-

[89] *Dramatic Opinions and Essays*, II, 70.

[90] Quoted in Henderson, *His Life and Works*, p. 211. See also *William Morris As I Knew Him*.

[91] *Self Sketches*, p. 66.

posed collaboration in a drama he had planned along the technical lines of the "well made" plays of Scribe and the French School, Shaw produced "two acts so defiant of these lines . . . that he cried off." Thus began the career of Shaw the dramatist. With no aid to speak of from schools, and with only some from people, Shaw taught himself how to write, read music, play the piano, and speak in public. In London he acquired a broad knowledge of politics, economics, art, literature, and music. Shaw learned to think, write, and speak in an atmosphere of passionate controversy. Perhaps it would be oversimplification to say art and controversy were the great and direct educators in his life, but he was, as his critical and polemical work testify, very much aware of the potent influences of great works of art, and of the intellectual open-mindedness which may be developed by controversial discussion.

Art and controversy are virtually inseparable for Shaw; he had a vast contempt for people who experienced art from books rather than from real life. Of Wilde he once said: "We did not refer to Art, about which, excluding literature from the definition, he knew only what could be picked up by reading about it." [92] And in a letter to Archibald Henderson: ". . . I have lived instead of dreaming and feeding myself with artistic confectionery. With a little more courage and a little more energy I could have done much more; and I lacked these because in my boyhood I lived on my imagination instead of my work." [93] The program he formulated for the education of children is geared in such a way as to enable a child to live in a real rather than in an artificial world.

His contempt for the academic mind derived partly from these bitter experiences with teachers and schools, and partly

[92] Quoted in Harris, *Oscar Wilde, His Life and Confessions,* p. 390.
[93] *Playboy and Prophet,* p. 7.

from his conclusions as a socialist, concerning the limitations of a capitalist society. His frequent vilifications of teachers as monsters and schools as prisons amount to a total condemnation of education in the usual sense. Some commentators seem to think he got most of his ideas out of Dickens, Squeers being the stereotype of a teacher in his mind.[94] This contention must be dismissed as literary guesswork, for Shaw has written quite realistically about teachers and schools. In "Biographers' Blunders Corrected" (*Self Sketches*) he points out that H. C. Duffin in his *The Quintessence of Bernard Shaw* (1939) is mistaken about his being unteachable.

You say I was an unschoolable boy at a bad school. But what is an unschoolable boy? I was greedy for knowledge, and interested in everything . . . I was probably the most teachable boy in Ireland; and if school taught me nothing except that school is a prison and not a place of teaching, the conclusion is that pedagogy is not yet a science.

A similar condemnation of our teachers and schools could be written today. His attacks on doctors and statesmen only lead him to demand better doctors and better statesmen; and his attacks on teachers and schools end in demanding better teachers and better schools. His fundamental belief that the infinite perfectibility of children could be realized under a superior social scheme provoked these assaults on the methods and values of teachers and schools under capitalism.

[94] See Irvine, *The Universe of G.B.S.*, p. 279.

3 The art of polemics and the polemics of art

To UNDERSTAND the nature of Shaw's thundering about education as it exists, it is essential to grasp not only his socialism and evolution but the methods he employs as a specialized kind of artist-philosopher and polemicist. Many of his statements about politics, morals, science, education—in fact about almost every phase of modern life—are slanted for a purpose. Eric Bentley aptly puts it: "What he says is always determined by the thought: what can I do to this audience? not by the thought: what is the most objective statement about this subject?" [1] If the Shavian theater was designed to make people think, so were the techniques of overstatement and exaggeration. Conducting a moral, political, and philosophic campaign as a passionate reformer, Shaw adopted a strategy that was meant to jolt or shock people into seeing the urgent need of something or other. For example, when Shaw quotes William Morris to the effect that parents are the worst people to be put in charge of children, he admits that Morris was "overstating his case," and then adds: "It is always necessary to

[1] *Bernard Shaw*, p. 24.

overstate a case startlingly to make people sit up and listen to it, and to frighten them into acting on it. I do this myself habitually and deliberately." [2] With reference to Henry Salt's autobiography *Seventy Years Among Savages,* Shaw remarked: "Of course this was an overstatement, as all statements must be if they are to receive attention." [3] Well known are his quips about democracy, Shakespeare, carnivorousness, the General Medical Council, or about himself. Concerning the famous G.B.S., who was always uttering the most outrageous perversities, Shaw once said: "In order to gain a hearing it was necessary for me to attain the footing of a privileged lunatic with the license of a jester. My method is to take the utmost trouble to find the right thing to say and then say it with the utmost levity." [4] Perhaps Keegan's "Every jest is an earnest in the womb of time" (*John Bull's Other Island*) meant that the real joke was that he, Shaw himself, was in earnest. For it was all deliberately planned strategy to educate us—that is, to change our minds, save our stereotyped souls, and reshape society according to the Shavian image.

The rhetorical techniques of exaggeration, epigram,[5] and paradox abound in Shaw's writings about education. Probably the most famous quip is the one about teachers in "The Revolutionist's Handbook" appended to *Man and Superman:* "He who can, does. He who cannot, teaches." Actually it is not Shaw but John Tanner who is the author. Widely quoted, particularly by teachers who despise teaching, this epigrammatic half-truth does not reflect Shaw's real sentiments about teachers, for he

[2] *Everybody's Political What's What,* p. 49.
[3] *Ibid.,* p. 175.
[4] Clarence Rook, "George Bernard Shaw," *The Chap-Book,* V (November 1, 1896), 539.
[5] See Irvine, *The Universe of G.B.S.,* p. 106: "Shavian epigram is in one sense but the rhetorical form of Shavian permeation."

did respect them and he did understand how important they are in a growing society. This overstatement (assuming it to be Shaw's for the moment and not Tanner's) is primarily designed to shock us into doing a little thinking about teachers and education in general. A glance at "The Revolutionist's Handbook" under the title "Education" will reveal numerous such examples, as will many of the plays. When Shaw states that "honest education is dangerous to tyranny and privilege" [6] and that "nobody knows the way a child should go. All the ways discovered so far lead to the horrors of our existing civilizations" [7] and that "the educated man is a greater nuisance than the uneducated one," [8] he is trying to stir us into thinking about a part of the truth which has largely been ignored. Fugitive pieces written for magazine and press reveal even more jolting statements such as: "Civilization is dying of what it calls education. . . . [9] Great communities are built by men who sign with a mark: they are wrecked by men who write Latin verses." [10] This is simply Shaw's way of calling attention to the inadequacies of the traditional classical curriculum and of educational methods or ideals. Practically all of Shaw's shock-statements connote political, social, philosophic, religious, or educational ideals which he wants people to believe in and act upon.

He was a master of the art of polemics not only for such ideals as he may have had in mind, but also for certain methods of thinking about them, particularly in the areas of art, science, and religion. He frequently stated in one way or another that "by profession I am what is called an original thinker, my business being to question and test all the established creeds and codes to see how far they are still valid and

---

[6] *What's What*, p. 169.
[8] Preface to *Back to Methuselah*.
[10] *Ibid.*, p. 342.

[7] Preface to *Misalliance*.
[9] *Doctors' Delusions*, p. 337.

how far worn out or superseded, and even to draft new creeds and codes." [11] Assuming this was Shaw's role, one may rightly ask what Shaw meant by the word "test." Did he at all adhere to what is called scientific method? Did he put a premium on intuition or reasoning, or on both sides in the Aristotelian sense? If Shaw's concepts about the nature of the individual and his growth, about the educative process, and about the meaning of life are to be grasped, it is essential to understand his polemical devices and their implications, and his methods as an avowed artist-philosopher.

Although Shaw did not deny the value of reason, he believed that it may sometimes "lead to grave error when intuitive wisdom jumps instantly to the right conclusion." And he adds:

Intellect can blunder disastrously; but so can intuition when it is ignorant. Neither of them can reach sound conclusions without authentic facts; and if the known facts are too few, or, being imaginary, are not facts at all, the inferences and guesses will be alike unsound. [12]

And even facts may provoke "vindictive resentments, sentimental leniences, hopes and fears, prejudices and cupidities" that sweep away every vestige of reason. What Shaw calls "evolutionary guessing" takes precedence over rational inference, since the "desire for the effect sometimes in defiance of all reason and prudence, is itself the cause, and we escape from the Determinist dungeon of Giant Despair to the path that leads to the Celestial City." [13] In repudiating Darwinism and accepting Lamarckian purpose in the universe, Shaw compared himself to Goethe, who jumped over the facts to the conclusions. In the mind of a great man there can take place "so rapid and intuitive an integration of the [logical] processes

<hr>

[11] *The Intelligent Woman's Guide*, p. 336.
[12] *What's What*, p. 271.   [13] *Ibid.*, p. 321.

62   *Polemics and art*

. . . that we get the inspired guess of the man of genius." [14]
Shaw to some extent like Aristotle and Einstein believed that
there is no essential contradiction between scientific method
and evolutionary or intuitive guessing; these, he held, must be
based on knowledge.

Despite Shaw's many attacks on modern science, he thought
that "art, science, and religion are really identical in their foundations." [15] In the Preface to *Back to Methuselah* he emphasized that, although his "own Irish eighteenth-centuryism made
it impossible for me to believe anything until I could conceive
it as a scientific hypothesis," he was compelled, in view of the
"impostures, venalities, credulities, and delusions of the camp
followers of science . . . all sedulously inculcated by modern
secondary education," to make a verbal distinction between
science and knowledge for fear of misleading his readers. Presumably, this distinction involved whatever differences there
were between Darwinism, which abolished mind and purpose
in the universe, and Creative Evolution, which recognized such
ends. Not a Baconian, science meant nothing to him except as
an ally of philosophy or a special brand of mysticism. He mistrusted laboratory methods, believing that too frequently "evidence is manufactured . . . or remanufactured until it proves
what the laboratory controller wants to prove." [16] As Pearson
remarks: "The truth was that the scientists were not scientific
enough for Shaw." [17] Eric Bentley has pointed out that Shaw
frequently uses the word "science" just as he uses the word
"democracy" in almost opposite senses.[18] To understand Shaw's
"religion is always right and science always wrong," [19] one must

[14] Preface to *Misalliance*.   [15] *What's What*, p. 188.
[16] *Ibid.*, p. 190.   [17] *G.B.S.: A Full Length Portrait*, p. 231.
[18] *Bernard Shaw*, p. 72. See also p. 48 where the author states Shaw's
thinking is anti-rationalistic, but not anti-scientific.
[19] *What's What*, p. 295.

see that religion, which he identifies with his doctrine of Creative Evolution, is not orthodox in the traditional sense, but rather a mystical concept that lies beyond the bounds of empirical proof. If religion represents the ideals people live by, then it is certainly more important than the mere facts science provides. In the light of this, the following overstatement by Shaw can perhaps be better understood:

"Modern" education differs from Dr. Johnson's education only in substituting Jenner and Pasteur for Plato and Euripides as academic idols, and replacing the recognition of a purpose in the world, and the investigation of that purpose, by a conception of the universe as the accidental result of a senseless raging of mechanical forces, and by a boundless credulity, not outdone in dirt, cruelty, and stupidity, by any known savage tribe.[20]

Shaw's attacks on modern science involve no repudiation of logic and intellect (glorified in a number of plays) as guides to ethical conduct and as a means of educating people.

In the "Epistle Dedicatory" to *Man and Superman* Shaw declares that such artist-philosophers as Bunyan, Blake, Goethe, Shelley, Schopenhauer, Wagner, Tolstoy, and Nietzsche are "the only sort of artists I take quite seriously." Dickens and Shakespeare are eliminated because "their pregnant observations and demonstrations of life are not coordinated into any philosophy or religion." What Shaw sought in art and philosophy was inspiration toward better conduct; therefore, he called Dickens and Shakespeare irreligious and anarchical since they are concerned "with the diversities of the world instead of with its unities." Shaw expressed contempt for bellettrists who uphold art for art's sake. "For art's sake alone I would not face the toil of writing a single sentence." Art must be essentially didactic, Shaw insisted, for art is the great

[20] *Doctors' Delusions,* p. 339.

teacher; and the artist-philosopher produces the highest kind
of art because he identifies himself with purpose in the world
and seeks to create better human beings. Comparing the artist-
philosopher's workshop to that of the scientist, Shaw states:

The artist's workshop is the whole universe as far as he can comprehend it; and he can neither contrive nor dictate what happens there:
he can only observe and interpret events that are beyond his control. A laboratory may be a fool's paradise or a pessimistic inferno.
. . . Its door may be shut against metaphysics, including consciousness, purpose, mind, evolution, creation, choice (free will). . . .
In short science may reduce itself to absurdity in the name of science with a large S. Fine art is allowed no such license.[21]

Yet he warned that just as science can be put to evil purposes so can fine art, which "is equally subject to his [the artist's] prejudices, his ignorances, his blunders, and much more
to his corruption by the public taste." In this sense, Shaw admits that the medium of art is as contrived and controlled by
the artist as the laboratory experiment by the scientist. "Idolatry of artists is as dangerous as idolatry of scientists." This concept enters into Shaw's program for art education in the
schools.

[21] *What's What*, p. 190.

4   *Human nature and human progress*

THE INTELLIGENT WOMAN'S GUIDE contains a forthright accusation that "capitalist mankind in the lump is detestable." [1] Shaw hates the poor and pities the rich, looking
forward, as he had done in his contribution to *Fabian Essays*
forty years earlier, to the extermination of both groups. Taking
great pains to deny that he is a misanthrope, Shaw insists that
"there is nothing that can be changed more completely than
human nature when the job is taken in hand early enough." [2]
If a civilized state is the aim, then humans are not "to be picked
up in the slums: they have to be cultivated very carefully
and expensively." The goal of society should be that of increasing the percentage of individuals who are carefully bred
and nurtured, "even to finally making the most of every man
and woman born." [3] To those who maintain that human nature

[1] *The Intelligent Woman's Guide*, p. 456. See also p. 459: "We can
despair of Democracy and of Capitalism without despairing of human
nature."
[2] Preface to *On the Rocks.*
[3] "Notes to Caesar and Cleopatra," *Three Plays for Puritans.* See *The
Perfect Wagnerite*, p. 68: "No serious progress will be made until we
address ourselves earnestly and scientifically to the task of producing
trustworthy human material for society." See also "The Revolutionist's
Handbook," *Man and Superman*, p. 241: "Civilization is a disease produced by the practice of building society with rotten material."

cannot be changed, Shaw replies: "Not only are they changeable, but if left alone they change themselves so much faster
than we change our minds that our haphazard governments
are never able to keep our institutions up to date. The most
staggering of our failures to change our institutions synchron-
ically with the changes in the social and natural facts is our
school system." [4] That we must finally adapt our institutions
to human nature is a basic contention. In the Preface to *Getting Married* he said: "In the long run our present plan of trying to force human nature into a mould of existing abuses,
superstitions, and corrupt interests, produces the explosive
forces that wreck civilization."

To those who insist that human nature has improved in the
last few centuries, Shaw replies that there has not been any
real moral progress in the last few thousand years, for "all the
savagery, barbarism . . . of which we have any record as
existing in the past exists at the present moment." [5] "The Revolutionist's Handbook" relentlessly enumerates the primitivisms
of modern man. The modern European who invaded Africa "in
search of ivory, gold, diamonds, and sport . . . is the same
beast of prey that formerly marched to the conquest of new
worlds under Alexander and Pizarro." "Flogging is still an institution in the public school, in the military prison, on the training ship, and in that school of littleness called the home." Many
illustrations of man's beastliness are cited, and Shaw (or Tanner) concludes that "unless we are replaced by a more highly
evolved animal—in short, by the Superman—the world must
remain a den of dangerous animals among whom our few accidental supermen, our Shakespeares, Goethes, Shelleys and
their like, must live as precariously as lion tamers do."

[4] *Everybody's Political What's What,* p. 146.
[5] "Notes to Caesar and Cleopatra," *Three Plays for Puritans.*

Shaw builds up the thesis that there is always in any civilization an illusion of progress, particularly moral progress. If the poor man is given a vote, if laws are passed to mitigate sweating, if schooling is made free and compulsory, if public steps are taken to house people decently—all this, even though some changes are gains, produces "an illusion of bustling progress; and the reading class infers from them that the abuses of the early Victorian period no longer exist except as amusing pages in the novels of Dickens." Whatever changes are made are mostly "changes that money makes," and the moment one looks for reforms due to a fundamental change in human nature "we are disillusioned." In effect, man as he exists is incapable of real moral change, for he "will return to his idols and his cupidities, in spite of all 'movements,' and all revolutions until his nature is changed."

As a socialist and as an educator, Shaw argued that "even a child must be taught . . . that men must reform society before they can reform themselves." [6] The difficulty was that unless man was changed he would refuse to change society. In a desperate attempt to solve this dilemma, Shaw clutched at the idea of the eugenic breeding of Supermen. "The only fundamental and possible Socialism," Shaw-Tanner declares in "The Revolutionist's Handbook," "is the socialization of the selective breeding of Man: in other terms of human evolution." And in the "Epistle Dedicatory" to A. B. Walkley in *Man and Superman,* to which the "Handbook" is appended, he expresses complete disillusionment with the processes of education as a means of bettering human nature.

I do not know whether you have any illusions left on the subject of education, progress, and so forth. I have none. . . . My nurse

[6] Preface to Workers' Educational Association *Year Book* for 1918 in *Doctors' Delusions.*

was fond of remarking that you cannot make a silk purse out of a sow's ear; and the more I see of the efforts of our churches and universities and literary sages to raise the mass above its own level, the more convinced I am that my nurse was right. Progress can do nothing but make the most of us as we are, and that most would clearly not be enough.

This desperate recourse to eugenic breeding was not exactly a practical proposal; perhaps it was a way of shocking people into realizing the need for superior people. One does not find anything about eugenic breeding in Shaw's later work—it is but one of a number of ideas to improve mankind. For example, the idea of longevity, the increase of our span of life to 300 years, is explored in *Back to Methuselah*. Although the concept of Superman is a constantly recurring theme in Shaw's works, and seems to many bound up with his tenative proposals for selective breeding, it does have a different place and purpose in Shaw's ideas about growth.

Like Shelley and Shakespeare, Mill and Owen, Shaw thinks little of human nature as it exists, but has great hopes for what it may become.

Robert Owen made desperate efforts to convince England that her criminals, her drunkards, her ignorant and stupid masses, were the victims of circumstance: that if we would only establish his new moral world we should find that the masses born into an educated and moralized community would be themselves moralized and educated.[7]

That circumstances do not govern character is an assumption that Shaw attacks in the Preface to *Back to Methuselah*. The artist-philosopher in Shaw prompts him to dispose of the problem of inadequate humans by simply saying that all habits are acquired, thus ridding himself of the Darwinist muddle of

[7] Preface to *Back to Methuselah*.

inherited and acquired characteristics.[8] In the later Preface to *The Simpleton of the Unexpected Isles,* Shaw approves of Livingston, who did not say to the savages: "There is between me and thee a gulf that nothing can fill: He proposed to fill it by instructing the tribesman on the assumption that the tribesman was as capable mentally as himself, but ignorant." And Shaw adds that his main reason for writing prefaces is based on the same premise. What is wrong with the average person, as with Livingston's tribesmen, is that he is largely ignorant "of facts, creating a vacuum into which all sorts of romantic antiquarian junk and cast-off primitive religion rushes." [9] Thus, what the average person needs is adequate instruction in a civilized community which would be more likely to produce civilized individuals. Evil tendencies in man, Shaw believed, are encouraged only because the state and its schools are not sufficiently concerned with man as he might become. Human nature, being largely the product of existing social, political, economic, and moral institutions, can be molded in many desirable directions provided there is an adequate social and educational philosophy. Despite his disillusionment with education at the time he wrote *Man and Superman,* Shaw continued to pin his faith on a regenerated society and more effective processes of education.

The scope of human possibility, hope, and attainment is endless for Shaw. The fact that "apparent freaks called Great Men" have existed—Shaw cites among others Mozart, Descartes, Kant, Butler, Bergson, Wagner, Marx, Ruskin, and Morris—seems to prove "that though we in the mass are only child Yahoos it is possible for creatures built exactly like us, bred from our unions and developed from our seeds, to reach the heights of these towering heads." Yet he reminds us re-

[8] *What's What,* p. 189.   [9] Preface to *Geneva.*

peatedly that since evolution is still creative, "man may have
to be scrapped and replaced by some new and higher creation, just as man himself was created to supply the deficiencies
of the lower animals." [10]

Similar concepts about the potential in human nature
emerge in some of the plays. While the "Epistle Dedicatory"
is sceptical about education as a means of transforming man,
the dream-sequence in the play dramatizes what ought to be
the future development of man. Even the Devil, who is in
conflict with Juan about the essential nature of man, asserts
that "in the arts of life man invents nothing; but in the arts
of death he outdoes Nature herself." He goes on to tell the
story of the bricklayer's wife with seven children who spent
the seventeen pounds club money on her husband's funeral
"and went into the workhouse with the children the next day.
She would not have spent sevenpence on her children's schooling . . . but on death she spent all she had." The Devil's
cynicism is countered by Juan's expression of faith in man's
potential. "You take man at his own valuation," Juan tells
him. Properly enlightened, "men will die for human perfection," Juan argues as he presents the case for the philosophic
man of the future.

In *Back to Methuselah* (1921) and *The Simpleton of the
Unexpected Isles* (1934), prophetic plays dealing with the
future of human life, scenes are found that dramatize the
"ought" and "is" with regard to the education of the individual. In *As Far as Thought Can Reach*, the last play of the
Metabiological Pentateuch, Pygmalion has discovered the secret of the "high potential life-force" and has succeeded in
creating two human beings. Unfortunately they turn out to be
creatures who are at the mercy of their reflexes, mere autom-

[10] *Sixteen Self Sketches*, p. 186.

ata or specimens of twentieth-century man. Pygmalion explains to the assembled group: "You can provoke them to tell any silly lie. . . . Give them a clip in their appetites or vanities or any of their lusts and greeds, and they will boast and lie, and affirm and deny, and hate and love without the slightest regard for the facts that are staring them in the face." Finally, in a temper the female figure bites Pygmalion and he dies. Significant are the words of the female as both are led away to be executed: "Is it my fault if I was not made properly?"

A parallel theme is communicated in the later *The Simpleton.* Four children are the result of a eugenic experiment in miscegenation, a union of the East and West involving four British subjects and the oriental priest and priestess, Pra and Prola. At one point when the children, symbols [11] of Love, Pride, Heroism, and Empire, have finished uttering all sorts of platitudes, their group parents discuss their education:

PRA. We have taught them everything except common sense.
LADY FARWATERS. We have taught them everything except how to work for their daily bread instead of praying for it.
PROLA. It is dangerous to educate fools.
PRA. It is still more dangerous to leave them uneducated.
MRS. HYERING. There just shouldnt be any fools. They werent born fools. We made fools of them.
PRA. We must stop making fools.

To Pra's prophecy that "the coming race will not be like them," Prola expresses a poetic faith in the potential of all children, of all human beings:

I tell you this is a world of miracles, not of jigsaw puzzles. For me every day must have its miracles, and no child be born like any

[11] See the Preface to this play: "I have introduced it [group marriage] only to bring into the story the four lovely phantasms who embody all the artistic, romantic, and military ideals of our cultured suburbs."

child that ever was born before. And to witness this miracle of the
children I will abide the uttermost evil and carry through it the
seed of the uttermost good.

The play ends with Pra and Prola expressing an abiding faith
in "the life to come."

Shaw maintained that people are not born either good or
bad; every individual is a bundle of potentialities—unique
potentialities—but all are primarily dependent upon the social and cultural environment for development. The criterion
of progress is not the advance of science which gives us ma-
terialistic comforts and conveniences, but the growth of the
spirit of man, the development of his nobler faculties. Consequently he saw no progress to speak of in the last few thousand years. Convinced of the bankruptcy of education as it
exists today, he denied that the essentially plastic nature of
the individual can be developed by its processes.

5   Education and the state

That education in a capitalist society is primarily designed to preserve an undesirable social, political, and economic status quo—in short "to keep us willing slaves instead of rebellious ones" [1] is an assumption upon which Shaw built a superstructure of denunciation of education as it exists. The investigation of such an assumption demands a discussion of his ideas about democracy, socialism, fascism, and communism in relation to education. Moreover, Shaw's ideas about these "isms" frequently overlap and confuse: capitalist democracy is distinguished from democracy or "genuine democracy," and the latter may suddenly become synonymous with socialism or communism—a complex of semantic confusions which must be resolved if Shaw's educational program is to be understood. Since the relation between the state and education is a crucial one in any society, it is important to determine whether the school in Shaw's state could have any degree of autonomy in order to fulfill its purpose; whether the schools and teachers could become uncritical instruments of state policy; and whether an all-powerful state, even though subscribing to so-called desirable ends,

[1] *The Intelligent Woman*, p. 64.

could be reconciled with individual freedom of action in the
spheres of culture and thought—a problem central to our
present society.

Shaw defined capitalism as "the system by which the wealth
of the country is in the hands, not of the nation, but of private
persons called landlords or financiers or industrialists." [2] This
system produces an enormous inequality of income, cheapens
labor as the population increases, and brings with it an "ap-
palling spread of discontent, misery, crime, disease." The
private ownership of property must lead to commercial competition and overproduction, followed by an ever recurring
cycle of crises, depressions, and recoveries. [3] The main motive in commerce becomes the accumulation of "the biggest
profit regardless of the ruin of rival profiteers or the starvation of the proletariat." And Shaw quotes Bunyan's "What is
this but trading without conscience?" [4] The institution of inherited wealth has lead to a "misdistribution of national income so outrageous . . . that babies are millionaires and
workers worn out by a lifetime of toil." [5]

Shaw denounced the argument that this system "must be
faced because human nature is so essentially selfish, so in-
accessible to any motive except pecuniary gain that no other
practicable way of building up a great modern civilization is
open to us." [6] The final aim in life for most people, Shaw
charged, is to become a member of the leisure classes, living
on the labor of others and enabling their children to do the
same. The tragedy is that a nation urgently needing better
housing, clothing, and education expends its labor on "fancy
goods (mostly entirely unnecessary rubbish) . . . for the
parasites." [7]

[2] *Ibid.*, p. 100.   [3] *Everybody's Political What's What*, p. 142.
[4] *Ibid.*, p. 168.   [5] *Ibid.*, p. 100.
[6] *Intelligent Woman*, p. 101.   [7] *What's What*, p. 100.

In the essay, "The Impossibilities of Anarchism," there is a violent diatribe against capitalist society. Admitting that the anarchist analysis is correct, Shaw sees modern society as conspiracy and hypocrisy:

I fully admit and vehemently urge that the State is at present a huge machine for robbing and slave-driving the poor by brute force. You may, if you are a stupid or comfortably off person, think that the policeman . . . is the guardian of law and order. . . . But the primary function of the policeman is to see that you do not lie down to sleep in this country without paying an idler for the privilege; that you do not taste bread until you have paid the idler's toll. . . . Attempt any of these things and you will be haled off and tortured in the name of law and order, honesty, social equilibrium, safety of property and person, public duty, Christianity, morality, and what not, as a vagrant, a thief and a rioter. . . . Members of Parliament, whose sole qualifications for election were 1000 pounds loose cash, an independent income, and a vulgar strain of ambition; parsons quoting scripture for the purpose of the squire; lawyers selling their services to the highest bidder at the bar, and maintaining the supremacy of the money class on the bench. . . . University professors elaborating the process known as the education of a gentleman; artists striving to tickle the fancy or flatter the vanity of the aristocrat or plutocrat; workmen doing their work as badly and slowly as they dare so as to make the most of their job; employers starving and overworking their hands and adulterating their goods as much as they dare: these are the actual living material of those imposing abstractions known as the State, the Church, the Law, the Constitution, Education, the Fine Arts, and Industry. . . . The ordinary man is insensible to the fraud just as he is insensible to the taste of water, which being constantly in contact with his mucous membrane, seems to have no taste at all.[8]

That these imposing abstractions are rarely penetrated by either the educated or the uneducated is a basic contention

[8] James Fuchs, editor, *The Socialism of Shaw*, pp. 140–41. Originally this essay was published in 1893 by the Fabian Society as *Fabian Tract, No. 45*.

in his two major social and political tracts, *The Intelligent Woman's Guide to Socialism and Capitalism* and *Everybody's Political What's What.* The result is, Shaw insists, that a superstructure of false beliefs and ideals is gradually built up in such a way as to permeate morals, religion, philosophy— in fact every phase of civilized life. Since the school cannot function independently of society and reflects mainly the philosophy of the world from which it draws its substance, Shaw arrives at the conclusion that education is primarily a means of perpetuating these false doctrines.

> There will inevitably spring up a body of biassed teaching and practice in medicine, law, religion, and government that will become established and standardized as scientifically, legally, religiously, constitutionally, and morally sound, taught as such to all young persons entering these professions, stamping those who dare dissent as outcast quacks, heretics, sedition mongers, and traitors.[9]

This corruption, Shaw argues, extends from the morality taught in the elementary schools to the "most abstruse and philosophic teaching in the universities." [10] The teaching of science "becomes a propaganda of quack cures, manufactured by companies in which the rich hold shares"; the teaching of political economy "becomes an impudent demonstration that without the idle rich we should perish for lack of capital and employment." Thus the poor are kept poor by their ignorance, and those who are well off enough "to receive what is called a complete education are taught so many flat lies that their false knowledge is more dangerous than the untutored natural wit of savages." Since capitalism cannot develop its possibilities "without genuine technical education, it must confine its obfuscation to the cultural side." [11]

[9] *Intelligent Woman*, p. 461.   [10] *Ibid.*, p. 63.
[11] *What's What*, p. 169. See also Preface to *Back to Methuselah:* "The

Shaw concluded that "honest government is impossible without honest schools, for honest schools are illegal under dishonest governments." [12] "Honest education" which he momentarily equates with "democratic education" is not only dangerous to tyranny and privilege but must inevitably lead to communism, "against which capitalism has to defend itself by systematic propagation of capitalist doctrine and vilification of communist teachers." Shaw's conclusion led him to draw a parallel between the capitalist system and the systems of Napoleon, Bismarck, the Kaiser, Mussolini, and Hitler, all of whom realized that the principles they stood for "must be inculcated in the schools as fundamental in education." Although Shaw admits that no system of government can exist unless the children are taught basic principles, he points out that "the definitions of flower and weed and vermin" are in the hands of the rulers.

Character, conduct, and mind-development are important to Shaw, not the accumulation of money. In the Preface to *The Millionairess* he tells us that unless we control those whose specific talents are for moneymaking, they will rule the world. The world's welfare depends on those higher intellectual operations by which no individual can make money. The Preface to *Major Barbara* contains a bitter indictment of the commercial millionaires who easily surpass in villainy "the worst that has even been imagined of the buccaneers of the Spanish Main." To Shaw, the meanest creature can become rich if he devotes his life to it, and profoundly educated people with

---

public schoolboy who is carefully blinded, duped, and corrupted as to the nature of a society based on profiteering" is carefully instructed in the use of weapons of destruction. "Instruction . . . is quite genuine: the instructors know their business, and really mean the learners to succeed."

[12] *What's What*, p. 169.

wider and more generous interests remain poor. The tragedy is that "the baser human currency drives out the nobler coinage." The method of controlling this baser currency involves genuine education in the nobler areas.

The play, *The Millionairess* (1935), dramatizes the views put forth in its Preface. Epifania has not been educated into discovering suitable outlets for her energies and abilities to direct, manage, and dominate. Consequently she accepts money as the symbol of power and pleasure. When the Egyptian doctor rebukes her for the ruthless way in which she "has preyed on the poverty of the poor" in the sweatshop, Epifania replies, "I have to take the world as I find it." The doctor raises the problem, treated fully in the Preface, as to why the most learned, the most useful people, die poor. "The wrath of Allah," he concludes, "shall overtake those who leave the world no better than they found it." The Preface helps the reader to understand more clearly the implications of the play, namely, that society and its educational facilities fail to provide more constructive activities for people with mind, energy, and a will to dominance.

Shaw saw capitalism, with its emphasis on discovering new markets, as a stimulus to modern international warfare. The Preface to *Heartbreak House* paints the cultural degeneration wrought by war. A kind of stoppage of civilization is realized in wartime since all pretenses about fine art and culture must be flung off as intolerable affectation, and the picture galleries and museums and schools are closed or occupied by war workers. The brutal "legal lawlessness" permeates civilization and corrupts human nature to such an extent that no amount of education for generations to come can redeem it. Shaw said that a society which thus kills many of its potential Platos and Shakespeares is headed for destruction. In 1918 he warned prophetically that the human tools by which conquerors become great men must be educated anew, for "another generation of secondary education at our ancient public schools and the cheaper institutions that ape them will be quite sufficient to keep the two [victor and vanquished] going until the next war." During World War II, Shaw declared that "war is not necessarily a culmination of human depravity: it is now a romantic superstition rooted in courage and generosity." [13] Through education, society must use these virtues for peace, not for war, because "in science, in politics, in exploration and research of all kinds there is now infinitely greater scope for the restless courage of the young . . . than in mere homicide and destruction."

Unlike capitalism, socialism insists that the first duty of the government is "to nationalize the means of production, distribution, and exchange" [14] so that the "nation's welfare" may become the predominant consideration. Comparing the state to the most efficient kind of insurance company which can "put the profit into the public treasury for the general good," [15] Shaw believed:

It is quite possible to organize society in such a manner as to enable every ablebodied and ableminded person to produce enough not only to pay their way but to repay the cost of twenty years education and training, making it a first-rate investment for the community, besides providing for the longest interval between disablement by old age and natural death.

Using the words socialism and communism synonymously, Shaw stated that "communism is a highly respectable way of sharing our wealth." [16] He was a socialist of the most extreme type in that, unlike Marx and other socialists, he de-

[13] *Ibid.*, p. 130.   [14] *Ibid.*, p. 250.
[15] *Ibid.*, p. 114.   [16] *Intelligent Woman*, p. 14.

manded absolute equality of income. Even a child is to inherit a fixed income from the state, and the state in turn must see that it is eventually earned. In this way, reasoned Shaw, socialism which "abhors poverty would abolish the poor, for a hearty dislike of poor people as such is the first qualification of a good Equalizer." [17] The basic income to be aimed at, Shaw writes in the Preface to *Farfetched Fables*, "must be sufficient to establish culture in every home." His assumption is that if there were true equality of income, all the work necessary to society could be more equally allotted and consequently done in half the time, thus "leaving the other half free for art and science and learning and playing and roaming and experimenting and recreation of all sorts." [18] Liberty means leisure for Shaw and socialism can produce the leisure without which there can be no culture. Again and again Shaw attacked the oligarchic argument that there is an advantage in providing society with a wealthy upper class able to cultivate themselves by an expensive education. As for the poor, Shaw suggested: "If a nation turns its rough mill hands into well-educated, well-dressed, well spoken . . . mill officials, properly respected and given a fair share of the wealth they produce, the nation is the stronger, the richer, the happier, and the holier for the change." [19]

Such a condition of economic equality would make it necessary to educate children to look at their country's affairs in a new way. They would be trained to understand the fundamentals of equality "just as under Capitalism children are educated to regard success in life as meaning more money than anyone else and no work to do for it." [20] Shaw saw no

[17] *Ibid.*, p. 95.　　　　[18] *Ibid.*, p. 39.
[19] *Ibid.*, p. 146.　　　　[20] *Ibid.*, p. 392.

future for a society whose citizens were not educated politically and economically to be socialists.

The alleged conflict between socialism and individualism,
Shaw maintained, is false and question-begging. "Socialism
is merely individualism rationalized, organized, clothed and
in its right mind." [21] Quite aware that an enormous extension
of state power carries with it a formidable extension of its
possible abuse, Shaw warns us to reject belief in any automatic earthly paradise and to understand that all systems,
particularly socialism, demand "eternal vigilance." Fundamentally, he denies that there can be any individual liberty without complete economic equality. But without law, there can
be no secure leisure. "The people who shout for freedom
without understanding its limitations, and call socialism . . .
slavery because it involves new laws as well as new liberties
are obstructive to the extension of leisure and liberty." [22] In
his essay on "Imprisonment" Shaw refuted Rousseau's dictum
that man is born free, maintaining that a civilized state must
regard its citizens as born in debt and that not until that debt
is paid in the form of social service to the community can any
freedom or leisure begin. [23]

Shaw, however, never succeeds in reconciling individual
liberty with the all-powerful socialist state he has in mind,
and this gap in his thinking had profound impact upon his
ideas about education. In much of his work during the thirties
he spoke glibly about euthanasia and liquidation of society's
incorrigibles. The Preface to *On the Rocks* proposes that
everyone be asked: "Are you pulling your weight in the so-

[21] Quoted in Henderson, *George Bernard Shaw: His Life and Works*,
p. 189.
[22] *Intelligent Woman*, p. 330.   [23] *Doctors' Delusions*, p. 219.

cial boat? are you giving more trouble than you are worth? have you earned the privilege of living in a civilized society?" Shaw's extremism is evident in his justification of the Russian Cheka whose purpose it was "to go into these questions and liquidate persons who could not answer them satisfactorily."

We need a greatly increased intolerance of socially injurious conduct and an uncompromising abandonment of punishments and its cruelties together with sufficient school inculcation of social responsibility to make every citizen conscious that if his life costs more than it is worth to the community, the community may painlessly extinguish it.

An "abandonment of punishments and its cruelties" obviously jars with the last words of this passage. While he later admits in the Preface to *The Simpleton of the Unexpected Isles* that the Russians may have gone to extremes in the emergencies following the revolution, Shaw here too justifies their demands that everyone be "public spirited enough to live in a Communist society." Shaw's reasoning runs like this:

A new social creed involves a new heresy. A new heresy involves an Inquisition. The precedents established by the Inquisition furnish the material for a new legal code. Codification enables the work of the Inquisition to be done by an ordinary court of law. Thereupon the Inquisition, as such, disappears precisely as the Tcheka disappeared.

The assumption that the inquisition disappeared in Russia (in 1934), or that it will disappear in any new society that begins with it, is questionable. Yet he can say: "Progress depends on our refusal to use brutal means even when they are efficacious."[24] What Shaw does make clear, despite contradictions and inconsistencies, is that an inquisition that makes

[24] Quoted in Pearson, *G.B.S.: A Full Length Portrait*, p. 322.

for what he calls a high order of civilization should be tolerated. What Shaw does not consider is that inquisition as a method, whatever the ultimate purpose, may never bring a high order of civilization into being. He never evaluates the problem of means and ends; and this lack in his thinking is most conspicuous when he writes about education: "In the meantime the terror will act as a sort of social conscience which is dangerously lacking at present, and which none of our model educational establishments ever dreams of inculcating." No qualification is added to these last words of the Preface to *On the Rocks,* and one is forced to conclude that Shaw would substitute this sort of "terror" in the schools for the terror of those pedagogic monsters he so eloquently denounced. Shaw has frequently expressed a maniacal hatred of cruelty in all its forms, but he never really comes to grips with the potential cruelty of an all-powerful state.

The Simpleton of the Unexpected Isles (1934) dramatizes the concept that in a living society every day is a day of judgment and that the recognition of this principle is the beginning of real civilization. An Angel of Judgment appears, complete with thunder and flaming sword for the purpose of "weeding the human garden." [25] As Hyering puts it: "The useless people, the mischievous people, the selfish somebodies and the noisy nobodies are dissolving into space." And Prola, the native priestess, adds:

The lives which have no use, no purpose, will fade out. We shall have to justify our existences or perish. We shall live under a constant sense of that responsibility. If the angels fail us we shall set up tribunals of our own from which worthless people will not come out alive. When men no longer fear the judgment of God, they must learn to judge themselves.

[25] See Preface to *On the Rocks:* "liquidation by the Ogpu is not punishment: it is only 'weeding the garden.'"

When Hyering wants to know what is judgment, Pra, Prola's husband, replies: "Judgment is valuation. Civilizations live by their valuations. If the valuations are false, the civilization perishes as all the ancient ones we know of did. We are not being punished to-day: we are being valued." Pra learns over the telephone that Judgment Day in England has caused the disappearance of most of the members of the stock exchange, Parliament, and the medical profession, including a noted Cambridge professor. Hyering, uneasy about being made to disappear, says: "What we have learned here to-day is that the day of judgment is not the end of the world but the beginning of real human responsibility." Prola's closing speech, full of mystic overtones, does little to clarify further Shaw's ideas about valuation and punishment. She concludes: "Let every day be a day of wonder for me and I shall not fear the Day of Judgment."

Although the Sergeant in *Too True To Be Good* (1932) carries a Bible and *The Pilgrim's Progress* at all times and denounces the cruelties of modern war, he communicates a philosophy of extermination which parallels what Shaw says in the Preface. He tells the Patient:

You see, miss, the great principle of soldiering, I take it, is that the world is kept going by the people who want the right thing killing the people who want the wrong thing. When the soldier is doing that, he is doing the work of God . . . But that's a very different thing from killing a man because he's a German and he killing you because you're an Englishman. We were not killing the right people in 1915.

Commissar Posky in *Geneva* (1938), who rationalizes the need for liquidating undesirables, denies that his "hands are . . . bloodstained." He explains: "You see, a Communist State is only possible for highly civilized people, trained to

Communism from their childhood. The people we shoot are gangsters and speculators and exploiters and scoundrels of all sorts who are encouraged in other countries in the name of liberty and democracy." [26] While few would dispute Shaw's aim of inculcating a sense of human responsibility in people, the fact remains that these plays and prefaces suggest that violent means be used to bring about a desirable end which is subjectively derived—a process which Shaw fails to justify.

The question arises whether Shaw would advocate such violent means in effecting the transition from capitalism to socialism. As a constitutional Fabian, Shaw believes that "socialism will come by prosaic instalments of public regulation . . . enacted by ordinary parliaments . . . parish councils, school boards, and the like; and that not one of these instalments will amount to a revolution." [27] Although Shaw has reluctantly conceded in his "In Praise of Guy Fawkes" that if "our property system . . . is defended by violence it will be overthrown by violence," [28] and that "at the end of the fighting we shall all be the poorer, none the wiser," he supports in his major social and political tracts a thesis of peaceful transition. Violence is primarily the product of capitalism because "we have recklessly taught our children to glorify pugnacity and to identify gentility and honor with the keeping down of the poor and the keeping up with the rich." [29] Socialism, on the other hand, "is neither a battle cry nor an election catchword but an elaborate arrangement of our production and distribution of wealth." [30] Even after a legalized

[26] See Preface to *The Apple Cart:* "Had we not better teach our children to be better citizens. We are not doing that at present. The Russians are."
[27] "The Illusions of Socialism" as quoted by Henderson, *Bernard Shaw: Playboy and Prophet,* p. 239.
[28] *Where Stands Socialism Today?* p. 204.
[29] *Intelligent Woman,* p. 380.   [30] *Ibid.,* p. 377.

transition from capitalism to socialism, an elaborate preparation by a trained body of civil servants would be needed. Shaw cites the French and Russian revolutions as attempts to impose a new order on a people not sufficiently educated or prepared for it. "The first thing civilized people have to learn politically is that they must not take the law into their own hands. Socialism is from beginning to end a matter of law." [31] Hopefully he looked forward to a constitutional realization of socialism, because the proletarian parents are a huge majority of the electorate: "If only it were possible for us to cease corrupting our children our political superstitions and prejudices would die with us; and the next generation would bring down the walls of Jericho." [32]

"Democracy," as defined by Shaw, "means the organization of society for the benefit and at the expense of everybody indiscriminately and not for the benefit of a privileged class." [33] A major obstacle in the way of its realization "is the delusion that the way of securing it is to give votes to everybody." Universal adult suffrage leads not to democracy, but "mobocracy," since most people "do not want liberty and have not been educated to want it." [34] In respect of government of the people and for the people, Shaw was a democrat; but on the subject of government by the people he was uncompromising, maintaining that Lincoln failed to understand that votes to anybody and votes for everybody nullified any hopes of political or social progress.[35] Shaw would remove the higher functions of government from direct popular control, proposing educational programs and tests in political science and public affairs not only for possible leaders but for voters as

---

[31] *Ibid.*, p. 98.   [32] *Ibid.*, p. 392.
[33] *What's What*, p. 40.   [34] Preface to *Misalliance*.
[35] Preface to *The Apple Cart*.

well. Shaw makes provision for those voters who are incapable of passing any tests: they would be given opportunity "to squeal their complaints, agitate for pet remedies . . . draft bills and call on the government to enact them, and criticize the government to their utmost with impunity." [36] Everyone in Shaw's hierarchical state would be allowed freedom of thought, freedom of speech and freedom of congress.

Genuine democracy can never be realized until the whole population is educated politically and socially and is capable of accepting all the responsibilities involved. This ideal, according to Shaw, has not been realized in any modern democracy. When he stated that democracy required a population of Supermen, he meant that democracy required a population of adequately educated humans—which capitalism or capitalist democracy was incapable of bringing about. For Shaw, democracy in its advanced state, or what he calls genuine democracy, is synonymous with socialism or democratic socialism.

Shaw's despair of democracy and his belief in a powerful socialist state partly explains his praise of such modern dictators as Stalin, Mussolini, and, with some reservations, even Hitler. Essentially his analysis of fascism as state capitalism is Marxist. State control, however, without socialist distribution —that is, equality of income—is to Shaw camouflaged tyranny all over again. In 1928 he challenged even the Soviet Union, "where the children are taught the Christian morality of Communism instead of the Mammonist morality of Capitalism," [37] for its failure to equalize incomes; yet in 1944, he hailed the "genuine democratic socialism of the U.S.S.R." [38] Despite the many contradictions and inconsistencies to be

[36] *What's What*, p. 52.   [37] *Intelligent Woman*, p. 374.
[38] *What's What*, p. 265.

found in his speeches and articles for magazine and press, undoubtedly designed to jolt a stolid public into doing a little thinking, there emerges a pattern of praise for all dictators, right as well as left. Lenin is hailed because he believed that in this world "things are done by men who have convictions and who are prepared . . . to impose appropriate institutions on the vast majority who are themselves incapable of making the institutions"; [39] Stalin, in one of his last prefaces, as deserving "the best right to the vacant Nobel peace prize"; [40] Mussolini for "substituting civilization for savagery" [41] in Abyssinia; and Hitler "for the ability with which he has undone our wicked work" at Versailles, although this praise is tempered in the Preface to *Geneva* by an attack on the Nazi "madman." Shaw's distrust of parliamentary procedures and faith in efficient action once led him to write to Lady Astor: "If you take thirty years to do an hour's work, you will presently have to do thirty years' work in half an hour, which will be a very bloody business." [42] Henderson suggests that Shaw supported dictatorial seizures "partly as expedients in emergencies, and partly as demonstrations of what can be done by realists in politics." [43] Eric Bentley maintains that for Shaw "liberalism and fascism are rival masks of capitalism and fascism is in some ways the better of the two" since it attacked individualism and advocated putting the community first; and further suggests that Shaw, being an artist in propaganda, was not so much concerned with being a systematic political thinker as with irritating people into thinking, into undermining their complacency.[44]

----

[39] An address before the Ruskin Centenary Council in 1921. Quoted by Rattray, *Bernard Shaw: A Chronicle*, p. 20.
[40] Preface to *Farfetched Fables.*   [41] Preface to *Geneva.*
[42] Pearson, *A Full Length Portrait*, p. 376.
[43] *Playboy and Prophet*, p. 231.   [44] *Bernard Shaw*, pp. 24, 29.

Linking Shaw with Rousseau, Jacques Barzun suggests that Shaw's attempted fusion of extreme individualism with a strong collective discipline illustrates his love, like that of many great romantic thinkers, for dramatic opposition and "dialectical opposites;" and that his postwar totalitarianism, which he did not qualify sufficiently, derived from his impatience to realize an ordered, civilized state. Even if partly true, these hypotheses suggested by Henderson, Bentley, and Barzun must be rejected: praise of dictatorial seizures and cruelties illustrates again Shaw's failure to grapple with the end-means complex, and vitiates to a great extent his earlier concepts about genuine democracy or democratic socialism.

In *Geneva*, written just before the outbreak of World War II, Shaw's approval of dictatorship in varying degree becomes apparent. Bombardone, the Italian dictator, comes to the World Court, proclaiming that his "will is part of the world's will." He tells the Newcomer, a middle-class Englishman who heckles him about democracy, that democracy is "mob law, lynching law, gangster law: in short, American democracy. I have rescued my country from all that by my leadership." While Bombardone does not go unchallenged, Shaw does use him as a spokesman for his own favorite denunciations of democracy. Although General Flanco and Ernest Battler (Franco and Hitler) air opinions antagonistic to Shaw's, the Commissar, with the aid of the Judge, spotlights Shaw's Russophilia. "Russia," says the Commissar, "will save the soul of the world by teaching it to feed its people instead of robbing them." It is significant that the Judge supports the Commissar by saying:

Why not bring your economics, your religion, your history, your political philosophy up to date? Russia has made a gigantic effort to do this; and now her politicians are only about fifty years behind

her philosophers and saints whilst the rest of the civilized world is
from five hundred to five thousand behind it. In the west the vested
interests in ignorance and superstition are so overwhelming that no
teacher can tell his young pupils the truth without finding himself
starving in the street.

The Judge's final, "Your objective is domination: your weapons fire and poison, starvation and ruin, extermination by
every means known to science," seems levelled at the de-
mocracies and the fascists rather than at Russia. The Judge
seems to overlook the work of the Cheka, which Shaw defends in a number of prefaces.

On the Rocks (1933) must also be regarded as a eulogy of
dictatorship. Hipney, an old labor leader, is a thinly disguised
Shaw lecturing Chavender, the Prime Minister, about the
futilities of democracy. When Chavender defends the inexorable laws of political economy, Hipney says: "That stuff
you learnt at college . . . won't go down with my lot." The
ideas of the Preface are put in Hipney's mouth: "Democracy
at first was a dream and a vision, a hope and faith and a
promise. It lasted until they dragged it down to earth, and
made it a reality by giving everybody votes . . . and now I'm
for any Napoleon or Mussolini or Lenin or Chavender [who
has now been educated into advocating a centralized socialist state] that has the stuff in him to take both the people
and their oppressors by the scruffs of their silly necks and
just sling them into the way they should go with as many
kicks as may be needful." Accused of advocating dictatorship,
Hipney replies: "Better one dictator standing up responsible
before the world for the good and evil he does than a dirty
little dictator in every street responsible to nobody to turn
you out of your house if you don't pay him for the right to
exist on earth, or to fire you out of your job if you stand up

to him as a man and an equal." While Hipney-Shaw would
give the people "a choice between qualified men," it becomes
apparent that this slight concession to democracy does little
to obviate the terrifying implications of dictatorship for good
or for evil.

Chavender is educated by a lady doctor into being a
champion of socialism and dictatorship. Stealing noiselessly
into his room and "contemplating him gravely and pityingly,"
she informs him that he is a sick man "suffering from that very
common English complaint, an underworked brain." "My life,"
Chavender objects, "has been a completely intellectual life,
and my training the finest intellectual training in the world.
First rate preparatory school. Harrow. Oxford. Parliament
. . . Intellect, intellect, all the time." The doctor, disagreeing
with his defense "of our great educational system," finally persuades him to visit her retreat with a suitcase of books by
"Marx, Lenin, Trotsky, Stalin and people like that." The result is that on his return from the Welsh retreat Chavender
has been transformed into a "Bolshy premier" who now proposes nationalization of everything in sight with an efficient
dictator at the top.

Shaw believed in socialism because he thought it would
create a more honorable way of life by removing the induce-
ments to selfishness, anti-social behavior, and irresponsible
individualism. Money values would be superseded by cultural and ethical values, thus making it possible for people
to develop their higher faculties rather than their acquisitive
instincts. Socialism is a means of evolving a superior type of
individual who would regard the betterment of the community
as more important than his own selfish interests. And since
people have to be educated into such attitudes, Shaw felt that
this type of education could never be realized in capitalism.

The growth of the individual is possible only in a socialist state, for "legislators and administrators, managers and scholars, lawyers and doctors and clergymen, artists and philosophers . . . cost education, culture, gentle nurture, decency and some leisure," [45] and only in a socialist state can these be adequately provided for.

A fair conclusion from these remarks would be that Shaw, democratic socialist and defender of individual liberty though he claimed to be, has said much for one reason or another to exalt the ideal of the dictator. While he insisted that only the virtuous and educated shall become the powerful, he fails to convince us of the positive outcomes of the severe collective discipline he would impose—a discipline which could easily enslave rather than free the individual. Such statist centralization of power could easily lead to totalitarian disciplines in the schools and to a commandeering of teachers and curricula for the purpose of perpetuating a status quo that Shaw would be the first to attack. While he advocated educating the young to want liberty, he also insisted that unless they fit themselves to live in a civilized society they cannot be allowed to live at all. In his program of painless liquidation of the unfit (he never really defines these), Shaw fails to clarify the end-means complex—a failure which could easily carry over into the administration of the schools in a Shavian state.

[45] *What's What*, p. 55.

6 *Growth of personality*

Because he was not a professional educator, Shaw did not conveniently title a chapter or book "Growth of Personality" and present specific recipes for implementing and measuring growth. If, however, socialism was for Shaw a way of realizing the great potential in human nature, his religious and philosophic doctrine of Creative Evolution, which outcrops in so much of his work, is itself virtually a philosophy of human growth, and will have to be considered as it touches upon areas in education.

Shaw charged that all the evils of modern society

are the result of an educational system which, instead of guiding the natural change from childhood to adolescence and maturity, arrests juvenile development at its most mischievous stage, and forces the experienced statesman to treat the country as an orphanage in which the age limit is fourteen, and the orphans as its mentally defective inmates.[1]

In contrast to this dismal state of affairs, Shaw proposes in the Preface to *Misalliance* this ideal of human growth:

. . . there is only one belief that can rob death of its sting and the grave of its victory; and that is the belief that we can lay down the burden of our wretched little makeshift personalities for ever at

[1] *What's What*, p. 79.

each lift towards the goal of evolution, which can only be a being that cannot be improved upon . . . Therefore let us . . . rejoice in death as we rejoice in birth; for without death we cannot be born again; and the man who does not wish to be born again and born better is fit only to represent the City of London in Parliament, or perhaps the university of Oxford.

Urging society to rid itself of its Jehovah-like creeds, particularly their "attributions of infallibility," Shaw suggests acceptance of his own creed which "is not infallible." [2]

. . . the Élan Vital, the Divine Spark, the Life Force, the Power that makes for righteousness (call it what you will) . . . proceeds by trial and error; and its errors are called the problem of evil. It is not omnipotent . . . and can only act through its creations. . . . It has neither body nor parts; but it has, or rather is, what we call a soul or passion, for ever urging us to obtain greater power over our circumstances and greater knowledge and understanding of what we are doing. It is also an appetite for truth (correspondence of belief to facts), for beauty, for justice, for mercy.

Shaw rejected the idea of a personal omnipotent God and accepted the idea of an imperfect God who drives experimentally, by means of His own imperfect creations, toward greater knowledge and power and completer intelligence. Such a concept of an imperfect deity explains for Shaw the existence of evil and suffering which are unexplainable in many other religious beliefs. In an address "The Religion of the British Empire," Shaw said:

When you are asked, "Where is God? Who is God?" stand up and say, "I am God and here is God," not as yet completed, but still advancing towards completion, just in so much as I am working for the purpose of the universe, working for the good of the whole of society and the whole world, instead of merely looking after my personal ends. [3]

[2] *Ibid.*, p. 232.
[3] *The Christian Commonwealth* (November 29, 1906). See also "Mr.

Here one begins to see the threads of Shaw's socialism fusing with those of his evolutionary theories and his educational ideals which would make for limitless growth. His concept of the Life Force attempts to make use of every individual's contribution (by means of effective educational processes) to the cause of evolutionary progress.

Since the universe is God in the act of making or completing Himself with the aid of His upward-striving creations, mind, will, and purpose become for Shaw the prime necessities for growth. Man, Shaw warns repeatedly, is not necessarily the ultimate aim of this striving will in the universe, but only a stage in the scale of evolution; and unless man wills greater knowledge and power over circumstances, in harmony with this universal will, he cannot change or grow. Shaw agrees with Lamarck that living organisms change only because they want to change. In relatively simple organisms such as plants and animals, this will is unconscious and instinctive, whereas in man it is, or should be, highly self-conscious, rational as well as instinctive, developed by an inward mystical sense and cultivated by contemplation. The tragedy for Shaw is that the average man, although he learns to stand or walk or cycle "by going through the wanting, trying process," not only does not consciously want or consciously try to develop other more difficult or complex habits, such as contemplation, but "actually consciously objects very strongly." [4] Despairing since "most of us are ungovernable by abstract thought," Shaw looked forward to the cultivation of people "to whom eating, drinking, and reproduction are irksome necessities in comparison with the urge to wider and

---

Bernard Shaw Explains His Religion" in *The Freethinker* (November 1, 1908); "What Is My Religious Faith?" *Sixteen Self Sketches*, pp. 119–28.
[4] Preface to *Back to Methuselah.*

deeper knowledge, better understanding." [5] He even suggested that the pleasures derived at present from thought or creative work are "as yet far from being as intense as the sexual orgasm or the ecstasy of a Saint, though future cortical evolution may leave them far behind." [6] Shaw emphasized his contention that "intellect is a passion" and that people, if they are to grow, must become "passion beings" who are possessed "of an overwhelming impulse towards a more abundant life." [7] Believing as a Lamarckian in the inheritance of acquired characteristics, Shaw maintained that not only can man be educated into cultivating such passions, but that he can pass on such acquisitions to the next generation.

A careful reading of the plays which dramatize the goals of evolution, particularly *Man and Superman* and *Back to Methuselah,* reveals that they actually say more about growth and education than their prefaces or Shaw's other nondramatic work. In *Man and Superman* (1903) one finds for the first time in Shaw's work a conception of the Life Force as will striving through the mind and instincts of humans. In the multiplex conflict of ideas which takes place in the eternity of hell, Juan asserts the indomitable will of the Life Force, the unlimited potential of the human brain. No longer obsessed with art and sex, Juan now strives toward unlimited growth, saying:

[5] *What's What,* p. 327.

[6] Preface to *Buoyant Billions.* See *Self Sketches,* p. 178: "I valued sexual experience because of its power of producing a celestial flood of emotion and exaltation which, however momentary, gave me a sample of the ecstacy that may one day be the normal condition of conscious intellectual activity." See also Preface to *Back to Methuselah:* "the most prolonged and difficult operations of our minds may yet become instantaneous, or . . . instinctive."

[7] Preface to Workers' Educational Association *Year Book* for 1918 in *Doctors' Delusions.* See also C. E. M. Joad, "Shaw's Philosophy," S. Winsten, editor, *G.B.S. 90,* p. 92: For Shaw, "the operations of the intellect are the goals of evolution."

I would think more, therefore I must be more. . . . I tell you that as long as I can conceive something better than myself I cannot be easy unless I am striving to bring it into existence or clearing the way for it. This is the law of my life. This is the working within me of Life's incessant aspiration to higher organization, wider, deeper, intenser self-consciousness, and clearer self-understanding. It was the supremacy of this purpose that reduced love for me to the mere pleasure of the moment, art for me to the mere schooling of my faculties.

Repudiating the vulgar pursuit of happiness, Juan wants "to spend my aeons in contemplation." To the Statue who glorifies the military man Juan replies: "I sing, not arms and the hero, but the philosophic man: he who seeks in contemplation to discover the inner will of the world, in invention to discover the means of fulfilling that will, and in action to do that will by the so-discovered means." That man can be ennobled "by simply putting an idea into his head" and that men "will die for human perfection" is Juan's credo. "Life was driving at brains—at its darling object: an organ by which it can attain not only self-consciousness but self-understanding." Anticipating the Ancients in *Back to Methuselah* Juan declares: "My brain labors at a knowledge which does nothing for me personally but makes my body bitter to me and my decay and death a calamity."

It becomes clear that the heaven Juan aspires to is accessible to everyone if the cultivation of the mind is willed. When Juan asks the Devil whether one can really leave hell and go to heaven, he is told: "Have you any canonical authority for assuming that there is any barrier between our circle and the other one?" The Devil explains that "a parable must not be taken literally," adding:

The gulf is the difference between the angelic and diabolic temperament. What more impassable gulf could you have? Think of what you have seen on earth. There is no physical gulf between the philosopher's class room and the bull ring; but the bull fighters do not come to the class room for all that. . . . And the classical concert is admitted to be a higher, more cultivated, poetic, intellectual, ennobling place than the race course. But do the lovers of racing desert their sport and flock to the concert room? Not they.

The Devil concludes that people "are free to do whatever the Government and public opinion allow them to do" for it is the "gulf of dislike which is impassable and eternal." Finally, when Juan requests the Commander to show him the way to heaven (where he can practice his ideal of contemplation) he is told that "the frontier is only the difference between two ways of looking at things," and that any road will get him there.

Implicit in this dialogue is that the "gulf of dislike" can be bridged by the cultivation of the will and the mind. These must be nourished by a society vitally interested in such a process. Only then can the "difference between the angelic and the diabolic temperament" be resolved and growth realized.

If *Man and Superman* explores the possibilities of the philosophic man, "nature's pilot," *Back to Methuselah* (1921), clarifies the ultimate direction of man's growth. In the first play, *In the Beginning*, Adam fears the horror of "having to be with myself forever. . . . I want to be different, to be better; to begin again and again; to shed myself as a snake sheds its skin." The serpent, however, prefers Eve as the more promising student and instructs her in the mysteries of birth, life, desire, and will. Communicating what Lilith, "who came before Adam and Eve," had taught him, the serpent advises Eve "that the imagination is the beginning of creation. You imagine what you desire; you will what you imagine; and at last you create what you will." In this way Lilith, the serpent relates, had conceived Adam and Eve though there was no man. Adam, despite his apparent desire to change and grow, is lazy and bored, a slave to certainty. But the serpent fears certainty as Adam fears uncertainty. "If I bind the future," Adam is told, "I bind my will. If I bind my will I strangle creation." And Eve, agreeing, adds: "I will create though I tear myself to pieces in the act." For this reason Eve, centuries later, denounces her warlike, destructive son, Cain, who would conquer and enslave other people rather than create. "Through him and his like, death is gaining on life. Already most of our grandchildren die before they have sense enough to know how to live." Disillusioned with her spinning and Adam's eternal digging for a living, Eve ends the play with: "Man need not always live by bread alone. There is something else. We do not yet know what it is; but some day we shall find out; and then we will live on that alone; and there shall be no more digging nor spinning, nor fighting nor killing."

In the *Gospel of the Brothers Barnabas*, the second play, the concept of unlimited growth is presented by the brothers, Conrad and Franklyn. "Greater power and greater knowledge: these are what we are all pursuing," Franklyn says. "Evolution is that pursuit. . . . It is the path of godhead." The recipe for easing this pursuit is longevity: man must live longer—at least three hundred years—for, as Conrad puts it, "the political and social problems raised by our civilization cannot be solved by mere human mushrooms who decay and die when they are just beginning to have a glimmer of wisdom and knowledge." The serpent's imagining, willing, creating is now transmuted into Franklyn's belief that if man wills a longer life he will realize it. And Franklyn's "as there is no limit to power and knowledge there can be no end" anticipates Lilith's vision at the close of the fifth play.

It does happen in *The Thing Happens.* Some longlivers
like Mrs. Lutestring and the Archbishop are well in their
third century. Imported educated Negresses and Chinese
rule the government. Confucius sounds a hopeful note for real
growth:

> We are just a lot of schoolboys. . . . Talk to an Englishman about
> anything serious, and he listens to you curiously for a moment just
> as he listens to a chap playing classical music. Then he goes back
> to his marine golf, or motoring, or flying, or women . . . We are
> only in our infancy. . . . But some day we'll grow up.

By 3000 A. D. society has grown considerably. In *The
Tragedy of an Elderly Gentleman* a group of shortlivers have
come from Baghdad, the capital of the British Commonwealth, to consult the oracle. One of the party, the Elderly
Gentleman, being unable to withstand the electric shock of
Fusima's and Zozim's mental fields, is assigned to Zoo, a child
of fifty. He is completely shattered to discover in a long
conversation with Zoo that his most advanced ideas make
no impression. Aghast at Zoo's charge that "contact with
truth hurts and frightens you" he tries to defend his shortlived civilization with the very ideals Shaw always attacks. As
he insists that "human nature is human nature, longlived
or shortlived, and always will be," Zoo tries to explain that
"if I knew I had to die in twenty years it would not be worth
my while to educate myself" and goes on to describe her
education under the "tertiaries."

> Like all young things I rebelled against them; and in their hunger
> for new lights and new ideas they listened to me and encouraged
> me to rebel. But my ways did not work; and theirs did; and they
> were able to tell me why. They have no power over me except that
> power: they refuse all other power; and the consequence is that
> there are no limits to their power except the limits they set them-
> selves.

The Elderly Gentleman's despair at being called a child by Zoo is eventually climaxed by his inability to withstand the electric shock of the Oracle's mental field, and he falls dead.

In the thirty-second millennium of *As Far As Thought Can Reach* people are immortal, except for physical accidents, and children are egg-born, entering the world in what we call their late teens. Pygmalion, the scientist, explains that the Newly Born, just hatched, knows by instinct what the greatest physicists and mathematicians of the past "could hardly arrive at by forty years of strenuous study." The Newly Born who "feels the need of education" is given her first lesson by a She-Ancient. The child is horrified to learn that if there had been anything wrong with her at birth she would have been quickly and humanely killed. The She-Ancient continues her lesson:

You began by being several sorts of creatures that no longer exist. . . . Then you became human; and you passed in fifteen months through a development that once cost human beings twenty years of awkward stumbling immaturity after they were born. They had to spend fifty years more in the sort of childhood you will complete in four years.

Yet the young do not understand the Ancients; they ridicule them and their way of life. But as the young approach the end of their fourth year they grow up and lose their interest in love and art. For example, the Maiden wants "to get away from our eternal dancing and music and just sit down and think about numbers . . . wandering about the woods, thinking, thinking, thinking; grasping the world, taking it to pieces; building it up again; devising methods; planning experiments to test the methods. . . ." But young Strephon is revolted by this as "cold and uncomfortable." Although growing up is the only solution to the problem of youth in any civilization, the process of maturation, Shaw thought, must be eased by a civilized society. It is significant that the Ancients put up with the taunts of the young and grant them complete freedom of thought. The Newly Born who invites an Ancient to play with her is told: "When you play with one another you play with your bodies, and that makes you supple and strong; but if we played with you we should play with your minds, and perhaps deform them." Presumably, this is what Shaw meant when he said "nobody knows the way a child should go."

The Ancients live in a vortex of thought. As the young Acis says: "Most of them have forgotten how to speak: the ones that attend to us have to brush up their knowledge of the language." The mocking Strephon is rebuked by the He-Ancient: "Infant, one moment of the ecstacy of life as we live it would strike you dead." Acis informs the Newly Born that the Ancients can alter themselves in marvellous ways. The human body has become a flexible tool of pure willed thought; and even the body is to be discarded eventually. "But still I am the slave of this slave, my body," complains the She-Ancient. "How am I to be delivered from it?" And the He-Ancient tells the Newly Born he would like to become a "vortex." To Acis's question, "If life is thought, can you live without a head?" the He-Ancient replies, "Not now perhaps. But pre-historic men thought they could not live without tails. I can live without a tail. Why should I not live without a head?" The Ancients believe that their bodies "imprison us on this petty planet and forbid us to range through the stars."

The ghostly voices of Cain, Adam and Eve, the serpent, and Lilith are now heard discussing the growth the Ancients have achieved. "There is no place for me on earth any longer," says the disappointed Cain as he vanishes. Despite his original desire to grow, Adam is still complacent. "They are dissatisfied because they cannot be bothered with their bodies. Foolishness, I call it," he pronounces and disappears. But Eve and the serpent are satisfied. "My clever ones have inherited the earth. All's well," says Eve and fades away. The stage is now left to Lilith who soliloquizes at great length on the deeds and misdeeds of the human race:

I had patience with them for many ages: they tried me sorely. . . . They have redeemed themselves from their vileness, and turned away from their sins. Best of all they are still not satisfied. . . . After passing a million goals they press on to the goal of redemption from the flesh, to the vortex freed from matter, to the whirlpool in pure intelligence. . . . I say, let them dread, of all things, stagnation. . . . Of Life only is there no end. . . . And for what may be beyond, the eyesight of Lilith is too short. It is enough that there is a beyond.

This allegory of human growth is developed further in the later *Farfetched Fables* (1948). The scene in the "Fifth Fable" is in a Genetic Institute in the distant future. Two men, Thistle and Shamrock, a woman, Rose, and Hermaphrodite are discussing the past and future of the human race. With regard to sex practices of the past, Rose observes: "Strangest of all, they seem to have experienced in such contacts the ecstacies which are normal with us in our pursuit of knowledge and power." It is soon revealed that the problem confronting them is to create the "Just Man Made Perfect" about whom there is no agreement as to the "exact prescription of the necessary protoplasms, hormones, vitamins, enzymes, and the rest." The crux of the dispute concerns the "last milligram of each ingredient . . . that determines whether the resulting product will be a poet or a mathematician." Opposing chemical formulas, Hermaphrodite insists that "we must get rid of our physical bodies altogether. . . . I want to be a mind and noth-

ing but a mind." Rose, however, complicates the issue further
by pointing out that "we should still be unable to agree on
what sort of mind we needed." While she would also be a
mind without a body, Rose suggests that at present there is no
choice but peopling the world in biochemical laboratories. To
Hermaphrodite's insistence that the desire to get rid of his
body was not manufactured in a laboratory, Rose replies,
"When we know even that it will be only another grain of sand
on the seashore." And to Shamrock's "In the infinity of time,
when the oceans dry up and make no more sand, we shall pick
them all up. What then?" Rose answers, "The pursuit of knowledge and power will never end."

In the "Sixth and Last Fable" some men have already
evolved into pure thought. The scene is on the Isle of Wight in
a Sixth Form School to which three youths and two maidens
have just been promoted. When the students demand an explanation of how "thoughts come into our heads" and question the
existence of the disembodied, the teacher explains: "People
actually did get rid of their bodies. They got rid of their tails,
of their fur, their teeth. They acquired thumbs and enlarged
their brains. They seem to have done what they liked with
their bodies." The sceptical students are told that the "Disembodied Races still exist as Thought Vortexes, and are penetrating our thick skulls in their continual pursuit of knowledge
and power, since they need our hands and brains as tools in
that pursuit." As the students continue to question whether the
vortexes are well meaning, the teacher further explains that
"even the vortexes have to do their work by trial and error."
Since the students have been taught that theirs is the "most
advanced civilization yet evolved," the teacher reveals that
their civilization is really "atavistic." "We are ourselves a
throw-back to the twentieth century, and may be killed as

idiots and savages if we meet a later and higher civilization."
And she cites "those children of ours who cannot get beyond
the First Form, and grow up to be idiots or savages."

A youth, Raphael, suddenly appears "clothed in feathers like
a bird" and announces he is an "embodied thought." "Evolution," he tells the astounded class (even the teacher is uncon-
vinced), "can go backwards as well as forwards. If the body can
become a vortex, the vortex can also become a body." Questioned whether he actually lives as a human with passions,
Raphael replies that physical passions such as "your eating and
drinking and reproductive methods" have been replaced by
"intellectual passion, mathematical passion,[8] passion for discovery and exploration: the mightiest of all the passions."

Buoyant Billions (1947) dramatizes the need for passion
beings dedicated this time to "world bettering" and mathematics. Inspired by the Life Force to do good, young Junius
informs his prosperous, middle-class father of his plans to
practice the profession of world-betterer because "living in a
world of poor and unhappy people is like living in hell." Junius
would emulate such world-betterers as "Ruskin, Morris, Confucius, Jesus, Mahomet, Marx, Lenin, and Stalin," but his
father insists on the need for practical men and advises him to
better himself before he betters the world. Junius counters:
"And until I better the world I cannot better myself." The
Native, whom Junius meets in the tropics, educates him into
understanding the deity, Hoochlipoochli. "Something within
me," says the Native, "makes me hunger and thirst for righteousness. That something must be Hoochlipoochli." Although
at the end of the play, Junius marries a billionaire's daughter
and compromises his ideals to some extent, it soon becomes

---

[8] In his old age Shaw became interested in mathematics, particularly
biometrics, as the Preface to *Farfetched Fables* testifies.

clear that the Secondborn, a member of the wealthy Buoyant family, is Shaw's mouthpiece. Hailing "mathematical perception, the noblest of all the faculties," he cites "Bruno, Copernicus, Galileo, Newton, Descartes, Rutherford, Einstein, all of them far seeing guessers carried away by the passion for measuring truth and knowledge." Mathematical passion, concludes the Secondborn, after a diatribe against the state of higher education, "promises a development in which life will be an intellectual ecstasy surpassing the ecstasies of saints." A disciple of Hoochlipoochli, he insists that leaving it to God is wrong for "we do not know what God is, and are still seeking a general mathematical theory expressing him.[9] All we know is He leaves much of it to us; and we make a shocking mess of it."

If these plays are to be regarded as dramatic treatises on human development, it is clear that Shaw provides no practical or consistent method whereby growth may be realized. In *Man and Superman* it is desire to grow philosophically and eugenic breeding; in *Back to Methuselah* it is also will to grow and longevity. One cannot find practical recipes in these plays. He intended them as dramatic allegories designed to educate audiences into understanding the urgent need to grow. Shaw is consistent about the will to grow. It is clear that man can decide to change himself and society for the better if he wills such alteration with sufficient intensity. Society and its educational machinery must be concerned with the individual's potential. The will to grow must be an educated one.

In the Preface to *Misalliance*, one of Shaw's longest pieces about education, the thesis is developed that maturity and

    [9] See Preface to the play: "The scientist who solves the problem of the prophet Daniel and John of Patmos, and incidentally of Shakespeare and myself, will make a longer stride ahead than any solver of physical problems."

growth in our society can hardly be realized, because society, parents, teachers, and schools pervert the "precious and sacred thing the child's conscience into an instrument of our own convenience."

From curates and governesses . . . to parents and nurserymaids and schoolteachers and wiseacres generally, there are scores of thousands of human insects groping through our darkness by the feeble phosphorescence of their own tails, yet ready at a moment's notice to reveal the will of God on every possible subject; to explain how and why the universe was made (in my youth they added the exact date) and the circumstances under which it will cease to exist; to lay down precise rules of right and wrong conduct. . . . As to children, who shall say what canings . . . and threats of hell fire and impositions and humiliations and petty imprisonings . . . they have suffered because their parents and guardians and teachers knew everything so much better than Socrates or Solon?

To teach a child false ideals, false religions, and false ethical values is to hinder the process of growth which the Life Force may intend in its drive toward perfection. Shaw suggests that if we proceeded on human assumptions and not on academic ones, and that if parents and teachers were to admit that they do not know what the purposes of the Life Force are, genuine growth would be the rule rather than the exception. He would even enact a law that "any person dictating a piece of conduct to a child or to anyone as the will of God, or as absolutely right, should be dealt with as a blasphemer." That a child feels the drive of the Life Force and that an adult or a teacher "cannot feel it for him" is a mystical assumption of Shaw. He meant that since most people are ignorant, uneducated, and victims of the static, stereotyped institutions of society, they cannot possibly know "what a human being ought to be."

The precise formula for the Superman, The Just Man Made Perfect, has not yet been discovered. Until it is, every birth is an experiment in the Great Research which is being conducted by the Life Force to discover that formula.

Anyone "who believes that he has more than a provisional hypothesis to go upon is a born fool." In this context, Shaw's controversial statement, "Now nobody knows the way a child should go. All the ways discovered so far lead to the horrors of our existing civilizations," may become somewhat clearer.

A number of writers have misunderstood Shaw's religion of the Life Force because they have ignored his program of education. For example, William Irvine suggests that Shaw's concept of the Life Force does not make for sound ethics, since telling a man that "his instincts and impulses are divine intimations does not encourage him in consistency, moderation, or justice." [10] Shaw's Schopenhauerian tendency to lump instinct and impulse together with will, Irvine holds, confuses the distinction between morality and animality or between rational free will and mechanistic fatalism. Although this criticism is important and well made, Irvine does not fully consider Shaw's qualifications. The point is that Shaw was fundamentally a mystical optimist who identified all life with the upward driving will of the Life Force, and who refused, despite its trial-and-error mistakes (the fault of people themselves and society), to regard this will as ultimately evil. He did not say that an individual, rationalizing his instincts and impulses as being divine, may with impunity ignore the distinctions between morality and animality or between a sense of responsibility and an unrestricted interpretation of his instincts and passions. An important aim of education for Shaw was the training of the individual to understand and practice moral responsibility, not only for himself, but for the sake of the community. If Shaw believed as Ibsen did that

[10] *The Universe of G.B.S.*, p. 246.

the expression of our individuality is our first duty, he also meant that this expression, cultivated by education, will not conflict with the ideals of good citizenship. As Henderson suggested in his earlier biography, "Shaw has evolved a philosophy for the naturally good man, for the strong man who realizes that freedom connotes, not license, but responsibility." [11] Shaw's thinking can be better evaluated if his socialism and evolution are considered together with the important role played by the third corner of the triangle, namely, education.

Socialism, honest education, evolutionary progress—these are Shaw's prescriptions for achieving human growth. He called for an immediate reorganization of society and its educational facilities and objectives; and he looked forward hopefully to evolutionary progress as allegorized in the plays. There is no certainty that man will grow, for this depends on his intelligent use of the cause of evolution; this he must be taught to understand. If man does not regard himself as responsible to that in him which calls for growth, he may retrogress and be scrapped as an instrument for evolutionary progress. Not only the schools, but also the social and economic circumstances together with counterfeit values, nullify any will to growth. As Joseph Wood Krutch said in his "Open Letter" to Shaw: "You would have proclaimed again that the great dynamic forces of evolution are two: the Imagination which can see what might be and the Will which can bring the might-be about." [12]

[11] *George Bernard Shaw: His Life and Works*, p. 468.
[12] *The Saturday Review* XXXIX (July 21, 1956), 12–13.

7 *Ways and aims*

To comprehend Shaw's theory of education it is necessary to understand not only the goals of education which would guide the development of human excellence, but also those concepts and activities which would stimulate learning. In view of Shaw's endeavors as a critic of music and the theater, and as a social thinker or propagandist, one realizes why he saw the educative process in the light of these experiences. An examination of Shaw's writings about education suggests the hypothesis that the educative process involves experiences primarily in the fields of art, controversy, and the theater.

Shaw had in mind some definite aims for education. "The object of a sane state is to make good citizens of its children: that is, to make them productive or serviceable members of the community." [1] In the Preface to *On the Rocks* he suggested that the "time cannot be far off when the education authorities will have to consider which set of beliefs is the better qualification for citizenship in Utopia." If a community does not make provision for this teaching of citizenship, it will presently be confronted with the "impossible task of maintaining civilization with savages instead of citizens." [2] The or-

---

[1] *What's What*, p. 79.   [2] *Ibid.*, p. 149.

dinary citizen, "politically uneducated and undisciplined," [3] regards public service not as a responsible job imposed by duty and honor, but as something which paves the way for corruption. To root out such cynicism, Shaw advocated the most intense kind of civic and political education, which, he admitted, is more difficult to inculcate than any other kind of education. All of Shaw's major pieces about education show his preoccupation with the ideal of public service in a socialist society.

The production of such citizens will be impeded unless it is a prime purpose of education to eliminate mass ignorance which gives rise to dictators, bosses, or what Shaw called the "dominators."

Armies, fanatical sects and mobs . . . have consisted mostly of people who should not exist in civilized society. . . . The soldiers of Marlborough and Wellington were never-do-wells, mental defectives, and laborers with the minds and habits of serfs. . . . Our public school and university education equips armies of this kind with appropriate staffs of officers. When both are extinct we shall be able to breathe more freely.[4]

This mass ignorance is primarily due to the failure of the schools and universities to teach people constitutional history, law, political science, and economics, without which it is impossible to maintain freedom in any state no matter how perfect its constitution may be.

In Shaw's socialist state all religious creeds would be fused into a common morality inculcated by "enlightened" leaders.

citizenship . . . is impossible without a common fundamental religion; and this had better be inculcated by a democratic state with a strong interest in tolerance and free-thought than by parents divided into hundreds of sects, each persuaded that it has a monopoly

[3] *Ibid.*, p. 272.   [4] Preface to *The Millionairess*.

of salvation and that any sceptical criticism of its tenets is impious and should be proscribed as heresy. Children brought up in such sects produce such incidents as The Thirty Years War about Transubstantiation just as they produce World Wars when they are brought up in nations each of which regards itself as The Chosen Race or Herrenvolk appointed by God to own and rule all the others.[5]

In the Preface to *On the Rocks* Shaw warns: "No future education authority, unless it is as badly educated as our present ones, will imagine that it has any final and eternal truths to inculcate." He also suggests his creed of Creative Evolution as a "provisional hypothesis" because of "its greater credibility and its more exact conformity to the facts alleged by our scientific workers, who have somehow won that faith in their infallibility formerly enjoyed by our priests." Admitting that all provisional hypotheses may be illusions, Shaw advises their acceptance if they conduce to beneficial conduct, at least until better ones arrive. He formulated a program of religious education designed to bring about greater tolerance and understanding of creeds other than one's own.

Education must be reconciled with liberty. Shaw systematically attacked with endless repetition what he called the "fundamental vice of imposing as education a system of imprisonment and 'breaking in' which has no reference to education at all." [6] In the Preface to *Misalliance* he protested:

Soon everybody will be schooled, mentally and physically, from the cradle to the end of the term of adult compulsory military service, and finally of compulsory civil service lasting until the age of superannuation. Always more schooling, more compulsion. We are to be cured by an excess of the dose that has poisoned us.

[5] *What's What*, p. 82.
[6] Preface to Workers' Educational Association *Year Book* for 1918, *Doctors' Delusions*.

Theoretically at least, Shaw demanded that the school population, particularly children, be granted "the elementary rights of human beings." In his essay on "Imprisonment" he declares his credo of liberty for everyone in a condition of tutelage:

No one who has not a profound instinctive respect for the right of all living creatures to moral and religious liberty: that is, to liberty of moral and religious experiment on themselves, limited only by their obligations not to become unduly burdensome to others, should be let come within ten miles of a child, a criminal, or any person in a condition of tutelage.[7]

Another important objective is the "communal training, the apprenticeship to society, the lessons in holding one's own among people of all sorts." [8] All parents, from the coster to the duke, are anxious about the manners of their children:

Laborers who are contemptuously anti-clerical will send their daughters to the convent school because the nuns teach them some sort of gentleness of speech and behavior. And peers who tell you that our public schools are rotten through and through . . . send their sons to Eton and Oxford, Harrow and Cambridge, not only because there is nothing else to be done, but because these places, though they turn out blackguards and ignoramuses and boobies galore, turn them out with the habits and manners of the society they belong to. Bad as those manners are in many respects, they are better than no manners at all. They can be acquired only by living in an organized community in which they are traditional.

It is communal living that "educates the will socially." Most Englishmen, Shaw declared, are given to a general quarrelsomeness because they have not been taught either to tolerate differences of opinion or to consider other people's wills. "Merely criticized or opposed in committee, or invited to consider anybody's views but his own, he feels personally insulted and wants to resign or leave the room unless he is apolo-

[7] *Ibid.*, p. 229. [8] Preface to *Misalliance*.

gized to." Shaw advocated communal living in all schools which would inculcate manners and intellectual attitudes compatible with the "democratic introduction of a high civilization."

The individual must be prepared for some useful vocation in life so that he can make his contribution as a citizen. In Shaw's socialist society, with its well-organized superstructure of guidance facilities, everyone would be enabled to discover what he is fitted for. Such guidance in the schools, Shaw hoped, would eliminate idling as a cherished way of life and abolish the present universal distaste for work in general. Although he admits that all states at present, democratic or plutocratic, have elaborate educational facilities "for confining practice in the trades and professions to persons who have qualified themselves by years of study and exercise," [9] he suggests that—as a result of capitalism—chaos rather than efficiency is now the rule. The success of a business or a nation depends "on its operators being vocationally the right persons in their natural places." [10]

Since genuine democracy cannot function properly without able leaders, one objective of education must be the training of such persons. "In no other way," he suggests in the Preface to *Too True To Be Good*, "can our hackneyed phrase 'responsible government' acquire any real meaning." Shaw has outlined a tentative program for the education of leaders in aesthetic, philosophic, political, and economic areas, and for testing and selecting them.

Shaw believed that the length of people's lives "varies according to their circumstances and education, both of which are controllable by the State." [11] In his frequent attacks on

[9] *What's What*, p. 51.   [10] *Ibid.*, p. 47.
[11] *Ibid.*, p. 235.

vaccination as a disease preventive, he praised Sir Almroth Wright for pointing out that the triumph of sanitation is a triumph of aestheticism.

Smallpox, typhus, cholera, tuberculosis, and the Black Death follow dirt, ugliness, stink and squalor, meanness and poverty as surely as they vanish before beauty and cleanliness and seemliness and sweet sootless air. What offends and degrades the mind, whether through the senses or the intellect, degrades the body. It is true also that what injures the body may injure the mind. . . . A sane Ministry of Public Health must assume that it is the mind that makes the body and not the body the mind.[12]

At this point the "Health Ministry becomes an Education Ministry." People need "agreeable surroundings, the satisfaction of physical cravings before they become mental anxieties, poetry, music, pictures, books, and leisure to enjoy them." In effect, sanitation, art, and leisure are thus the safeguards of mental and, consequently, physical health. Furthermore, such a Health Ministry must eliminate ignorances about food, drugs, alcoholism, and sex.

Not only is the cultivation of aesthetic tastes related to health, but it also to a great extent dominates the educative process; it must therefore be an important aim of education. For Shaw, art "has become an instrument of culture, a method of schooling, a form of science, an indispensable adjunct of religion." [13] In the Preface to *Misalliance* he states that it is art "which alone can educate us in grace of body and soul" and that "we all grow up stupid and mad to just the extent to which we have not been artistically educated." Discussing the methods and character of Jesus in the Preface to *Androcles and the Lion*, Shaw remarks: "When reproached, as Bunyan was, for resorting to the art of fiction when teaching in para-

[12] *Ibid.*, p. 247.　　　　[13] *Ibid.*, p. 188.

bles, he justifies himself on the ground that art is the only way in which people can be taught." The processes of education fail to function without art, for life itself is impossible without art.[14]

Because technological advances have reduced the working hours for most people, education must concern itself with how leisure time is spent. "But leisure without aesthetic education is ruinous." Although the leisure classes do have their musical, literary, theatrical, and artistic sets, yet "in the lump they . . . despise art as epicene instead of valuing it on that account." [15] Shaw asserted that these people with uncultivated minds and plenty of unearned money know of no other pleasures but "eating, drinking, sexual intercourse, fighting, killing, hunting, and gambling." [16] And the workers "ape them even more savagely, being not only without aesthetic education but living ugly lives in ugly quarters." [17] There is among the lower classes the widely spread notion that fine art is "self indulgent, unproductive, unnecessary, effeminate, unpolitical, unscientific, and highly suspicious morally." Shaw invokes his socialist principles to explain the economic reasons for such misconceptions, and adds:

. . . association with drunkenness, gambling, and fornication, and with nothing else, produces a conditioned reflex which makes the poor proletarian identify enjoyment with vice and sin, and art, being enjoyable, with smut and wickedness. Inevitably the poor proletarian educates his child as he trains his dog, by the whip, and

[14] *Ibid.*, p. 183.   [15] *Ibid.*, p. 175.
[16] *What's What*, p. 174. See also "The Religion of the Pianoforte," *Fortnightly Review* 61 (February, 1894), 255–66: "as life becomes more intense with the upward evolution of the race, it requires a degree of pleasure which cannot be extracted from the alimentary, predatory, and amatory instincts without ruinous perversions of them."
[17] *What's What*, p. 184.

punishes aestheticism as corruption, thereby making aesthetic education impossible.

Many of Shaw's muscial criticisms during the eighties in *London Music* [18] assert his conclusion that art and poverty are irreconcilable. Shaw would use all the resources of art for the betterment of the individual, but would not countenance art for its own sake while people remain as they are. Art for art's sake was never enough for Shaw because he believed that the "substitution of sensuous ecstasy for intellectual activity and honesty is the very devil." [19] Art, for Shaw, was a way aiming at the illumination and the intensification of living. Leaning heavily on Ruskin and Morris, Shaw adapted Pater's gem-like flame to his own purposes. In *The Sanity of Art,* which was an eloquent reply to Max Nordau's *Entartung,* Shaw wrote a definition of the nature and function of art which carefully qualifies the impact of art upon individual conduct and the development of character. It is interesting to see how Shaw distinguished between refinement of our senses for a purpose and the "idolatry of sensuousness" for its own sake.

The claim of art to our respect must stand or fall with the validity of its pretension to cultivate and refine our senses and faculties until seeing, hearing, feeling, smelling, and tasting become highly conscious and critical acts with us, protesting vehemently against ugliness, noise, discordant speech, frowzy clothing, and rebreathed air, and taking keen interest and pleasure in beauty, in music, and in nature. . . . Further, art should refine our sense of character and conduct, of justice and sympathy, greatly heightening our self-knowledge, self-control, precision of action, and considerateness, and making us intolerant of baseness, cruelty, injustice, and

[18] See for example, p. 138.
[19] Preface to *Three Plays for Puritans.*

intellectual superficiality or vulgarity. The worthy artist or crafts-
man is he who serves the physical and moral senses by feeding
them with pictures, musical compositions, pleasant houses and
gardens, good clothes and fine implements, poems, fictions, essays,
and dramas which call the heightened senses and ennobled faculties
into pleasurable activity. The great artist is he who goes a step
beyond the demand, and, by supplying works of higher beauty and
a higher interest than have yet been perceived, succeeds, after a
brief struggle with its strangeness, in adding this fresh extension of
sense to the heritage of the race.

If art is the device by which life achieves its purpose, lifting
itself to a higher level of awareness, the great artist or genius
is the instrument created for the fulfilment of that purpose. In
discussing geniuses and saints in the Preface to *Saint Joan*,
Shaw defines a genius as a "person who, seeing further and
probing deeper than other people, has a different set of ethical
valuations from theirs, and has energy enough to give effect to
this extra vision and its valuations in whatever manner best
suits his or her specific talents." Thus a Beethoven, a Shelley,
a Wagner, or an Ibsen outrage not only accepted concepts of
form and style and taste, but ethical, moral, and philosophic
concepts as well. Eventually this new and original valuation
embodied in a work of art will be accepted. Consequently,
the higher works of art are "instruments of evolution which
dare to criticize public opinion and existing institutions" [20]
and therefore contribute to the upward evolution of mankind.
And only a society whose schools are vitally concerned with
the creations of its great artists can attain to a high degree of
civilization.

Shaw's characterizations of artists in some of the plays may
puzzle readers who are not familiar with his theories about
art. For example, Praed in *Mrs. Warren's Profession* (1893),

[20] *What's What,* p. 194.

though he is an architect, can be interpreted as a reflection of Shaw's contempt for the artist who venerates conventional beauty and romance. He is horrified when Vivie Warren confesses she likes working for money, and when fatigued, "a cigar, a little whisky, and a novel with a good detective story in it." In a frenzy of repudiation he cries out, "I am an artist; and I can't believe it. . . . You haven't discovered yet what a wonderful world art can open for you." Apparently Vivie has not been artistically educated at Newnham College and at Cambridge, where she has already distinguished herself in mathematics. She tells Praed that one of her college chums "took me to the National Gallery, to the opera, and to a concert where the band played Beethoven and Wagner. I wouldn't go through that experience again for anything." What comes clear at the end is that Vivie, a realist, repudiates "with a shudder" Praed's trite suggestion that she "saturate [herself] with beauty and romance." Shaw is obviously attacking the romantic, would-be artist in this characterization of Praed.

Octavius in *Man and Superman* (1903) is also portrayed as a weak specimen of an artist. His devotion to Ann stamps him as a victim of romantic, idealistic woman-worship. He wants desperately to be a poet, "to write a great play" with Ann as his inspiration. It becomes necessary for Tanner to explain to him that the true "artist's work is to shew us ourselves as we really are . . . and he who adds a jot to such knowledge creates new mind as surely as woman creates new men." Painting that remorseless struggle between the artist-man, "a child-robber, a blood-sucker, a hypocrite and a cheat," and the mother-woman, Tanner ridicules Octavius' "romanticist cant" that they love one another. Tanner's conception of the artist is extended in the dream sequence of the play. Tracing

the history of his intellectual life, Juan explains the role that
art played in his development:

Then came [after the professors, the doctors of divinity and the
politicians] the romantic man, the Artist, with his love songs and
his paintings and his poems; and with him I had great delight for
many years, and some profit; for I cultivated my senses for his
sake; and his songs taught me to hear better, his paintings to see
better, and his poems to feel more deeply. But he led me at last into
the worship of Woman.

Elaborating further, Juan tells of his final disillusionment with
women as, in Ana's words, "lovely incarnations of music
and painting and poetry." Although he admits that woman
taught him much, in fact "she interpreted all the other teaching for me," the ideals of art and women were eventually shattered. They have now become merely a means to attaining the
goal of the philosopher. For Juan it is now, "I would think
more; therefore I must be more."

The relation between art and thought is pursued further in
Back to Methuselah (1921). In the first play, *In the Beginning*, Eve rebukes the destructive Cain who imagines "a
glorious poem of many men . . . killing, killing," reminding
him that her sons and sons' sons are not all fighters, but musicians, poets, sculptors, scientists, priests. "When they come,
there is always some new wonder, or some new hope. . . .
They . . . are always learning and always creating either
things or wisdom, or at least dreaming of them." In the last
play, *As Far As Thought Can Reach*, Eve's elevation of cre-
ativity becomes transmuted into a glorification of a direct
sense of life so that only thought is left. At the birth of the
Newly Born, a She-Ancient instructs her in the progress of her
life for the first four years. "Your companions here will teach

you how to keep up an imitation of happiness by what they call arts and sports and pleasures. . . . They have many pretty toys: a playhouse, pictures, images, flowers, bright fabrics, music. . . . At the end of four years, your mind will change." Later at the Festival of the Artists the young people debate about art and life. Ecrasia insists that the business of the artist is to create, something the Ancients do not seem to understand. Arjillax, sensing the futility of the "pretty-pretty confectionery you call sculpture," argues in favor of realism in art such as that "intensity of mind that is stamped" on the Ancients, and cites the work of the great Archangel Michael (Michelangelo). But Martellus, an older artist, reveals that he has long since graduated from this stage. He, too, has modelled Ancients, but he has destroyed his work "because you cannot give them life. . . . Anything alive is better than anything that is only pretending to be alive." Martellus concludes that "in the end the intellectual conscience that tore you away from the fleeting in art to the eternal must tear you away from art altogether because art is false and life alone is true." Martellus now reveals that the scientist, Pygmalion, has created the two most wonderful works of art in the world, two living human beings. Both Martellus and Pygmalion, however, admit failure when it turns out that the "synthetic couple" are all reflexes, mere automata responding only to external stimuli.

The Ancients then instruct the youths at the festival to be content in their present immaturity with creating dolls, not human beings. Ecrasia who still insists that art is superior to life is told:

Yes, child: art is the magic mirror you make to reflect your invisible dreams in visible pictures. . . . But we who are older use neither glass mirrors nor works of art. We have a direct sense of life. When you gain that you will put aside your mirrors and statues, your toys and your dolls.

And the She-Ancient concludes: "It was to myself I turned as to the final reality. Here, and here alone, I could shape and create."

In *In Good King Charles's Golden Days* (1939) a different view of art is to be found. The Dutch artist, Godfrey Kneller,[21] argues at great length with Newton about straight lines and curves, maintaining that God as an artist had created a curved universe. Subordinating philosophy and science to art, Kneller tells Charles:

The world must learn from its artists because God made the world as an artist. Your philosophers steal all their boasted discoveries from the artists; and then pretend they have deduced them from figures which they call equations, invented for that dishonest purpose. . . . Artists do not prove things. . . . They *know* them.

And to George Fox, "who is dumbfounded by this strange and ungodly talk" about the hand of the artist being the hand of God, Kneller says: "The hand that can draw the images of God and reveal the soul in them . . . is not his hand the hand used by God, who, being a spirit without body, parts or passions, has no hands . . . ?" Kneller, it must be assumed, is Shaw's mouthpiece since his arguments against science which appear in the Preface are easily recognizable as the author's. Philosophy—Juan's and the Ancients' means to attaining a direct sense of life—is ranked below art in Kneller's scheme. Since *Man and Superman* and *Back to Methuselah* establish the function of art as a means to further growth, it is clear that

---

[21] See the Preface to this play where Shaw explains that Kneller is only a substitute for Hogarth who "could not by any magic be fitted into the year 1680."

Shaw regarded art as a major building block of the educative process.

Because conformity and standardization, particularly with regard to the higher operations of the intellect, signify a kind of death for civilization, Shaw formulated this important objective for education:

One of the main objects of education is to prevent people from defeating their own civilization by refusing to tolerate novelties and heresies which history proves that they had better tolerate. Therefore it is of extraordinary importance that all citizens should be educated in liberty, toleration, and the theory of natural rights. At present they are taught nothing but an idiotic demonstration that natural rights are a fiction of the vulgar imagination, because, forsooth natural rights *are* natural and not derived or acquired: in short, not logical.[22]

True liberty for Shaw was the "freedom to preach sedition and immorality, to utter blasphemy" against commonly accepted valuations in any society. In the Preface to *The Shewing-Up of Blanco Posnet*,[23] which is an attack on censorship in general, immorality is defined as follows: "Whatever is contrary to established manners and customs is immoral. An immoral act or doctrine is not necessarily a sinful one: on the contrary, every advance in thought and conduct is by definition immoral until it has converted the majority." For that reason immorality must be protected "against the attacks of those who have no standard except the standard of custom, and who regard any attack on custom—that is, on morals—as an attack on society, religion, and on virtue." Since there is no need to tolerate what is accepted as enlightened, tolera-

---

[22] Preface to W.E.A. *Year Book* in *Doctors' Delusions* (Shaw's italics).
[23] See "The Rejected Statement, Part I." See also *The Author's Apology from Mrs. Warren's Profession*, p. 40: "All censorships exist to prevent anyone from challenging current conceptions and existing institutions."

tion and liberty do not make sense except as toleration of opinions that are considered heretical. Consequently, it is "immorality, not morality, that needs protection," for most people tolerate what the majority considers right. Presenting many examples to prove that toleration of unpopular ideas may not always be a golden rule if the rights of others are threatened, Shaw concluded that "toleration is a matter of degree: we all draw the line somewhere; and nothing will shift that line except education."[24]

Shaw's method for implementing the aim of educating people in liberty and toleration is what he calls "controversial education."

The only solution of the difficulty is controversial education. That is what all the real education we have at present is. The student must be warned that religion, science, and philosophy are all fiercely controversial subjects, and that if he feels interested he must hear champions of the opposed views fighting it out in debate, and be permitted to question them afterwards.[25]

Although a student may, like a jury, be unable to reach a verdict—"it may even take him forty years to arrive at one"— he will have learned a lot in absorbing the clash of intellectual opinion, for a "controversially educated person with an open mind is better educated than a dogmatically educated one with a closed mind."[26] Shaw does not mean to say that every difference of opinion must involve the indefinite postponement of coming to decisions. The young must be trained to

[24] Preface to W.E.A. *Year Book* in *Doctors' Delusions.*
[25] Preface to W.E.A. *Year Book* in *Doctors' Delusions.* See Henderson, *Playboy and Prophet,* p. 686 where the author suggests that one of Shaw's earliest influences was Mill's essay *On Liberty* which states: "Since the general or prevailing opinion on any subject is rarely or never the whole truth, it is only by the collision of adverse opinion that the remainder of the truth has any chance of being supplied."
[26] Preface to W.E.A. *Year Book* in *Doctors' Delusions.*

understand that "there is a vast field of human action in which something must be done immediately and they must all agree to do the same thing without stopping to argue about it." Furthermore, he specifies that if an individual thinks he knows the road to improvement, he must "be educated to understand that his business is to persuade the authorities to make the new road and plough up the old, and not immediately to trample and trespass along his pet line as if the business concerned himself alone."

Learning can not take place if people are protected "against shocks to their opinions and convictions, moral, political, or religious." [27] Controversial education is the only kind of education, Shaw argued, which can teach people the nature and processes of thought involved in critical thinking. If people could be educated into understanding such processes of thought, and consequently the variety of intellectual alternatives always present in any controversy, they would more readily understand the teacher of new truths, the man of genius who contributes to society's progress. Even those whose opinions seem evil to us must be tolerated not only because they may be on the right track for all we know, but also because "it is in the conflict of opinion that we win knowledge and wisdom." People must be taught to respect their intellectual enemies and to evaluate immoral ideas fairly, for men who know their intellectual opponents and understand their views "quite commonly respect and like them, and always learn something from them." A fine teacher, too, can be dangerous in the classroom, because "the abler a schoolmaster is, the more dangerous he is to his pupils unless they have the fullest opportunity of hearing another equally able person do his utmost to shake his authority and convict him of error."

[27] Preface to *Misalliance*.

Shaw is assuming that an able teacher tells his class what to think instead of instructing them how to think. His program is concerned with a frontal attack on intellectual prejudice in general. Shaw believes that the reason "such teaching . . . does not exist in the schools" is that it "would tear away the camouflage from commercial civilization." [28]

The Preface to *Saint Joan* paves the way for the play. That we must "make it a point of honor to privilege heresy to the last bearable degree on the simple ground that all evolution in thought and conduct must at first appear as heresy and misconduct" qualifies the theme of the drama. The law of God, he argues, is the law of change, and if "churches and schools and governments set themselves against change as such, they are setting themselves against the law of God." Discussing Joan's illiteracy ("yet she understood the political and military situation in France much better than most of our newspaper-fed university women graduates understand the corresponding situation of their own country to-day"), Shaw states that her "want of academic education disabled her when she had to deal with such artificial structures as the great ecclesiastical and social institutions of the Middle Ages. She had a horror of heretics without suspecting that she was herself a heresiarch." Comparing the intolerance of the Middle Ages with that of to-day, Shaw concluded that Joan, tried today, "would be treated with no more toleration than Mrs. Sylvia Pankhurst, or the Peculiar People, or the parents who keep their children from the elementary school, or any of the others who cross the line we have to draw, rightly or wrongly, between the tolerable and the intolerable." The reason is the mental and spiritual giants suffer in our society because "their fellows hate mental giants and would like to destroy them . . . because it frightens

[28] Preface to W.E.A. *Year Book* in *Doctors' Delusions*.

them." The schools, Shaw charged, glorify the military and political scoundrels, not the saints and artists.

The epilogue of the play is a bitter commentary on the state of the world and man. A clerical gentleman clothed in the fashion of 1920 appears and announces that Joan of Arc has been canonized as a saint. All who had combined to bring about her execution—Cauchon, Dunois, the Archbishop, Warwick, De Stogumber, Charles—kneel and voice their praise. And when Joan suggests, "Shall I rise from the dead and come back to you a living woman?" they all spring to their feet in consternation. Cauchon says: "The heretic is always better dead and mortal eyes cannot distinguish the saint from the heretic." And Dunois: "Forgive us, Joan: we are not yet good enough for you." Each in turn begs to be excused and leaves. Joan's final words are: "O God that madest this beautiful earth, when will it be ready to receive thy saints? How long, O Lord, how long."

Many people have testified to Shaw's role as a teacher in the Aristophanes–Molière tradition. Albert Einstein has stated: "I salute with sincere emotion the supreme master of this method, who has delighted—and educated—us all." [29] Aldous Huxley, linking Shaw with Erasmus and Voltaire, suggests that "instead of just applauding Mr. Shaw's plays and chuckling over his prefaces, we had also paid some serious attention to his teaching, what remains of our civilization might not now be lying under sentence of death." [30] Harold Laski thinks Shaw "has been the greatest teacher of his generation." [31] Laurence Housman believes the "difference between the well-educated mind of the twentieth century and the less well-educated mind of the

[29] *The World As I See It*, p. 37.
[30] "A Birthday Wish," S. Winsten, editor, *G.B.S. 90*.
[31] "Four Literary Portraits," *Living Age* 339 (November, 1930), pp. 289–92.

nineteenth century to be very largely of Shaw's production," [32] and compares Shaw with the great teacher, Socrates. That Shaw, having succeeded as an artist, may also enjoy some success as a teacher is Eric Bentley's belief.[33] Although there have been as many detractors as enthusiasts, the point is that Shaw did use the theater for his own pedagogical purposes.

These purposes of the Shavian theater were frequently admitted by Shaw. When Ellen Terry complained that she did not like *Captain Brassbound's Conversion*, the play he had written for her, he replied: "I must educate a new generation with my pen from childhood up—audience, actors and all." [34] In discussing flogging in the schools, he states: "I must really ask whether I, who am, for good or evil, a genuine teacher by a highly skilled method, am to admit as my equal a person whose 'profession' it is to hit a boy half his size." [35] In the Preface to *Geneva* he declares that "when I am not writing plays . . . I write political school books." And in the Preface to *The Shewing-Up of Blanco Posnet* he admits himself "to be a specialist in immoral and heretical plays . . . with the deliberate object of converting the nation" to his system of morals.

In order to educate the public to appreciate serious drama, Shaw attacked the frivolous, stereotyped, romantic drama and denied that the playwright must be "a mere purveyor of pleasure." Repeatedly he denounced the fashion of people going to the theater, as to church, to display their best clothes, to have something to talk about at dinner parties, "in short for any and every reason except interest in dramatic art as such." [36]

[32] "G.B.S. and the Victorians," S. Winsten, editor, *G.B.S. 90.*
[33] Foreword, *Bernard Shaw.*
[34] *Ellen Terry and Bernard Shaw: A Correspondence,* p. 246.
[35] Preface to W.E.A. *Year Book* in *Doctors' Delusions.*
[36] Preface to *Saint Joan.*

Shaw declared that the well-made plays of Scribe and Sardou succeeded because the formula for such plays was developed in the days when "the spread of elementary schooling produced a huge mass of playgoers sufficiently educated to want plays instead of dogfights, but not educated enough to enjoy or understand the masterpieces of dramatic art." [37] The Preface to *Three Plays for Puritans* emphasizes the impact of literature upon personal codes of morality:

The worst of it is that since man's intellectual consciousness of himself is derived from descriptions of him in books, a persistent representation of humanity in literature gets finally accepted upon. . . . If the conditions of romance are only insisted on long enough and uniformly enough, then, for the huge School Board taught masses who read romance and nothing else, these conventions will become the law of personal honor.

It would be much better, Shaw believed, if people were left to their former ignorance and superstition. "Ten years of cheap reading have changed the English from the most stolid nation in Europe to the most theatrical and hysterical." And the majority of critics and playwrights who feed the uneducated masses artificial concepts of life are themselves, Shaw charged, "as to education all but illiterate." His conclusion was that "the box office would never become an English influence until the theater turns from the drama of romance and sensuality to the drama of education."

This type of drama was invested by Shaw with ethical, moral, and intellectual purposes. Not only must the serious playwright —and Shaw cites Euripides, Aristophanes, Molière, Brieux— attack and destroy stereotyped concepts of life, but he must be

[37] Preface to *Three Plays by Brieux.* Of *Les Hannetons* by Brieux, Shaw suggests: "To witness a performance might very wisely be made part of the curriculum of every university college and polytechnic in the country."

a "ruthless revealer of hidden truth and a mighty destroyer of idols." [38] Like Meredith, Shaw believes that the function of comedy is nothing less than the destruction of old-established morals. Such revelations can be communicated only in a work of dramatic art that stirs audiences, takes them outside of themselves, makes them suffer and think. In the "Epistle Dedicatory" to *Man and Superman* he states: "It annoys me to see people comfortable when they ought to be uncomfortable; and I insist on making them think in order to bring them to a conviction of sin." Shaw would have people leave the theater with a very disquieting sense that they are somehow involved in a problem and that they must find a way out if civilization is to be tolerable. In this respect he cites his own plays which "are built to induce, not voluptuous reverie but intellectual interest, not romantic rhapsody but humane concern." [39] The contemporary theater, which Shaw compared to the Church in the Middle Ages, must become a "factory of thought, a prompter of conscience, an elucidator of social conduct . . . and a temple of the Ascent of Man." [40] If art is a method of schooling, then drama, a form of art, must stimulate people to learn more about life as it really is, to improve themselves ethically and morally.

I am convinced that fine art is the subtlest, the most effective means of propaganda in the world, excepting only the example of personal conduct; and I waive even this exception in favor of the art of the stage because it works by exhibiting examples of personal conduct made intelligible and moving to crowds of unobservant, unreflecting people to whom real life means nothing.[41]

Speaking of his own plays, Shaw warned repeatedly that if people were to be edified by his kind of drama they must be

[38] Preface to *Three Plays by Brieux*.
[39] *The Author's Apology from Mrs. Warren's Profession*, p. 43.
[40] "The Author's Apology," *Dramatic Opinions and Essays*, I.
[41] *The Author's Apology from Mrs. Warren's Profession*, p. 25.

aware that "my attacks are directed against themselves not against my stage figures." [42] The guilt of defective social organization does not lie with individuals such as Sartorius or Mrs. Warren, who evidence unusual capacities and virtues, but with the whole body of citizens. The average person, badly educated in the understanding of dramatic art, will laugh at the stage puppets but never at himself.[43] Vital participation in a problem play, coupled with the knowledge of the immense importance of the drama as a means of enlightenment and self-criticism, is lacking because the theater has always been regarded as a place of superficial amusement.

Bad theaters are as mischievous as bad schools; for modern civilization is rapidly multiplying the numbers to whom the theater is both School and Church. Public and private life become daily more theatrical: the Emperor is the "leading man" on the stage of his country; all great newspapers are now edited dramatically; the records of our law courts show that the spread of dramatic consciousness is affecting personal conduct to an unprecedented extent, and affecting by no means for the worse, except in so far as the dramatic education of the persons concerned has been romantic; that is, spurious, cheap and vulgar. In the face of such conditions there can be no question that the commercial limits should be overstepped, and that the highest prestige, with a personal position of reasonable security and comfort, should be attainable in theatrical management by keeping the public in constant touch with the highest achievements of dramatic art.[44]

Shaw's concept of the theater as both a school and a church leads up to this suggestion:

Performance should be in the order of academic courses, designed to take audiences over the whole ground as Ibsen and his successors took them; so that the exposition may be consecutive. Otherwise

[42] Preface to *Plays: Pleasant and Unpleasant*, I.
[43] See Shaw on *Saint Joan*, The New York *Times* (April 13, 1924): "My method of education is to teach people how to laugh at themselves."
[44] Preface to *Plays: Pleasant and Unpleasant*, II.

the doctrine will not be interesting, and the audiences will not come regularly.[45]

Apparently Shaw would suspend his usual condemnation of academic methods if genuine training of audiences in the nature and function of true dramatic art were possible. The passage emphasizes the obvious need for viewing experiences in the theater as vital constituents of the educative process.

This theme is apparent in *The Dark Lady of the Sonnets* written in 1910 to help the fund for establishing a National Theater. Shakespeare is shown stealing into the Palace at Whitehall for a secret rendezvous with the Dark Lady. Queen Elizabeth, walking in her sleep and speaking like Lady Macbeth, is mistaken by Shakespeare for his mistress, Mary, who suddenly arrives and sends both of them sprawling. It all ends with Shakespeare making a lengthy plea to Elizabeth for a "National Theater for the better instruction and gracing of your Majesty's subjects." Attacking the commercial theater of his day, Shakespeare tells Elizabeth that only when "there is a matter of murder, or a pretty youth in petticoats, or some naughty tale of wantonness, will your subjects pay the great cost of good players." Admitting he wrote "two filthy pieces," *As You Like It* and *Much Ado About Nothing,* in order to make money, Shakespeare begs the Queen "to give order that a theater be endowed . . . for the playing of those pieces of mine which no merchant will touch." And adds:

Thereby you shall also encourage other men to undertake the writing of plays who do now despise it and leave it wholly to those whose counsels will work little good to your realm. For this writing of plays is a great matter, forming as it does the minds and affections of men in such sort that whatsoever they see done in show on

[45] *The Quintessence of Ibsenism: Now Completed to the Death of Ibsen,* p. 239.

the stage, they will presently be doing in earnest in the world, which is but a larger stage. Therefore now must your Majesty take up the good work that your Church hath abandoned, and restore the art of playing to its former use and dignity.

Predicting that "it will be three hundred years or more before my subjects learn that man cannot live by bread alone," Elizabeth tells Shakespeare that England will do only what "she seeth everybody else doing."

The Beefeater, representing the average playgoer, says when he is offered a pass to the theater: "I care not for these newfangled plays. No man can understand a word of them. Will you not give me a pass for *The Spanish Tragedy*?"

The theater, for Shaw, must be a means of educating people in controversy, that is in liberty, toleration, and in the theory of natural rights. He denounced the censors of plays who set out to "suppress heresy and challenges to morality in their serious and avowed forms," yet set out to approve "frivolous and even pornographic plays." [46] Shaw's program of controversial education which, to him, eased the path of the educative process, also applies to the theater.

[46] Preface to *Three Plays by Brieux*.

8   *Planning the schools*

SHAW's socialist and evolutionary ideals would largely determine the aims, content, and methods of the schools, from the nursery to the university. "Though proletarian orthodoxy will differ from capitalist orthodoxy, it will be inculcated in the schools and enforced in the courts just as our present capitalist orthodoxy is at Eton and the Old Bailey. And its legislation will not take the Whig direction of less government interference." [1] Shaw is admitting that his socialist society would have to create in its schools a vast propaganda machine to insure its existence. He is quick, however, to point out that the "orthodoxy" to be taught in the schools does not cover the whole field of human conduct and that there "would always be a Nomansland ahead in which morals are disputable and changeable." Presumably, this qualification is designed to guard his program of "controversial education" which would "keep all our moral measures open to discussion."

THE CURRICULUM

The function of the schools is to help realize the goals of the educative process. Citizenship, being a major aim, can-

[1] *What's What*, p. 171.

not be taught unless the schools "inculcate political principles, manners, morals, and religion." [2] It would be the obligation of the state "not only to make all knowledge accessible to those who seek it, but to impose some knowledge on those who do all they can to escape it." [3] The state "must determine the point at which compulsory education shall stop and voluntary education and voluntary ignorance begins." The point is to be reached quite early in the education of a child, but it is a time which must be reached "for there is in hard fact an irreducible minimum of knowledge without which men cannot live in civilized society; consequently its acquisition must take precedence of their liberties and eccentricities." It is evident that Shaw's rejection of modern compulsory education involves a system of compulsion with socialist implications.

What Shaw calls technical education is a qualification for living in society. "Being necessary to life, it justifies itself by its results even to those who acquire it with difficulty and repugnance, and exercise its accomplishments without pleasure for ulterior objects." [4] Citizenship involves not only the mastery of fundamentals as reading and writing, but a knowledge of moral, religious, and intellectual concepts.[5] Science would also be required and would include political science, "not only in its elementary branch of police regulation, but in its modern constitutional developments as industrial democracy and Socialism." [6] These subjects "in a modern democratic state" (the same as a socialist state to Shaw) are "to be as compulsory, up to the limit of the scholar's capacity for them, as the multiplication table. . . . though we cannot make every

[2] *Ibid.*, p. 152.   [3] *Ibid.*, p. 165.
[4] Preface to *Year Book* for 1918, in *Doctors' Delusions.*
[5] See "Limits to Education," *Survey* 48 (May 6, 1922), p. 218. (Digest of a lecture).
[6] Preface to *Year Book* in *Doctors' Delusions.*

boy and girl a Sidney and Beatrice Webb we can at least save them from the democratic delusion that political capacity is not a scientific acquirement but an intuition which descends on every freeborn Briton at the age of twenty-one." This kind of civic education would be of particular importance in Shaw's state since nobody would be given the voting privilege unless certain "tests of technical qualification" were passed. As to methods of teaching political science and civic education Shaw specifies that no such education "is possible without discussion and controversy. The dogmatic schoolmaster, with his authoritative textbook and his sanction of the cane, or the imposition, or the keeping in, will not do here."

Differentiating between technical and liberal education, Shaw believed that the latter "which is really recreation" cannot be attained through compulsory schooling. "A liberal education cannot be acquired without interest and pleasure." He admitted that it would be difficult for a future state to draw a rigid line between technical and liberal education. "There are parts of liberal education which are as necessary in modern social life as reading and writing; and it is this that makes it so difficult to draw the line beyond which the State has no right to meddle with the child's mind or body without its free consent." [7] Shaw's discursiveness on this point makes it difficult to determine to what extent liberal education overlaps into technical education. Presumably he is referrring to the inclusion in the curriculum of such subjects as morals, religion, history, law, political science, economics, and art. Though he asks elsewhere "Is there an irreducible minimum of aesthetic education as there is of elementary [technical?] education?" [8] he qualifies an uncertain conclusion by suggesting that everybody should at least be given the chance of attaining creative

[7] *The Intelligent Woman*, p. 422.   [8] *What's What*, p. 173.

eminence. In general aesthetic education is part of liberal education and cannot be communicated through compulsion. Shaw would "throw the extremes of learning open to everyone so that no talent or capacity shall be thrown away for lack of training or opportunity." [9] But he thinks it unwise to "impose the highest education indiscriminately on average minds (let alone primitive ones)." [10]

People who are neither over nor under educated take their places in the world cheerfully, and are the first to admit that the notion that everybody can be taught at school to become a higher mathematician, a grammarian and epic poet writing in ancient Greek and Latin, an epoch-making philosopher . . . which is the theoretic aim of our Boards of Education . . . is pedantic poppycock.

While the statement that people neither over- nor undereduccated to extremes can take their places in the world seems acceptable in our own democracy, the statement that the Boards of Education (English or American) seek to make everyone into a poet, philosopher, or mathematician is, of course, questionable.[11] Written in 1944, this contention seems to indicate that Shaw was perhaps not too familiar with the "theoretic aims" as set forth in modern educational philosophies.

In a sense Shaw toys with what modern educational theorists call general education. At one point he states:

The educationists who think that everything should be taught to everybody are as bad as the "practical" people at the opposite end who think it sufficient to teach people the technical routine of the trades or professions by which they will have to earn their livings. Such education may produce efficient robots. It will not produce citizens.

[9] *Ibid.*, p. 164.   [10] *Ibid.*, p. 345.

[11] See *ibid.*, p. 172, where Shaw is critical of Russian education. The Soviets "aimed at making every little Russian a complete Marxist philosopher as madly as Eton aims at making every English boy a complete poet, theologian, and higher mathematician."

But immediately he wonders whether "there is something, after all, in the notion that everybody should be taught everything . . . for we should be savages if we knew nothing beyond the things we can do well." Aware of the potential in each individual, Shaw seems to suggest—his discursiveness obliterates certainty here—that a kind of general education (he never uses the term) might bring forth those tastes and capacities which poverty, ignorance, and lack of opportunity ordinarily extinguish. Earlier he had stated that "even the uneducated should know what education means. Such an epithet as 'half educated' should vanish from the language." [12] Shaw may have thought that his irreducible minimum of knowledge required of every individual constitutes a kind of general education, but he never quite says so.

Although Shaw considered it a "monstrous thing to force a child to learn Latin or Greek or mathematics on the ground that they are an indispensable gymnastic for the mental powers," [13] he admitted that dead languages not only have their uses—but that ignorance of them may close certain careers to people:

They will always be learned by people who want to learn them; and people will always want to learn them as long as they are of any importance in life: indeed the want will survive their importance: superstition is nowhere stronger than in the field of obsolete requirements. And they will never be learnt fruitfully by people who do not want to learn them either for their own sake or for use in necessary work.

Shaw points out that when Latin was a living language in the Middle Ages it had to be effectively taught so that students

[12] Preface to W.E.A. *Year Book* in *Doctors' Delusions.* See also "The Revolutionist's Handbook," *Man and Superman:* "No man can be a pure specialist without being in the strict sense an idiot."
[13] Preface to *Misalliance.*

could read it and write it. When the language went out of use it became a teaching subject "taught by each generation of teachers to the next generation so that the teaching profession might continue to make a living by teaching it, the pupils who did not become teachers learning it for no purpose whatever except to pass examinations in." [14] Since Latin had lost contact with life what was studied in the schools "was a spurious Latin . . . and never learnt by the vast majority of boys, even when they had been kept at it for ten years: enough to learn all the languages of Europe." As late as 1944 he could say: "Yet our school system still proceeds on the assumption that Latin is the language of literature and culture." [15]

A fundamental conviction of Shaw is that the schools must prepare an individual for the living experiences of life itself. The so-called educated people, saturated with the "unassimilated stuffing" or useless subjects taught in the schools, not only are "impenetrable to the lessons of life," but regard "intellectual exertion hateful instead of healthy and natural." [16] Shaw was keenly aware that the lessons of life and intellectual exertion do not necessarily derive from—though they may be stimulated by—great books which may not reflect the real world and its problems. In the "Epistle Dedicatory" to *Man and Superman* he wrote: "The world shewn us in books, whether the books be confessed epics or professed gospels, or in codes, or in political orations, or in philosophic systems, is not the main world at all: it is only the self-consciousness of certain abnormal people who have the specific artistic talent and temperament." *Man and Superman* and *Back to Methuselah* extend the concept that man's capacity for thought and for direct contact with life must take precedence over art and over

[14] *Doctors' Delusions*, p. 335.   [15] *What's What*, p. 146.
[16] *Doctors' Delusions*, p. 334.

any creations not deriving from the essences of life itself. Elevating the "contemporary real" over the world of books in this passage from the "Epistle Dedicatory," Shaw implies that it is the burden of the schools to bridge the gap between the world of books and culture, and the experiences of life itself:

And since what we call education and culture is for the most part nothing but the substitution of reading for experience, of literature for life, of the obsolete fictitious for the contemporary real, education, as you no doubt observed at Oxford, destroys, by supplantation, every mind that is not strong enough to see through the imposture and to use the great Masters of Arts as what they really are and no more: that is, patentees of highly questionable, and for the majority but the half valid representations of life. The schoolboy who uses his Homer to throw at his fellow's head makes perhaps the safest and most rational use of him; and I observe with reassurance that you occasionally do the same, in your prime, with your Aristotle.

Culture for Shaw (he does not seem to have defined it directly) implies not only knowledge of the greatest in art, literature, science, and philosophy, but also a rational understanding of the problems of life. University graduates having "half valid representations of life" and unable to penetrate the false abstractions inherent in society would not be considered cultured by Shaw.

Spurious culture is attacked in *Caesar and Cleopatra* (1898). When Caesar is informed by Theodotus that the library at Alexandria is in flames, he says, "Is that all?" And when Theodotus asks whether he is willing "to go down to posterity as a barbarous soldier too ignorant to know the value of books," Caesar replies: "I am an author myself; and I tell you it is better that the Egyptians should live their lives than dream them away with the help of books." This dialogue follows:

THEODOTUS (kneeling, with genuine literary emotion: the passion of the pedant). Caesar: once in ten generations of men, the world gains an immortal book.

CAESAR (inflexible). If it did not flatter mankind, the common executioner would burn it.

THEODOTUS. Without history, death would lay you beside your meanest soldier. . . . What is burning there is the memory of mankind.

CAESAR. A shameful memory. Let it burn.

THEODOTUS (wildly). Will you destroy the past?

CAESAR. Ay, and build the future with its ruins. . . . But harken, Theodotus, teacher of kings: you who valued Pompey's head no more than a shepherd values an onion, and who now kneel to me, with tears in your old eyes, to plead for a few sheepskins scrawled with errors. . . .

This is Shaw's way of making an audience realize the collective stupidity of mankind. Human life and civilized ethics are more important than a pedantic adoration of books. Caesar is unable to reconcile Theodotus' cruelty to Pompey with his passion for learning.

In *Major Barbara* (1905) the characterization of Cusins, the professor of Greek, illuminates some of Shaw's ideas about culture and the classics. "After all," says Lady Undershaft, the wife of Undershaft, the munitions manufacturer, "nobody can say a word against Greek: it stamps a man at once as an educated gentleman." When Undershaft admits, "I am not a gentleman; and I was never educated," Cusins suggests satirically:

Let me advise you to study Greek, Mr. Undershaft. Greek scholars are privileged men. Few of them know Greek; and none of them know anything else; but their position is unchallengeable. Other languages are the qualifications of waiters and commercial travellers: Greek is to a man of position what the hallmark is to silver.

Undershaft, considering Cusins as a possible son-in-law and successor to his munitions industry, objects at first because it is against the business tradition of the firm to consider an "educated man." At this point Cusins becomes Shaw: "Once in ten thousand times it happens that the schoolboy is a born master of what they try to teach him. Greek has not destroyed my mind: it has nourished it. Besides, I did not learn it at an English public school." Although Undershaft is won over, he attempts to drive a hard bargain, and objects to Cusins' demand for ten percent of the profits on the grounds that he is "not bringing any capital into the concern." Cusins' reply is in effect an attack on the business man's contempt for intellect and poetry.

What! no capital! Is my mastery of Greek no capital? Is my access to the subtlest thought, the loftiest poetry yet attained by humanity, no capital? My character! my intellect! my life! my career! what Barbara calls my soul! are these no capital? Say another word; and I double my salary.

THE EDUCATION OF YOUNG CHILDREN

To Mrs. Pat Campbell Shaw once wrote: "Parents and Children: that is the theme of my preface. The tears of countless children have fallen unrevenged. I will turn them into boiling vitriol and force it into the souls of their screaming oppressors." [17] In an essay "Killing for Sport" he made a Swiftian proposal to introduce the shooting of children as a sport since they would at least be preserved very carefully, like deer and pheasants, for ten months of the year.[18] Shaw's eloquent attacks

[17] *Bernard Shaw and Mrs. Patrick Campbell: Their Correspondence,* p. 59.
[18] Preface, Henry S. Salt, editor, *Killing for Sport: Essays by Various Writers.*

on the practice of imprisoning children physically are illustrated in this passage from the Preface to *Misalliance:*

With millions of acres of woods and valleys and hills and streams and fishes . . . or with streets and shop windows and crowds and vehicles and all sorts of city delights at the door, you are forced to sit, not in a room with some human grace and comfort . . . but in a stalled pound with a lot of other children, beaten if you talk, beaten if you move, beaten if you cannot prove by answering idiotic questions that even when you escaped from the pound and from the eye of your gaoler, you were still agonizing over his detestable sham books instead of daring to live.

In fact, Shaw insisted, all this is crueler than a prison where "they may torture your body, but not your brains" and where they at least "protect you against violence from your fellow prisoners." The Preface to the Workers' Educational Association *Year Book*, written some years after English law had already banned corporal punishment, states that "there are worse tortures, both physical and moral, in actual use . . . in schools where corporal punishment is not permitted." [19] Although Shaw was a pioneer in helping to abolish flogging, he was primarily concerned—even as late as 1944—with moral and intellectual laming and breaking of young spirits to the detriment of evolutionary progress.[20]

The function of the school is to qualify children "for their part in life as responsible citizens of a free state." [21] In order to implement this aim Shaw would establish a constitution of children's rights which,

being clearly those of any other human being, are summed up in the right to live. . . . And this right to live includes, and in fact is,

[19] See the many pieces about flogging, written for the press, in *Doctors' Delusions.*
[20] *What's What,* p. 155.   [21] Preface to *Misalliance.*

the right to be what the child likes and can, to do what it likes and can, to make what it likes and can, to think what it likes and can, to smash what it dislikes and can, and generally to behave in an altogether unaccountable manner within the limits imposed by the similar rights of its neighbors.

That Shaw does not mean the creation of an anarchic child world coexistent with the restrictions demanded of all adult members of a democratic socialist state should now be evident. In his desire to reconcile education with liberty he is suggesting that "what the child needs is not only a school and an adult home, but a child world of which it can be a little citizen, with laws, rights, duties and recreations suited to childish abilities and disabilities." [22] Such a child world would have to be carefully supervised by the state.

The production of responsible citizens would be accelerated if at the very outset a child were taught "the fundamental economic truth . . . that whoever consumes goods or services without producing by personal effort the equivalent of what he or she consumes, inflicts on the community precisely the same injury that a thief produces." [23] Shaw recommended that children be given the opportunity to work for the community at a very early age, even if only for half an hour a day. This sort of productive work "has the advantage that its discipline is the discipline of impersonal necessity, not that of wanton personal coercion." He suggested that the desire of most children to escape from school to the adult world is a natural eagerness to experience "the dignity of adult work, the exchange of the factitious personal tyranny of the schoolmaster, from which grown-ups are free, for the stern but entirely dignified Laws of Life to which all flesh is subject."

[22] *What's What*, p. 69.   [23] Preface to *Misalliance*.

The social creed must be imposed on us when we are children; for it is like riding, or reading music at sight: it can never become a second nature to those who try to learn it as adults; and the social creed, to be really effective, must be a second nature to us. It is quite easy to give people a second nature, however unnatural, if you catch them early enough.[24]

In the Preface to *Misalliance* Shaw has suggested the kind of subjects a child must master if he is to be granted liberties.

A child must know the rules of the road, be able to read placards and proclamations, fill voting papers, compose and send letters and telegrams, purchase food and clothing and railway tickets for itself, count money and give and take change, and, generally, know how many beans make five. It must know some law, were it only a simple set of commandments, some political economy, agriculture enough to shut the gates of fields with cattle in them and not to trample on growing crops, sanitation enough not to defile its haunts, and religion enough to have some idea of why it is allowed its rights and why it must respect the rights of others. And the rest of its education must consist of anything else it can pick up; for beyond this society cannot go with any certainty, and indeed can only go this far rather apologetically and provisionally, as doing the best it can on very uncertain ground.

This sort of curriculum Shaw calls "natural" education as distinguished from "school" education. He repeats emphatically that "teaching children subjects that do not interest them directly, or at least as necessary steps to the fulfilment of their hopes and desires, not only makes them unhappy but injures them both physically and mentally." [25]

Shaw recommends that when a pupil has no natural impulse to learn, and yet must not be left in ignorance, an "indirect motive" must be supplied. If a child cannot or refuses to learn the multiplication and pence table, for example, the problem is

[24] *Intelligent Woman*, p. 427.   [25] *What's What*, p. 163.

easily solved if the child can be persuaded to understand that it can never hope to be given pocket money until it knows its tables. "An adventurous boy with a craze for exploration or for the sea may have no mathematical turn; but he will tackle enough mathematics as a navigator as willingly as our air pilots tackle the Morse code, not in itself a very attractive study." [26] Here it is apparent that Shaw assumes, like so many modern progressive teachers, that demonstrating the imperative need for mastering a subject will by itself result in learning. Furthermore, in suggesting that child life should be so organized "as to create a strong collective opinion among children that there are certain things everyone must learn and know" [27] and that "learning should bring . . . privileges and liberties, status, and earnings," Shaw perhaps disposes of the learning complex too glibly. He believed that a "child has a right to finality as regards its compulsory lessons" [28] for the endless mountains of information ordinarily thrown at it merely serve to torture it. All that can be done is to prescribe certain definite acquirements and accomplishments as qualifications for certain employments and to provide certain privileges if these are mastered. There should be, Shaw suggests, a series of "Coming of Ages" for children:

The child should have its first coming of age when it is weaned, another when it can talk, another when it can walk, another when it can dress itself without assistance; and when it can read, write, count money, and pass an examination in going a simple errand involving a purchase and a journey by rail or other public method of locomotion, it should have quite a majority.

Although Shaw has not provided any specific techniques for the teaching of the compulsory requirements, he was to a great extent in the vanguard of those who championed pro-

[26] *Ibid.*, p. 164.   [27] *Ibid.*, p. 177.   [28] Preface to *Misalliance.*

gressive methods providing humane incentives for learning. What is more important than the school and the home is "the communal training, the apprenticeship to society" which only a socialist state can provide. This can be acquired early in life only by mixing with the world. Therefore it is important

. . . to give children variety of experience and company, the world to live in, homes to sleep in, communal halls to eat and associate in, safe cities to roam through and learn from the crowds and sights, and opportunity to hear every statement that can be made to them controversially criticized.[29]

Instead of being forbidden to do as they like, children should be compelled to dispense with adult guidance, and depend on themselves to the full limit of their resourcefulness. Child development in this area depends upon a state in which "children should find in every part of their native country, food, clothing, lodging, instruction, and parental guidance for the asking." [30]

The freedom to "roam" safely was to Shaw a most important part of a child's training. To those who object to a country in which children are roaming savages, Shaw replied that the condition of children today as "little caged savages" is much worse. He thinks it "pitiable to see men and women doing after the age of 45 all the travelling and sightseeing they should have done before they were 15." Distinguishing between vagabondage which is the misery of having nothing to do and nowhere to go, and purposive roaming which is particularly suited to children, Shaw emphasizes that "mere wondering and staring is an important part of a child's education."

If a child has its papers and its passports . . . from responsible agents of the community . . . and with some formal acknowledgment of the obligations it is incurring and a knowledge of the fact

---

[29] *Doctors' Delusions*, p. 343.   [30] Preface to *Misalliance*.

that these obligations are being recorded: if, further, certain qualifications are exacted before it is promoted from permission to go as far as its legs will carry it to using mechanical aids to locomotion, it can roam without much danger of gypsification.

Under such circumstances a child could be at home everywhere and never be lost. Shaw indulges perhaps in some shock treatment in suggesting that parents could drive disagreeable children out of doors, temporarily or permanently, without inhumanity. He is hopeful of the customs and institutions which would eventually evolve in societies of free children. "Child laws and child fashions, child manners and child morals are now not tolerated; but among free children there would certainly be surprising developments in this direction."

Shaw recommended disciplining children, from two to five years of age, by means of "pleasant lies," that is by "fables and legends and allegories and parables" [31] instead of by the cane and birch. Reasoning with children to the extent of their capacity and as adroitly as possible is desirable, and even when the reasons given are not the real reasons, when it has to be told fairy tales in short, "these lies should be pleasantly encouraging, uplifting, poetic fictions and not damned lies." [32] Shaw warned that the artificial threats of heaven and hell and angels and the like prolong the stage of immaturity. Although the "crudest nursemaids and the most bigoted governesses may be more immediately successful than the most profound philosophers specializing in child psychology," any moral or physical reign of terror "may make its victims nervous wrecks and mental cowards for life."

Citing his own education which "operated by a succession of eye-openers each involving the repudiation of some pre-

---

[31] *What's What*, p. 66.　　　　　　[32] *Ibid.*, p. 70.

viously held belief," [33] Shaw recommends that children be organized into age groups, from two to ten, and that promotion from one group to an older one be marked by a "ceremony of disillusion in which the novices should be informed that they may now scrap the childish part of their instruction as poppycock no longer suitable to their advancing years."

. . . it will be necessary, if they are to think honestly and seriously, to tell them frankly on their promotion and initiation to the ten-year-old division that the bear stories were baby talk suited to their infancy, and that they must now discard them for lessons in scientific natural history and astronomy which disprove them conclusively as records of possible facts.[34]

This might be interpreted as a practical application of what the Ancients tell the young in the last play of *Back to Methuselah*. Shaw quotes Paul who in the first century wrote that the putting off of childish things is a normal incident of growth, and warns that such ceremonies of disillusion be practiced frankly and systematically "so that we may get rid of our present tophamper of people with incalculable mixtures of childish superstitions which they have not put off with the mature conclusions of their adult experience and observation." [35] If a child is deliberately told a lie "to establish a conditioned reflex of good conduct in its childish mind," it should in all decency be disabused of the lie when it is mature enough to understand the truth of the matter. Since the capacity for truth "varies not only from individual to individual but from age to age," [36] Shaw saw it as an obligation of future Boards of Education, inspired by leaders educated for the job, to specify as clearly as possible the limits of both the immature

[33] *Ibid.*, p. 155.
[35] *Ibid.*, p. 155.
[34] *Ibid.*, p. 66.
[36] *Ibid.*, p. 176.

and grown-up groups, for children must not be taken out of their depths.

When the child has learned the social creed and is qualified to make his way about in city or country and do ordinary useful work, he should be left to find out for himself what he wants to do in the direction of higher cultivation. If the child refuses to be educated further he should be left alone. If he is a genius he will master the essential techniques "without having them shoved down his throat." [37] All that is necessary is that he should have access to books, teachers, art, theaters, or whatever he needs. "A child should begin to assert itself early, and shift for itself more and more not only in washing and dressing itself, but in opinions and conduct." [38] Shaw admits that "the problem of how far children or adults need guidance and coercion, and how far they should be left free to think and act for themselves is always a difficult one." [39]

The few writers who have commented about Shaw's educational theories are mostly concerned with what he says about the education of children. A. S. Neill in his essay, "Shaw and Education," [40] believes that what Shaw says about the education of children must be judged not by the standards of today, but by the standards of yesterday and that he had a purely intellectual rather than a practical conception of children. While Neill recognizes that "Shaw's big message is: Put this civilization in order and then talk about educating children," he does not sufficiently consider Shaw's socialism and evolution as the basis of his theories about the training of children. Edmund Fuller maintains that Shaw's tendency

[37] *Intelligent Woman*, p. 428. [38] Preface to *Misalliance*.
[39] *What's What*, p. 161. [40] S. Winsten, editor, *G.B.S.* 90.

to extended digression in his writings about education serves to obscure some fundamentally sound conclusions. "From it all emerges a concept that preceded the sweeping progressive craze in child nurture and which, if heeded, could have done much to avoid many excesses and errors now confessed publicly by a good number of psychiatrists and educators." [41] John L. Childs in his *Education and Morals* (1950) comments with respect to Shaw's statement that the "vilest abortionist is he who attempts to mold the mind of a child":

In this striking phrase he has summarized a view held by some who have been identified with the "child-centered" educational movement. Shaw, however, both mistakes and mis-states the issue. The primary fact is that the life and the mind of the child is necessarily molded, for it is through the nurture provided by other human beings that each child achieves its most distinctive human traits. . . . The real question is whether the development of the child is to come as a by-product of the accidents and pressures of his own unplanned and unguided interactions with his surroundings, or whether his growth is to come as the result of an experience in a special environment planned for this educational purpose. . . . If we really oppose any and all molding of the life of the child, we should in consistency repudiate the whole enterprise of deliberate education.

Shaw opposed molding the child's mind and life only after he had mastered the minimum of knowledge, which is in itself an important form of molding. While Childs presents a most pertinent argument, it is evident that in his disagreement he fails to consider Shaw's numerous qualifications, assuming that Shaw implies a kind of complete anarchy in his program for children. If Shaw's plan treads a tightrope between freedom for the child and necessity, his powerful state could easily

[41] *George Bernard Shaw: Critic of Western Morale,* p. 64.

lean toward such a thorough molding as to enslave the child's mind in the interests of a static, automatized community rather than toward a growing one.

FAMILY RELATIONS AND THE SCHOOLS

In view of Shaw's program what part should the family play in the education of the young? In *The Quintessence of Ibsenism* there is a long passage about marriage which ends with these words: "and finally to its disuse and disappearance as the responsibility for the maintenance and education of the rising generation is shifted from the parent to the community." [42] And more than fifty years later Shaw writes: "Parentage has already for the greater part shifted from the actual fathers and mothers at home to the teaching staff in the school: that is from the amateur to the professional." [43] Although the family would have a relatively weak voice in the education of the young, he denies, on the whole, that he wants the abolition of the family. But there are qualifications attuned to the practical needs of the present. A number of the plays fail to communicate the extremist, statist view which crops up in the Preface to *Misalliance* and in such a chapter as "The State and the Children" in *The Intelligent Woman.*

The Preface to *Getting Married* suggests that until poverty is abolished it is not possible "to push rational measures of any kind very far." He would make the parent justify his custody of the child, for if a "family is not achieving the purposes of a family it should be dissolved just as a marriage should be when it is not achieving the purposes of marriage." Shaw was careful to make recommendations in order that society might benefit from sound family relations. The natural course, he

[42] *The Quintessence of Ibsenism,* p. 36.   [43] *What's What,* p. 20.

advised, is for parents and children to cast off specific parental and filial relations when they are no longer necessary to one another, for when such relations persist beyond a certain point they are likely to become morbid. Children's feelings ought to take their natural course, for "dictated compulsory affection is . . . positively detrimental." [44] While condemning the narrowing influence of the family, "its petty tyrannies, its false social pretences . . . its sacrifice of the boy's future by setting him to earn money when he should be in training for his adult life (remember the boy Dickens and the blacking factory)," [45] Shaw carefully admits that "we cannot break up the facts of kinship nor eradicate its natural emotional consequences. What we can do . . . is to set people free to behave naturally and to change their behavior as circumstances change." [46]

Even though family relations were to be more rational, Shaw, looking forward to his future socialist state, suggested that at present the "division of a child's life between home and school can be changed; and as the changes take the child more and more from home into school life successive points are reached at which the school takes the place of the family, and the teachers of the parents." [47] He visualized "school welfare work" which would secure students against exploitation, domestic tyranny, and neglect. "Let it not be forgotten that in such a civilization the families . . . will cooperate with the schools, and retain the natural affection of their own children, without the reservations at present inevitable." The professional teacher and statesman of the future, Shaw said, will have "the experience of all relevant human history to guide

[44] Preface to *Misalliance.*   [45] Preface to *Getting Married.*
[46] Preface to *Misalliance.*
[47] *What's What*, p. 81. See also "Postscript," *Back to Methuselah:* "we must . . . re-educate the parents."

him, whereas parents begin without any experience at all,
and find their problems changing from year to year."

The early *You Never Can Tell* (1896) dramatizes the concept
that parents who refrain from demanding "compulsory affection" can realize greater compatibility with their children.
When Crampton, Mrs. Clandon's estranged husband for eighteen years, returns only to demand "duty, affection, respect,
obedience," he is repudiated by his scientifically educated
children, Gloria and the advanced twins, Dolly and Philip,
as a disagreeable clown. Of Dolly, Crampton says: "That's a
spoiled child . . . one of your modern products. When I was
her age, I had many a good hiding . . . to teach me manners."
When he is rejected by Gloria who reminds him that he once
bought "a whip to beat me with," Crampton wisely changes
his tactics and gains the esteem of his children by deserving
rather than demanding it.

When Ann Whitefield tells Tanner in *Man and.Superman*
that "I love my mother," she is lectured at great length on this
"vile abjection of youth to age." Tanner paints the conventional mother as a "cynical, cunning, avaricious, disillusioned,
ignorantly experienced, foul-minded old woman . . . whose
duty is to corrupt her [daughter's] mind and sell her to the
highest bidder." Pleading that the "law for father and son and
mother and daughter is not the law of love," Tanner calls for
the "final supercession of the old and worn-out by the young
and capable." And Tanner concludes: "The man who pleads
his father's authority is no man; the woman who pleads her
mother's authority is unfit to bear citizens to a free people."
Even Ann's mother, Mrs. Whitefield, admits to Tanner she
does not seem able to "care for Ann and Rhoda as I do for you
and Tavy and Violet."

The young people in *Fanny's First Play* (1911) react violently against the rigid respectability of home and school. Bobby Gilbey and his Darling Dora find themselves in prison after an intemperate night. So does Margaret Knox for drunkenness and for knocking out a policeman's teeth. This contact with reality, which is "pretty brutal and pretty filthy," is a necessary supplement, Margaret believes, to the "good conduct prize" she had won at school for three successive years. "When I was at home and at school," she explains, "I was what you call good, but I wasn't free. And when I got free I was what most people would call not good." Margaret's religious mother ("out of the mouth of Mrs. Knox I have delivered on them the judgment of her God," Shaw states in the Preface) says when the two families are gathered together:

We dont really know whats right and whats wrong. We're all right as long as things go on the way they always did. We bring our children up just as we were brought up; and we go to Church or chapel just as our parents did; and we say what everybody says; and it goes on all right until something out of the way happens. . . . We find out then that with all our respectability and piety, weve no real religion and no way of telling right from wrong.

This speech is consistent with the Preface which suggests that since there is no test of conduct except morality, the result is that the "young had better have their souls awakened by disgrace, capture by the police, a month's hard labor than drift along from their cradles to their graves doing what other people do . . . and knowing nothing of good and evil." A year earlier in the Preface to *Misalliance,* Shaw argued that the "moral and physical risks of education are enormous: every new power a child acquires . . . opens up immense new possibilities of mischief." His point is that instead of forbidding young people to walk near the "dangerous precipices" of evil, society should make these "dangerous places as safe as possible

and then boldly . . . allowing others to take the irreducible
minimum of risk." *Fanny's First Play* suggests that the home
and the school must assume the burden of teaching the young
the true nature of reality and morality.

Although the Preface to *Misalliance* champions the rights
and liberties of children, the play itself dramatizes the disastrous results of granting unlimited freedom to Hypatia Tarleton. Mr. Tarleton's recipe for his daughter's education is: "Let
her read what she likes. Let her do what she likes. Let her go
where she likes." Mrs. Tarleton had never agreed with her
husband in sending Hypatia to "an expensive school [where]
all the girls belonged to big business families like ourselves. It
takes all sorts to make a world; and I wanted [Hypatia] to see
a little of all sorts." Hypatia loathes controversial discussions,
lacks the artistic culture which Lina, the modern, independent
acrobat possesses, and is ignorant about problems of sex since
she was not permitted at school to "attend a physiology and
hygiene class." Undisciplined, uncultivated by either school,
society, or family, Hypatia ought not to be regarded as a product of the sort of education Shaw approved although she seems
to be when she exclaims: "Oh, home! home! parents! family!
duty! how I loathe them!" Revolted also at the "impassable,
eternal gulf" between parents and children, Mr. Tarleton
declares in rage at the end of the play: "Let the family be
rooted out of civilization. Let the human race be brought up in
institutions." And denouncing the young as "hard, coarse, shal-
low, cruel, selfish, dirty minded," he orders Hypatia out of the
house.

Joey Percival, pursued so shamelessly by Hypatia, has had
the kind of education Shaw approved of because he has had
three fathers: "the regulation natural chap," a philosopher,
and an Italian priest. As Bentley relates:

The whole three of them took charge of Joey's conscience. He used to hear them arguing like mad about everything. You see, the philosopher was a freethinker, and always believed in the latest thing. The priest didn't believe anything, because it was sure to get him into trouble. . . . And the natural father kept an open mind and believed whatever paid him best. Between the lot of them Joey got cultivated no end.[48]

Not having been subjected to the narrowing confines of a family with one father, Percival has been well educated in the complexities of social behavior. Disapproving of Hypatia's undisciplined behavior, he tries to explain the meaning of freedom to her:

Freedom, my good girl, means being able to count on how other people will behave. If every man who dislikes me is to throw a handful of mud in my face, and every woman is to behave like Potiphar's wife, then I shall be a slave: the slave of uncertainty: the slave of fear: the worst of all slaveries. . . . Give me the blessed protection of a good stiff conventionality among thoroughly well-brought up ladies and gentlemen.

Although the Preface supports such a concept of freedom— for freedom implies restriction—matters are confused somewhat by the inclusion of a "good stiff conventionality," an un-Shavian mode. Hypatia's reply that "men like conventions because men made them" makes it seem as if she is now educating Percival. Percival at last joins Hypatia in standing up to Mr. Tarleton to whom he says: "You must remember that Ive been educated to discuss human affairs with three fathers simultaneously. I'm an adult person. Patsy is an adult person.

[48] See *Sixteen Self Sketches*, p. 31: "Those who know my play *Misalliance* . . . will note that I also had a natural father and two supplementaries. This widened my outlook very considerably. Natural parents should bear in mind that the more supplementaries their children find, at school or elsewhere, the better they will know that it takes all sorts to make a world." The "supplementaries" are George Vandaleur Lee and his Uncle Walter.

You do not inspire me with veneration." To assume that the young people are the rebellious realists and the father the tyrant with a paternal complex is to mistake Shaw's intention. Actually Tarleton as a frustrated father and intellectual is drawn with greater sympathy than Hypatia. It is, in short, almost impossible to understand Shaw's ideas about family relations and education by reading the play without its Preface.

In *Too True To Be Good* (1932) the Patient, who is transformed from a wealthy, sickly parasite into a rational being desirous of constructive work, wants "a world without parents." Even her mother, Mrs. Mopply, admits the negative results of being too solicitous a mother bent on self-sacrifice. "But my daughter ran away," she states, "when I had sacrificed myself to her until I found myself wishing she would die like the others and leave me a little to myself." The obvious solution is for mother and daughter to regard each other as companions on trial and "forget that there are such miserable things in the world as mothers and daughters." ˙

Aubrey, the burglar-preacher, brings down the curtain in a long sermon on religion, war, society, and particularly the younger generation.

Our souls go in rags now; and the young are spying through the holes and getting glimpses of the reality that was hidden. . . . They exult in having found us out; and when we their elders desperately try to patch our torn clothes with scraps of the old material, the young lay violent hands on us and tear from us even the rags that were left to us. But when they have stripped themselves and us utterly naked, will they be able to bear the spectacle? . . . I stand midway between youth and age like a man who has missed his train: too late for the last and too early for the next. What am I to do? . . . I am by nature and destiny a preacher. . . . I must have affirmations to preach. Without them the young will not listen to me; for even the young grow tired of denials.

In the final stage directions Shaw admits that "fine words butter no parsnips," and calls for action rather than talk. What becomes clear in Aubrey's long speech is that—so far as the young are concerned—the conventional relationships between parents and children will not do, and that the older generation must inspire the younger with genuine, not stereotyped ideals with which to build a better world.

RELIGIOUS EDUCATION

Because everyone must be educated in the final sanctions of conduct in Shaw's state, religious training would be a necessary part of the technical or required education. Secular education for Shaw is therefore an impossibility. "Every attempt," he writes in the Preface to *On the Rocks*, "to banish religion from the schools proves that Nature abhors a vacuum." Elsewhere he writes:

Unless schooling is to include manners and morals—that is, applied religion—the teacher, in imparting the method of the three R's, must either allow complete anarchy in the classroom or else impose orderly conduct by mute brute force. As neither plan is humanly possible, children cannot be educated without metaphysical assumptions; and once you admit metaphysics it is vain to urge that they shall at least be unsectarian, that is, formless.[49]

Shaw assumed then that the nearest thing to secular education is "secular discipline in which conduct is governed wholly by fear of punishment and the desire to escape it." Since any sort of external coercion is usually reinforced by appeals to a child's sense of shame and disgrace—in short to conscience— this method, whether one admits it or not, becomes a religious method. He resolves the conflict between secular and religious education by asserting that it is really a conflict between dif-

[49] *Doctors' Delusions*, p. 360.

ferent forms of religious doctrine based on different histories
of the human race.

Secular education fails because children have a right of
access to all knowledge of which they are capable. They
should be made acquainted with all the forms of religion just
as they are made acquainted with geography and ethnog-
raphy.[50]

What confuses the issue and leads even highly intelligent religious
persons to advocate secular education as a means of rescuing children from the strife of rival proselytisers is the failure to distinguish
between the child's personal subjective need for a religion and its
right to an impartially communicated historical objective knowledge
of all the creeds and Churches. Just as a child, no matter what its
race and color may be, should know that there are black men and
brown men and yellow men . . . so it should know that there are
Christians and Mahometans and Buddhists and Shintoists and so
forth, and that they are on the average just as honest and well-
behaved as its own father.

A child in England, Shaw warned, should not be told that
Allah is a false god, but that some people think so and that
believers in Allah think the converse about our God. Such false
teaching, he suggested, is extremely dangerous in an empire
in which a great majority of the subjects do not profess the religion of the governing country.

Such objectivity, though intellectually honest, tells the child
what other peoples believe. What the child believes, Shaw
urged, is of vital importance.

The child must have a conscience and a code of honor (which is
the essence of religion) even if it be only a provisional one, to be
revised at its confirmation. For confirmation is meant to signalize a
spiritual coming of age and may be a repudiation. Really active

[50] Preface to *Misalliance*.

souls have many confirmations and repudiations as their life deepens and their knowledge widens. But what is to guide the child before its first confirmation?

Shaw's solution is that at the very start the schools must encourage the "child's appetite for perfection and teach it to attach a peculiar sacredness to it." His argument is that since the secularist is eventually compelled "to appeal to the child's vital impulse towards perfection," he might as well begin with such inculcation as soon as possible. Shaw believes that by means of a universal religion the state and its schools can proselytize more effectively than parents and their divided churches. "For school purposes a religion is a belief which affects conduct."

Since the Bible contains the ancient literature of a remarkable Oriental race and since "the imposition of this literature on our children left them more literate," Shaw, despite frequent denunciations,[51] would use the Bible in the schools for purposes of moral instruction. It also provides an excellent source of vastly entertaining stories which could be exploited as "poetic lies" to keep children in order, and which would eventually be outgrown. "The object of a moral instruction book is not to be rational, scientific, exact, proof against controversy, nor even credible: its object is to make children good." [52] For this reason Shaw recommended teaching children the stories of Jonah and the whale and Elisha and the bears, despite the fact that the temper of God in these stories is "shocking and blasphemous." Of Elisha and the bears he says:

[51] See *What's What*, p. 357: "the Bible being the work of many highly gifted authors and translators, rich in notable poems, proverbs, precepts . . . is yet a jumble of savage superstition, obsolete cosmology."
[52] Preface to *Misalliance*.

It interests a child because it is about bears; and it leaves the child with an impression that children who poke fun at an old gentleman and make rude remarks about bald heads are not nice children, which is a highly desirable impression, and just as much as a child is capable of receiving from the story.

Since Shaw held that no literature can be an instrument of education unless it is discussed with perfect freedom, both children and teachers must be permitted to say, if they wish, that the story of Noah's ark is manifestly a child's fairy tale. The Preface to *Back to Methuselah* attacks "those bigoted ignoramuses claiming infallibility for their interpretation of the Bible, which was regarded, not as a literature nor even as a book, but partly as an oracle which answered and settled all questions." One of Shaw's reasons for the exclusion of the Bible from the schools, was that its advocates wanted it sanctified as an infallible record of perfect truth and the supreme authority on conduct.

The difficulty is not evaded by the silly proposal to have the Bible read "without comment." If the book of Genesis is to be read without comment whilst the statement that the world stands on an elephant which stands on a tortoise is to be read with any comment the teacher or the pupils choose to make on it, then the Bible is clearly claiming superstitious privileges.[53]

To eliminate freedom of discussion, to teach Bible stories as literally true—and this is implied when the scriptures are read without comment—was, to Shaw, only a way of stimulating a child to later indifference toward any religion once he begins to question anything.[54] Shaw said in the Preface to *Back to*

[53] *Doctors' Delusions*, p. 365.
[54] See the Preface to *Back to Methuselah* where Shaw discusses the repudiation of the Bible by the educated and professional classes. See also *Pen Portraits and Reviews*, p. 8 where Shaw remarks of William Archer's refusing to read the Bible: "This was a very natural consequence of dosing a clever child prematurely with mental food that Ecumenical

Methuselah that although the legends, parables, dramas in the Bible are among the choicest treasures of mankind, "there is only one inexorable condition attached to their healthy enjoyment, which is that no one shall believe them literally." [55] The world, he suggested, must pool its legends of religious folklore on an honest basis so that man can enter into the heritage of all the faiths. "China would share her sages with Spain, and Spain her saints with China." [56] Religious prejudice and bigotry could best be fought on such a basis.

All the sweetness of religion is conveyed to the world by the hands of story-tellers and image makers. Without their fictions the truths of religion would for the multitude be neither intelligible nor even apprehensible; and the prophets would prophecy and the teachers teach in vain. And nothing stands between the people and the fictions except the silly falsehood that the fictions are literal truths, and that there is nothing in religion but fiction.

Shaw's conclusion is that the exclusion of the Bible from the schools is as monstrous as the exclusion of the works of Shakespeare or Milton or Shelley or Blake or Dickens. For without knowledge of what the Bible contains and the part it has played in history, no one can claim to be educated.

A section of the Preface to *Androcles and the Lion* specifies some methods for the teaching of Christianity to children who

Councils have before now failed to digest; and parents and school committees will do well to make a careful note of it."

[55] See "The Revolutionist's Handbook," *Man and Superman:* "Do not give your children moral and religious instruction unless you are quite sure they will not take it seriously." It is suggested that this Shavian paradox can only be grasped in the light of his ideas about religious education. See *The Adventures of the Black Girl in Her Search for God*, p. 65: "as we cannot get rid of the Bible, it will get rid of us unless we learn to read it in the proper spirit . . . of intellectual integrity . . . and to judge it exactly as they [honest thinkers] judge the Koran, the Upanishads, the Arabian Nights, this morning's leading article in *The Times*, or last week's cartoon in *Punch*."

[56] Preface to *Back to Methuselah*.

must be delivered from the "proselyting atheists on the one hand and the proselyting nuns in the convent school on the other."

The teacher of Christianity has to make known to the child, first the song of John Barleycorn, with the fields and seasons as witness to its eternal truth. Then as the child's mind matures, it can learn, as historical and psychological phenomena, the tradition of the scapegoat, the Redeemer, the Atonement, the Resurrection, the Second Coming, and how Jesus has been largely accepted as the long expected and often prophecied Redeemer, the Messiah, the Christ. It is open to the child also to accept him.[57]

The Preface also contains an elaborate summation of what Shaw called the revolutionary and communistic teaching of Christ which is never taught in the schools. And if the child accepts Christ, he will accept the interpretations demanded by Shaw.

Religious education is inseparable from art education. "The last ray of art is being cut off from our schools by the discontinuance of religious education." [58] In the Preface to *Back to Methuselah* he states:

It will be seen that the revival of religion on a scientific basis does not mean the death of art, but a glorious rebirth of it. Indeed art has never been great when it was not providing an iconography for a live religion. And it has never been quite contemptible except when imitating the iconography after the religion had become a superstition.

[57] See *Adventures of the Black Girl*, p. 74 where the missionary lifted the black girl "out of her native tribal fetichism into an unbiassed contemplation of the Bible with its series of gods marking stages in the development of the conception of God from the monster Bogey Man to the father; then to the spirit without body, parts, nor passions; and finally to the definition of that spirit in the words God is love." See p. 71: "And yet our children are taught . . . to believe that Micah's God and Job's God and Noah's God are one and the same."

[58] Preface to *Misalliance*.

What Shaw meant by the revival of religion on a scientific basis is the inculcation of his doctrine of Creative Evolution, "now unmistakably the religion of the twentieth century." But even Creative Evolution cannot become a popular religion until it has its legends, parables, and miracles, and these would have to be created by "writers, painters, sculptors, and artists of higher sorts," themselves highly educated in aesthetics and religion. Shaw warned that no child "can learn religion from a teacher or a book or by any academic process whatever. It is only by an unfettered access to the whole body of Fine Art: that is, to the whole body of inspired revelation, that we can build up that conception of divinity to which all virtue is an aspiration."

Although Shaw may have elaborated a program of religious education for a future socialist state, he yet saw the necessity of immediate "socially practicable alternatives." He recommended that all schools—church- as well as community-supported institutions—"be placed under the Education Department, and fully financed by the State." [59] He hailed the London Education Act of 1903 as a "magnificent piece of educational socialism" because it provided unlimited educational opportunities for children attending Board or Church Schools. Alderman A. Emil Davis in an essay, "G.B.S. and Local Government," in *G.B.S. 90* states that the election address of two Progressive candidates for the London County Council in 1903 was written by Shaw. The address makes a plea for tolerance with regard to the education of children, "without asking whether their parents be Established Churchmen, Free Churchmen, Roman Catholics, or Jews." Shaw is antagonistic to church schools, not so much because they inculcate a spe-

[59] *Doctors' Delusions*, p. 358. See *ibid.* for many articles on this subject for the press.

cific creed, but because the teachers are inadequate and underpaid, and the school buildings are inferior and unsanitary.
Shaw admitted that neither he nor the Fabians liked these
concessions to the Church and his primary concern was that
"the education of the hosts of children in the Church schools
shall no longer be starved by sectarian bigotry or postponed
until . . . a generous ideal of unsectarian education is realized." [60]

SECONDARY EDUCATION

Beyond required training Shaw did not approve of secondary education as we know it, but of voluntary "self-education."
Citing his own experiences in schools, he concludes that "the
extension of what is now called secondary education to the
age of eighteen or twenty for all classes would abolish the
little culture we now have and produce a generation of young
Goths and Vandals which would reduce all Europe to the
intellectual level of an officers' mess." [61] Shaw defined the self-
educated as "those who have taken advantage of the voluntary
associations, the summer schools, the professional societies,
the propagandist organizations which continually keep up a
supply of lectures and controversial discussions under free
conditions, and also of the access to literature and art and
music provided by our libraries, galleries, concerts, theaters,
and the like." [62] That any kind of education will flourish under
free conditions in a well-regulated society, particularly "sec-

[60] *Doctors' Delusions*, p. 363. See also Pearson, *G.B.S.: A Full Length
Portrait*, p. 159, where Shaw is quoted as saying to a nonconformist who
objected to granting money to Church schools: "Don't you know that
you pay taxes now for the support of the Roman Catholic Church in
the Island of Malta and for the prosecution of booksellers who expose
the Bible for sale in British India and North Africa?"
[61] Preface to W.E.A. *Year Book* in *Doctors' Delusions*.
[62] *Doctors' Delusions*, p. 324.

ondary self-education," is an assumption which perhaps derives from his own self-education.[63]

The nature of his proof is tenuous. He argued that many of our most cultivated people owe absolutely nothing to their schooling. As proof, he cites, among others, Ruskin and Dickens, and, of course, Shaw himself. "Though Ruskin took an Oxford degree," he states in the Preface to the *Year Book*, "he was never a schoolboy." And elaborating the same theme a generation later he adds that Ruskin's parents "instead of packing him off to preparatory school and afterwards to Eton or Harrow . . . made him learn the Bible verse by verse, and steeped him in the glories of European art and scenery instead of in the traditions of the public schools." [64] Of Dickens, he declares that it was "fortunate for him and for the world as he escaped the public school and university routine. . . . Better no schooling at all than the schooling of Rudyard Kipling and Winston Churchill." [65] Although Shaw is attacking in this context the traditions of the public schools, he denies his own arguments for self-education when he asserts elsewhere that "genius is finally irresistible in all classes," [66] or that the higher faculties of most people can hardly be developed in an atmosphere of poverty and ignorance. Of those who leave school early in their teens and begin earning their livings as "white collar or black coat employees," Shaw states that this "main body of the half educated, having no lucrative talent . . . have to stay as they are, poor, pretentious, unorganizable because they are on speaking terms neither with the laborers nor the leisured . . . that they are not only half educated but half bred." Yet at the same time he suggests:

[63] See Preface to *Immaturity* for an attack on secondary education.
[64] *What's What*, p. 179.
[65] Preface to Charles Dickens, *Great Expectations*.
[66] *What's What*, p. 158.

Middle class children brought up in a not unbearably overcrowded house with books and a piano and a few pictures in it, and taught to read and write easily, can pick up all the knowledge they are capable of and care for, a process which, as it goes on all their lives . . . leaves them much better educated than the average Bachelor of Arts. Their half education is the better half.

Citing in this context Shakespeare, Bunyan, Blake, Hogarth, Turner, Purcell, and Elgar, it is apparent that Shaw concentrated on the exception to the rule. What can be gathered from Shaw's inconsistencies is that he mistrusted secondary or any other kind of compulsory schooling because he believed that intellectual achievement could not be realized in an atmosphere devoid of freedom and a voluntary personal drive, and that the average individual would become all too easily the dupe of established ideals and institutions.

Although secondary education must be voluntary, it should not necessarily be free from government control. "Secondary schools must be provided even when no one is obliged to attend them." [67] Like colleges and universities they should be adequately financed and staffed and made available to anyone who may be interested.

In *Misalliance* (1910) the two examples of the self-educated seem to be contradictions of Shaw's own ideas. John Tarleton, the underwear manufacturer, reveres ideas, books (his hobby is donating libraries), and enlightenment. A self-educated, voracious reader, he advises people to read Darwin, Weismann, Ibsen, Butler, Whitman. To heal his paternal wounds— the result of giving unlimited freedom to his daughter, Hypatia—he turns in desperation to reading *King Lear*. "I ought to have been a writer," he says. "I'm essentially a man of ideas." And discontented with his family and business and

[67] *Ibid.*, p. 165.

unrealized intellectual ambitions, he vows "to chuck it all and try something that will give a scope to all my faculties." One's impression is that Tarleton is a victim of an educational system which never met his needs as a potential student of ideas.

This is also true of Gunner who breaks into Tarleton's home and tries to kill him because Tarleton had had an affair with Gunner's mother. Although Tarleton suspects that Gunner has cultivated a melodramatic view of life by reading trashy novels, he is mistaken. Actually Gunner has been educating himself, in the manner prescribed by Shaw, with books about Marx, Russia, and the new social experiments. In a long speech Gunner denounces his wretched life as a clerk-cashier. "I spend my days in a stuffy little den counting another man's money. I've an intellect: a mind and a brain and a soul." These attributes, he believes, need to be developed since he is "one of the intellectuals . . . a reading man, a thinking man." But how, he asks, is this possible for anyone doomed to "spend my days from nine to six" in a prison? Gunner is full of Marxist invective about class war, the rotten bourgeoisie, and the plunder of the poor. Lord Summerhays, a former colonial governor, declares that people of Gunner's sort and education "are a most serious problem"—one for the police. Gunner emerges as a pathetic, contemptible specimen of his own self-education. Shaw may have intended dramatizing the tragedy of a society which respects neither leisure nor opportunities for self-improvement.

The public schools fail disastrously as institutions of secondary learning for they are "partly a degenerate survival from the feudal system, in which class stratification was a necessary moral basis." [68] It was during the nineteenth century, when the feudal aristocracy associated and intermarried with

[68] *Ibid.*, p. 77.

the "purse-proud snob tradesmen," that the children of the rich
were sent to such schools "not to get scholarship and culture
. . . but solely to be hallmarked as members of the upper
class." While admitting that these schools have changed considerably in the last century—Rugby and Oundle for example
—Shaw maintained as late as 1944 that the older methods still
prevail enough "to make sure that the class enriched by our
property system is the one which commands the ruling majority in Parliament, and in the Upper Division of the Civil
Service." He even charged that these schools imperil the peace
of the world:

Take a boy . . . whose parents are rich. Graft on to him a tradition that trade and manual labor are degrading; that service in the
commissioned ranks of the army or in diplomacy are the only oc-
cupations worthy of a gentleman . . . ; accustom him to regard
religion as a matter of church going in his best clothes, mixed up
with ordering God to confound the politics . . . of his enemies, and
with devotion to an idolized sovereign or Leader who is the living
symbol of his country; and you get not only the familiar non-adult
plutocrat whose ideas rule this distressful country, but a national
God with imperial instincts and a completely prejudiced conviction
that the expensive public school is the supreme triumph of divine
education . . . ; and as the same thing occurs in all the plutocratic states, we get as many rival patriotisms as there are languages
and nations, making the peace in our time for which we pray impossible.

The most excellent minds, Shaw argued, cannot resist the influences of such plutocratic education. Of Dean Inge, who attended Eton, Shaw declares that "not even the Dean's wonderful mind has been able to resist that disastrously successful
swindle which we call secondary education." [69] And this is

[69] *Pen Portraits and Review*, p. 162. See "If I Were a Priest," *Atlantic*
185 (May, 1950), in which Shaw praises Inge's "original mind." See
also Pearson, *A Full Length Portrait*, p. 378.

followed by one of Shaw's most violent passages wherein he
"curses the inauspicious hour in which Inge went to Eton."
Shaw denied that the solution was to infiltrate these expensive institutions with elementary school scholarship win-
ners. Since a relatively small percentage of these poorer classes
would be admitted, "a cad unfortunate enough to be thrust
into a community of toffs must either transform himself into a
gentleman without the habits and accent to support that pretension, or else be as unhappy and out-of-place as a toff would
be in a school over-crowded with children from the slums." [70]
Shaw's remedy would be to abolish cads and toffs—both undesirable—by altering the distribution of the national income
so that "the Etonian standard of subsistence and culture will
come within the reach of the slum-dwellers." Until such a
condition is realized, Shaw recommended that the poor and
rich remain in separate schools, with the cads "intensely proud
of their dignity as workers, and fiercely contemptuous of the
parasitic rich." Although Shaw denied the Marxian doctrine
of the class struggle he seems—if he is at all serious—to uphold it where education is concerned.

Etonian toffs and Polytechnic cads should contact each other only
in street fights, the organization of which might be regarded as a
legitimate part of their physical exercise, or in the examination halls
or laboratories in which their capacities and pretensions will be
tested impartially. [71]

[70] *What's What*, p. 60.
[71] *Ibid.*, p. 61. See also *Self Sketches*, p. 49: "the remedy is not to
force all the sections into the old institutions, but to face the fact of
their segregation and tolerate proletarian schools, lower middle class
schools, Etonian caste schools, Jim Crow cars and the like, with the
difference that . . . they should 'keep themselves to themselves' and
assert, not their equality but their superiority as chosen races." This is
probably a deliberate overstatement designed for the complacent reader
since "chosen races" were anathema to Shaw.

Eventually the Etonian system will "die a natural death," and there will be no advantage in wearing an old school tie if one has "to share the social burden of labor and service." [72]

HIGHER EDUCATION

"What is the matter with our universities is that all the students are schoolboys, whereas it is of the very essence of university education that they should be men," Shaw declared in the Preface to *Misalliance*. Explaining that the function of a university "is not to teach things that can be taught as well or better by University Extension lectures or by private tutors or modern correspondence classes," he states these aims:

We go to them [universities] to be socialized; to acquire the hall mark of communal training; to become citizens of the world instead of inmates of the enlarged rabbit hutches we call homes; to learn manners and become unchallengeable ladies and gentlemen.

Such aims are not intended for a "barbarous rabble of half emancipated schoolboys and unemancipable pedants." He supposed that in a reasonable society the life experiences of most people would educate them more completely than any university now does so corruptly. Since the university "will always exist in some form as a community of persons . . . pursuing culture, talking culture, thinking culture, above all, criticizing culture," such people, "must know the world outside the university at least as well as the shopkeeper on High Street." Paraphrasing Kipling with "What do they know of Plato that only Plato know," Shaw concluded that those who had not earned a living for at least a few years ought to be excluded from any institution of higher learning. Elsewhere he adds:

[72] *What's What*, p. 80.

Academic degrees should not be obtainable by technical proficiency, nor technical proficiency be assumed on the strength of an academic degree. Nobody should be dubbed Master of Arts without specifying what arts, if any. The college don who knows everything and can do nothing should not be lumped in with the handy man who knows nothing and can do everything. To put it learnedly, the cognitive type should be distinguished from the conative as far as that can be done in view of the fact that as these extremes do not exist, real human persons can be placed only somewhere on the scale between them.[73]

"University schoolboyishness" is illustrated in *Misalliance* in the character of Bentley Summerhays. A failure at Cambridge, he is given to lying down and screaming for what he wants despite his pretensions to intellectual discussions. His father, Lord Summerhays, says of his son's education: "He was completely spoilt. When he was sent to a preparatory school he simply yelled until he was sent home. Harrow was out of the question; but we managed to tutor him into Cambridge. No use: he was sent down." While Lord Summerhays thinks Bentley "has a hard and penetrating intellect and a remarkable power of looking facts in the face," he is also aware that his son lacks manhood which, as Shaw states in the Preface, a university education should develop. Rejected by Hypatia as a mate, Bentley, in a fit of hysterics, is completely humiliated as he is carried off the stage by Lina, the manly Polish aviatrix.

In *Major Barbara*, Undershaft's son, Stephen, illustrates the negative effects of higher education. Undershaft's comments, as he catechizes Stephen about any special abilities he has been trained for, are quite Shavian. Stephen, who has attended Harrow and Cambridge, asserts: "I have nothing of the artist about me, either in faculty or character, thank Heaven." Admitting under further questioning that he knows nothing about

[73] *What's What*, p. 312.

literature, philosophy, religion, politics, or law, he insists that
he knows "the difference between right and wrong." "Right is
right; and wrong is wrong," Stephen had earlier told his
mother, "and if a man cannot distinguish them properly, he is
either a fool or a rascal." To which Lady Britomart had replied, "That's my own boy. Your father never could answer
that." But Undershaft does:

What! no capacity for business, no knowledge of law, no sympathy
with art, no pretension to philosophy; only a simple knowledge of
the secret that has puzzled all the philosophers, baffled all the lawyers, muddled all the men of business, and ruined most of the artists: the secret of right and wrong. Why, man, you're a genius, a
master of masters, a god!

Unperturbed, Stephen attributes his father's ideas to his power
for making money in munitions, saying:

But [money] has kept you in circles where you are valued for your
money and deferred to for it, instead of in the doubtless very old-
fashioned and behind-the-times public school and university where
I formed my habits of mind.

Village Wooing (1933), a minor work about a heroine pursuing a penny-a-line author of travelogues, still communicates
Shaw's ideas about life's experiences and responsibilities in
relation to higher education. The female, Z, spends all her
prize money on an ocean cruise during which she decides to
marry A, whom she has aggressively approached on the ship.
He is later drawn to her native village and buys the shop
where she works. The result is that he gives in to marriage and
to a useful life in the community. A now admits: "I now make
critical distinctions of the greatest subtlety, and value them in
terms of money. I am forced to admit that the shopkeeper is
enormously superior to the Marco Polo man and that I have
learnt more in three months in this shop than I learnt in three

years at Oxford." Formerly snobbish and preoccupied with
selfish ends, he is now friendly and actively concerned with
the practical affairs of life.

Buoyant Billions (1947) draws an uncomplimentary picture
of the state of higher education. Junius Smith, the would-be
world-betterer journeys to Panama where he meets the
daughter of Buoyant and her servant (the Native), with
whom he discusses religion and education:

HE. I would have you know that I am a Master of Arts of the Uni-
versity of Oxford, the centre of all the learning in the universe.
The possession of such a degree places the graduate on the high-
est mental plane attainable by humanity.
THE NATIVE. How did you obtain that degree, sir?
HE. By paying a solid twenty pounds for it.
THE NATIVE. It is impossible. Knowledge and wisdom cannot be
purchased like fashionable garments.
HE. In England they can. A sage teaches us all the questions our
examiners are likely to ask, and the answers they expect from us.
THE NATIVE. One answers questions truthfully only out of one's
own wisdom and knowledge.
HE. Not at Oxford. Unless you are a hundred years behindhand in
science and seven hundred in history you cannot hope for a
degree there.

The third act, set in a London drawing room which has been
converted into a Chinese temple, presents the educational
problems of the wealthy Buoyant family. The Secondborn,
who is Shaw's spokesman for mathematical and intellectual
passion, admits that his university education left him helpless
to earn his own living. A daughter, Darkie, affirms that "we
are a family of helpless duffers . . . with scraps of tastes and
talents for scholarship, painting, playing musical instruments,
writing, and talking." Darkie thinks it would have been better
if her parents had forced her "to learn life's lessons by break-

ing my shins against them. . . ." She envies the practical education of her sister in Panama, who learned to cook, make
beds, sweep and scrub, and sew her clothes before she was ten,
the result of being sent to a good ladies' school. What Shaw
says about the purposes of higher education in the Preface
to *Misalliance* is explained by the Secondborn to Sir Ferdi-
nand Flopper, Mr. Buoyant's lawyer:

SECONDBORN. We have all spent three years at college. Our father
    sent us there to acquire the social training the communal life of
    a university gives. But he insisted on our leaving without a de-
    gree.
SIR F. In Heaven's name, why?
S. One of his notions. He holds that dictated mental work on uncon-
    genial subjects is overwork which injures the brain permanently.
    So we are not university graduates; but we are university men
    none the less. If a man is known to have been at Oxford or Cam-
    bridge nobody ever asks whether he has taken a degree or not.
SIR F. But that does not justify false pretences.
THE YOUTH. University degrees are the falsest of pretences. Gradu-
    ates as a class are politically and scientifically obsolete and
    ignorant.

At the end of the act the Chinese Priest discusses the "pinks"
with the Native who is a Creative Evolutionist:

THE NATIVE. They have much to teach us.
THE PRIEST. Yes; but they are themselves unteachable, not under-
    standing what they teach.
THE NATIVE. True: they can teach; but they cannot learn.
THE PRIEST. Freaks. Dangerous freaks. The future is with the learn-
    ers.

Shaw's principle of voluntary self-learning is especially applicable in the areas of higher education.

That "A little learning is a dangerous thing" is true; but the proposed remedy "Drink deep, or taste not the Pierian spring" is not

advisable in more than a percentage of the cases. . . . By all means throw the extremes of learning open to everyone so that no talent or capacity shall be thrown away for lack of training and opportunity. Statesmen must know the importance of this, and see to it that whoever will and can shall have ways open for them to the utmost instruction.[74]

Shaw was ahead of his time in recommending state supported community colleges "within reach of everybody and forced on nobody." [75] Centralized higher education as illustrated by Oxford, Cambridge, or Yale ("What is Yale? They make locks, don't they?" [76]) would, he believed, defeat the purposes he had in mind. Henderson quotes him as saying: "We must replace them by local universities, and decentralize education." Of philanthropic contributions to famous universities Shaw wrote in "Socialism for Millionaires": "An intelligent millionaire, unless he is frankly an enemy of the human race, will do nothing to extend the method of caste initiation practiced under the mask of education at Oxford and Cambridge." [77] He adds that he would welcome contributions which would permit experiments in educational methods—particularly in such areas as technology, political science, economics, statistics, and industrial history.

METHODS OF TEACHING FINE ARTS

Keenly aware of the gap between the "pompous phrases about education and fine art and the actual facts of the school." [78] Shaw denied that the arts could be taught by traditional school methods. He advocated "plenty of books, plenty of picture postcards of masterpieces of design, plenty of good

[74] *What's What*, p. 164.   [75] *Ibid.*, p. 345.
[76] Quoted in Henderson, *Playboy and Prophet,* p. 21.
[77] Fuchs, *The Socialism of Shaw*, p. 98.
[78] Preface to W.E.A. *Year Book* in *Doctors' Delusions.*

performances of the best plays and the best music obtainable (not necessarily always in the heaviest genres), and plenty of rambles in the country," as well as free trips to the galleries. Shaw admired such unusual teachers as Jacques-Dalcroze who "like Plato believes in saturating his pupils with music. They walk to music, play to music, work to music, think to music, live to music." [79] Since such teachers are rare, music, painting, and other fine arts become "teaching subjects." The ordinary teacher tries "to make a boy appreciate Venetian painting by asking him the date of Tintoretto's birth." [80] Music becomes an academic subject which has little relationship to real music and which stimulates many a student to loathe the sight of musical notation or music itself as an instrument of culture.[81] It was a tragedy to Shaw that schools and teachers combine to destroy a love for the arts in people who were spontaneously attracted to them. "It is only when learning is made a slavery by tyrannical teachers that art becomes loathsome to the pupil." [82]

As early as 1894, in "The Religion of the Pianoforte," Shaw had suggested that teachers of the arts keep in mind that "it is feeling that sets a man thinking and not thought that sets him feeling."

The secret of the absurd failure of our universities and academic institutions in general to produce any real change in the students who are constantly passing through them is that their *method* is

[79] Preface to *Misalliance.*
[80] Preface to W.E.A. *Year Book* in *Doctors' Delusions.*
[81] See "Epistle Dedicatory," *Man and Superman:* "And so with your Doctors of Music [like men of letters], who with their collections of discords duly prepared and resolved or retarded or anticipated in the manner of the great composers, think they can learn the art of Palestrina from Cherubini's treatise. All this academic art is far worse than the trade in sham antique furniture."
[82] Preface to *Misalliance.*

invariably to attempt to lead their pupils to feeling by way of thought.

A student of music, for example, cannot be expected "to acquire a sense of the poetry of the Ninth Symphony by accumulating information as to . . . the compass of the contrafagotto, or the number of sharps in the key of D major."

All education, as distinct from technical instruction, must be education of the feeling; and such education must consist in the appeal of *actual* experiences to the senses, without which literary descriptions addressed to the imagination cannot be rightly interpreted.
. . . In educational institutions appeals to the senses can only take the form of performances of works of art, and the bringing of such performances to the highest perfection is the true business of our universities.

In attempting to define the actual nature of the aesthetic experience, Shaw is undoubtedly a forerunner of progressive teachers who understand that no student can ever appreciate the arts unless they become vitally bound with his life experiences. Although Shaw concluded in mature life that intellect is fundamentally a passion, he took great pains even in this early essay to show that high feeling, stimulated by great works of art, may eventually stimulate high thinking. Students, he concluded, can grasp the essence of an artistic work only in that order.

As he attacked censorship of plays and books, so he attacked censorship of students' tastes in the arts. "In art," he writes in the Preface to *Misalliance*, "children, like adults, will find their level if they are left free to find it, and not restricted to what adults think good for them." Since "young people are ripe for love long before they are ripe for religion," teachers must understand that the most dangerous art for young people is that which presents itself as religious ecstasy. The boy of fifteen, given the opportunity to wander in a well-stocked library, will soon discover for himself that *Treasure Island* or Byron's *Don Juan* or *Ivanhoe* or Pickwick—"the safest saint for us in our nonage"—are more absorbing than the *Imitation of Christ*. Shaw recalls that as a youth he had found a copy of the *Arabian Nights* and was devouring it avidly when a relative hid it from him "lest it should break my soul." A student's right to pick and choose books, music, and art for his own purposes must be recognized even when the choice "may often be rather disgusting to his elders who may want him to choose the best before he is ready for it." Shaw failed to present any constructive methodology for improving the tastes of students bombarded by vulgar, standardized forms of art. Regarding the craze for jazz rhythms, he did suggest that if students "had learnt what can be done with syncopation from Beethoven's third Leonora overture, they would enjoy the ragtimes all the more . . . and put them in their proper place as amusing vulgarities." [83] Shaw's conclusion is that in the schools there can be no "carefully regulated access to good art."

The practical moral is that we must read whatever stories, see whatever pictures, hear whatever songs and symphonies, go to whatever plays we like. We shall not like those which have nothing to say to us; and though everyone has a right to bias our choice, no one has a right to deprive us of it by keeping us from any work of art or any work of art from us. [84]

[83] See Reynolds, "Bernard Shaw on Art in the Schools," *Journal of Education* 78 (December, 1913), in which the author reports a lecture by Shaw, "Music and Drama in the Schools," delivered before an audience of teachers. Shaw is quoted: "I should seek to have a single motif from Mozart, Beethoven, or from other great composers played over and over on the piano until the children learned to love the masters. If this were done the halls where classic music is presented would not be abandoned for entertainment that is both cheap and vulgar."

[84] Preface to *Misalliance*.

It is the obligation of the schools, Shaw believed, to deliver "our children from the idolatry of the artist."

Nothing is more pitiably ridiculous than the wild worship of artists by those who have never been seasoned in youth to the enchantments of art. . . . The influence they [musicians, actors, writers] can exercise on young people who have been brought up in the darkness and wretchedness of a home without art, and in whom a natural bent towards art has always been baffled and snubbed, is incredible. He who reveals the world of art to them opens heaven to them. They become satellites, disciples, worshippers of the apostle. Now the apostle may be a voluptuary without much conscience.

If people were artistically educated in the schools they would not regard the artist "as in any way extraordinary apart from his actual achievements as an artist." [85]

The Doctor's Dilemma (1906) can perhaps be more readily understood if one observes Shaw's ideas about artist idolatry. Although the play is a comedic satire on doctors, it also considers the man of genius who in the normal relations of daily life is a scoundrel. A great painter but utterly unscrupulous about women, money, and morals, Louis Dubedat dies of tuberculosis. His last words are dedicated to "Michael Angelo, Velasquez, and Rembrandt . . . the redemption of all things by Beauty everlasting." Dr. Ridgeon observes after his death: "The most tragic thing in the world is a man of genius who is not also a man of honor." Jennifer, Dubedat's devoted wife, is

[85] See "Artstruck Englishman," *New Republic* 10 (February 17, 1917), 78–79, where Shaw attacks Dixon Scott's "The Innocence of Bernard Shaw" in his *Men of Letters*, for venerating style, not content: "To an Irishman there is always something indecent in the way an Englishman takes to art when he does take to it. He worships it, exalts its artifices above its inspirations; makes God of its frail and ridiculous human instruments; pontificates and persecutes in its name; and ends in delirium and drunkenness which seems to him the raptures of a saint's vigil."

steadfast in her belief that her husband, in his own words, had "never denied my faith, never been untrue to myself." And she justifies his unethical conduct outside his art to Ridgeon: "He was one of the men who know what women know: that self-sacrifice is vain and cowardly." Shaw leads one to believe that Louis, despite his dedication to art, has preyed on an innocent, devoted wife who has not herself been educated artistically in the prescribed manner.

ON TEACHERS AND TEACHING

Despite his contempt for the teaching profession, there is evidence that Shaw did admire and respect the capable instructor and looked forward to the time when skilled teaching would be the rule rather than the exception. Shaw saw the teacher enslaved like the industrial worker. Underpaid and despised, teachers are forced to work "in prisons instead of in heaven." [86] In *The Intelligent Woman* Shaw compares the teacher "shut in with a class of unwilling, hostile, restless children" [87] with a poor family living in a one-room tenement. "Modern psychological research . . . is forcing us to recognize how serious is the permanent harm that comes of this atmosphere of irritation on the one side and suppression, terror, and reactionary naughtiness on the other." In the Preface to *Misalliance* he suggests that the teachers hate school much more than the students, for "the ablest and most impatient of them were often so irritated by the awkward, slow-witted, slovenly boys: that is, the ones that required special consideration and patient treatment, that they vented their irritation on them ruthlessly." Furthermore, the ordinary teacher "does not devise the curriculum: he simply carries out a prearranged

[86] Preface to *Misalliance*.   [87] *The Intelligent Woman*, p. 416.

routine like the school charwoman." [88] In 1918 Shaw said that the "secret of the shameful poverty and low social status" of the teacher was that he was not trained professionally.

The remedy is not to give professional pay and status to unskilled men who cannot even pronounce the alphabet presentably, but to exact genuine professional qualifications from the schoolmaster and pay him their market value. His status will then take care of itself. I have not noticed that the genuine teachers who now undertake the care of children are at any disadvantage pecuniarily or socially in ordinary professional society. . . . The true teacher can leave the doctor, the lawyer, and even the parson nowhere in the rapidity with which he can gain respect and liking both in his school and out of it.

The good teacher requires "some natural vocation, a good deal of skill, experience and an honorable character." Good schools and genuine teachers, Shaw held, can only be realized "as part of a social synthesis which involves the reconstruction of many other institutions besides our schools." Socialism would abolish incompetent teachers by providing them "with less hateful and equally respectable employment. Nobody who had not a genuine vocation for teaching would adopt teaching as a profession." [89]

It must therefore be concluded that Shaw did not believe the statement attributed to John Tanner in "The Revolutionist's Handbook," namely: "He who can, does. He who cannot, teaches." C. E. M. Joad, discussing Shaw's pellets of thought, provides an interesting comment about this popular quotation:

[88] Preface to W.E.A. *Year Book* in *Doctors' Delusions.*
[89] *Intelligent Woman*, p. 415. See also the Preface to *Too True to Be Good* where Shaw, attacking the ideal of celibacy insisted upon by Boards of Education, defends mothers' rights "to have their children taught and handled by mothers."

Its meaning developed in the Preface to *Misalliance* is that the teaching profession in this country is usually embraced as a second best. Englishmen are by nature men of action; their natural mode of self expression is to play games, engage in field sports, explore deserts. . . . Failing these direct forms of self expression they start businesses and make money, or become executives or administrators and achieve power. It is only when in so far as they find themselves frustrated or prove themselves to be incompetent in regard to these, their natural spheres of activity, that they take to teaching, just as schoolboys, by and large, tend to be good at their books only when they are bad at their games.[90]

Shaw's maxim, in its barb of thought, implies an attack not so much on the teacher as on the material and moral values in our society. If Joad is correct, and he probably is, then the maxim would seem to have come from the very Philistine whom Shaw intended to attack. If Tanner's statement was intended to jolt people into thinking about the failure of the schools and teachers, it does not of itself communicate Shaw's ideas on the subject.

He opposed the schoolmaster's claim "to be organized and recognized as the medical profession" because he feared that, like the General Medical Council, an organization of teachers might become a "monstrous tyranny with legal powers of coercion over the rest of the community, and with unlimited power to dictate its own qualifications and to prevent anyone practising as a teacher without its authority."[91] What Shaw feared was the creation of an "omniscient and infallible" body of teachers which might perpetuate brutal methods of teaching. "By all means," he concludes, "let us have a register of teachers, but let the learners keep the key of it."

His plays generally reveal a complimentary view of the pro-

[90] *Shaw*, p. 83.
[91] Preface to W.E.A. *Year Book* in *Doctors' Delusions*.

fession. In *Major Barbara*, Undershaft, in his search for a suitable foundling as successor to his munitions industry, at first rejects Cusins, the professor of Greek, saying:

Every blessed foundling nowadays is snapped up in his infancy by . . . School Board officers . . . ; and if he shews the least ability, he is fastened on by schoolmasters; trained to win scholarships like a racehorse; crammed with secondhand ideas; drilled and disciplined in docility and what they call good taste; and lamed for life so that he is fit for nothing but teaching.

Cusins convinces Undershaft that he does not fall into such a category. In the second play of *Back to Methuselah*, Dr. Conrad Barnabas, Professor of Biology at Jarrowfields University, is a teacher after Shaw's own heart. Recognizing his limitations as a biologist because of his short life, he is convinced that if he "could count on nine hundred and sixty years I could make myself a real biologist instead of what I am now: a child trying to walk." He agrees with his brother, Franklyn, that we neither live long enough "to form a well instructed conscience," nor "to find out what life really means."

Perhaps the most famous of Shaw's teachers is Higgins in *Pygmalion* (1912), a professor of phonetics, who in the process of improving the cockney speech of Eliza, the flower girl, seems to overlook the gap between his theories and his practice. At his first meeting with Eliza he tells her: "Remember that you are a human being with a soul and the divine gift of articulate speech." At the same time he declares that "a woman who utters such depressing and disgusting sounds has no right to live." And this tallies with what Shaw tells us in the stage directions where Higgins is described as "the energetic, scientific type, heartily, even violently interested in everything that can be studied as a scientific subject, and careless about himself and other people, including their feelings." "If I decide to teach you," he tells Eliza, "I'll be worse than two fathers to you." Higgins' methodology is primarily that of intimidation and reward. Colonel Pickering, a student of Indian dialects who joins Higgins in rehabilitating Eliza's speech, tries to remind him that "the girl has some feelings." But Higgins believes that Eliza is "incapable of understanding anything" and outlines his methods of teaching to Pickering and his pupil:

No use explaining. As a military man you ought to know that. Give her orders: that's what she wants. Eliza: you are to live here for the next six months, learning how to speak beautifully. . . . If you're good and do whatever you're told, you shall sleep in a proper bedroom, and have lots to eat, and money to buy chocolates. . . . If you're naughty and idle you will sleep in the back kitchen among the black beetles, and be walloped by Mrs. Pearce with a broomstick.

When Pickering suggests that no illicit advantage be taken of the girl, Higgins replies: "That thing! Sacred, I assure you. You see she'll be a pupil; and teaching would be impossible unless pupils were sacred." Apparently Higgins' methods are at odds with his philosophy, for he is not even aware of the effects of his teaching. Having passed off Eliza as a lady at the garden party, he is blind to the new soul he has created. Eliza now demands to know what is to become of her, resents his attempt to dominate her and to treat her as a mechanical object—something to be taught and discarded. To Eliza this newly acquired distinction of speech and manners is a means to further development, something Higgins fails to understand. Contemptuous of her desire for independence as a newborn individual, Higgins says: "Independence? That's a middle class blasphemy. We are all dependent on one another, every soul of us on earth." If Shaw meant Higgins to propagandize for spiritual socialism, it should be noted that Higgins still seems unaware of the needs of one spirit, his pupil. Eliza, on the other hand, seeing their relations in a new light, shrewdly observes: "The difference between a lady and a flower girl is not how she behaves but how she's treated." Defending himself with what appear to be Shaw's ideas, Higgins replies: "The great secret, Eliza, is not having bad manners or good manners . . . but having the same manner for all human souls: in short, behaving as if you were in Heaven, where there are no third class carriages, and one soul is as good as another." It can be said in Higgins' favor that he does seem to treat everyone alike in his blunt, bullying way. To the pretentious Eynsford Hills he says: "You see, we're all savages, more or less. We're supposed to be civilized and cultured—to know all about poetry and philosophy and art and science, and so on; but how many of us know even the meanings of these names. . . . What the devil do you imagine I know of philosophy?" "Or of manners, Henry?" Mrs. Higgins observes with shrewd insight.

It is Colonel Pickering to whom Eliza owes the really important part of her education. Always understanding and polite, Pickering is aware of Eliza as a human soul—not as an "experiment." Eliza tells him that "what began my real education" was his calling her Miss Doolittle and showing her numerous courtesies. Presumably, Higgins, blessed with Pickering's manners, would have made the perfect Shavian teacher. That Shaw intended such a contrast of teaching methods seems a reasonable conclusion.

The Millionairess (1935) presents a contrast between a dominating moneymaker and a genuine teacher. The Egyptian doctor, who tries to educate Epifania away from her acquisitive instincts, tells her that he once read in a newspaper:

And behold! a paragraph headed Wills and Bequests. . . . Mrs. Somebody of Clapham Park, one hundred and twenty two thousand pounds. She had never done anything but live in Clapham Park. . . . But what was the next name? It was that of the teacher who changed my whole life and gave me a new soul by opening the world of science to me. I was his assistant for four years. He used to make his own apparatus for his experiments; and one day he needed a filament of metal that would resist a temperature that melted like sealing wax.

To Epifania's mercenary suggestion that he buy his teacher's patent for her, the Doctor replies: "He never took out a patent. He believed that knowledge is no man's property."

In the "Sixth and Last Fable" of *Farfetched Fables* (1948), the teacher of the Sixth Form School uses Shavian methodology in handling a class to which three youths and two maidens have just been promoted. Testing the class by asking "how and why the sixth form differs from the fifth," she gets a correct answer from one of the youths: "We shall explain nothing to you. If you are our teacher it is for us to question you: not for you to question us." The students have been so well trained with such methods in these classes of the future (the play is really a farcical sequel to *Back to Methuselah*) that another youth says: "If you do [question us], Mother Hubbard, you'll not have a happy time with us." Patiently permitting such informal replies, the teacher exhibits neither pompousness nor anger in the conversational give-and-take. When the students ask innumerable "why" questions, she advises them to "ask what, when, where, how, who, which; but never why. Only first form children, who think their parents know everything, ask why." A member of the disembodied races suddenly appears and congratulates the teacher on "your passion for teaching."

VOCATIONAL EDUCATION

In a sensibly organized society, "all the square pegs will not only find square holes but be forced by social pressure into them instead of out of them." [92] Socialism and all the educational facilities at its command will eliminate the problem of human maladjustments so that everyone will be enabled to discover the occupational niche that suits him. Since the citizen of the future will work from an early age and will be taught as a child that "all useful work may be equally honorable," [93] work, Shaw hoped, would eventually cease to be "the curse our schools and capitalist profit factories make it seem today, but a prime necessity of a tolerable existence." [94] Shaw would also like to eliminate the universal distaste for "dirty work."

We are so accustomed to see dirty work done by dirty and poorly paid people that we have come to think that it is disgraceful to do it, and that unless a dirty and disgraced class existed it would not be done at all. This is nonsense. Some of the dirtiest work in the world is done by titled surgeons and physicians who are highly educated, highly paid, and move in the best society. The nurses who assist them are often their equals in general education, and sometimes their superiors in rank.[95]

He suggested that it is not the dirty work that is objected to so much as its association with poverty and degradation; a great deal can be done by society and its schools by removing prejudices which distinguish between clean and dirty work, and between manual and mental labor. Shaw nevertheless deplored the fact that society makes the highest kinds of mental

[92] *What's What*, p. 51.
[94] Preface to *Misalliance*.
[93] *Intelligent Woman*, p. 76.
[95] *Intelligent Woman*, p. 74.

work so unremunerative as to render it impossible to make a living by them. He cites the "clergymen, doctors, lawyers, authors, actors, painters, sculptors, architects, schoolmasters, university professors" [96] who see that successful men of business are inferior in knowledge, talent, character, and public spirit, and make much more money. Shaw would equalize all incomes and nationalize "the rent of ability." Ultimately, the problem to be faced is not how soon people should be put to work in their appropriate places, but "how soon they should be released from any obligation of the kind." [97] Throughout *The Intelligent Woman* there are insistent reminders that only through socialism and genuine education can such a complex program be realized.

Henry Straker, Tanner's chauffeur in *Man and Superman,* represents the "new man" educated for a useful purpose. While Straker is tinkering with the motor of his car, Tanner says to Octavius: "But this chap has been educated. What's more, he knows that we haven't." When Straker explains that "it's not the Board School that does it: it's the Polytechnic," Tanner observes: "His university, Octavius. Not Oxford, Cambridge . . . mere shops for selling class limitations like ours." To Straker, Oxford is "a very nice sort of place. . . . They teach you to be a gentleman there. In the Polytechnic they teach you to be an engineer or such like." And when Octavius states that "I believe most intensely in the dignity of labor," Straker counters with, "That's because you never done any. My business is to do away with labor. You'll get more out of me and a machine than you will out of twenty laborers." Tanner's conclusion is that "we literary and cultured persons for years have been set-

[96] *Ibid.,* p. 169. See also "Art Workers and the State," *Atlantic* 180 (November, 1947) where Shaw suggests granting the artist a shorter work day in order that he may have more leisure time to create.
[97] Preface to *Misalliance.*

ting up a cry of the New Woman . . . and never noticing the advent of the New Man."

The prose sequel to *Pygmalion,* which should be considered as part of the play, relates that Eliza does not marry Higgins, but Freddy Eynsford Hill. Unfortunately, Freddy's mother, intent on achieving an air of gentility, had not made any effort "to procure any serious secondary education for her children, much less give the boy a profession." And Mrs. Hill's snobbery had prevented her daughter Clara "from getting educated, because the only education she could have afforded was education with the Earlscourt greengrocer's daughter." The result was that Freddy had no occupation and Clara, a victim of artist idolatry, "ran after painters and novelists . . . was, in short, an utter failure, an ignorant, incompetent, pretentious, unwelcome, penniless, useless little snob." Clara eventually outgrew her frailties and learned to work in a furniture shop. Freddy and Eliza, at the suggestion of Colonel Pickering, opened a flower shop which failed to prosper because Freddy "like all youths educated at cheap, pretentious, and thoroughly inefficient schools knew a little Latin and . . . nothing else." Neither Freddy nor Eliza had ever learned to write out a bill, and Pickering "had to explain what a cheque book and a bank account meant. And the pair were by no means easily teachable." Eventually, Eliza "grasped the fact that business, like phonetics, has to be learned."

On the piteous spectacle of the pair spending their evenings in shorthand schools and polytechnic classes, learning bookkeeping and typewriting with incipient junior clerks . . . from the elementary schools, let me not dwell. There were even classes at the London School of Economics, and a humble personal appeal to the director of that institution to recommend a course bearing on the flower business.

Success came at last, but only after a belated education in their vocation.

Too True To Be Good (1932) dramatizes the empty lives of the rich who, like the poor, are rarely trained to do useful work for the community. The hypochondriacal Patient with the aid of an educated burglar, Aubrey, and his accomplice, Sweetie, escapes her wealthy home and overindulgent mother. Transformed into a sunburnt, healthy woman, she now gives way to her "higher centers" and questions her place in the world. She complains: "The glories of nature dont last any decently active person a week, unless theyre professional naturalists or mathematicians or something. I want something sensible to do." Expressing her contempt for the clinging woman, she determines upon constructive work. Colonel Tallboys at first believes Private Meek to be an idiot but soon learns that Meek has mastered many vocations. Tallboys says:

How I envy him! . . . I have been driven to sketching in water colors because I may not use my hands in life's daily business. . . . I see this man Meek doing everything that is natural to a complete man: carpentering, painting, digging, pulling and hauling, fetching and carrying, helping himself and everybody else, whilst I . . . must loaf and loll, allowed to do nothing but read the papers and drink brandy . . . to prevent myself going mad.

The central theme of "The Third Fable" of *Farfetched Fables* involves the measuring and classifying of humans for the purpose of assigning work commensurate with their capacities and talents. All this is done in an "Anthropometric Laboratory" situated on a pleasant spot in the Isle of Wight. The Matron explains to a passing Tourist, whose "embroidered smock and trimmed beard proclaim the would-be artist," that "anthropometric work is what we do here. Classifying men and women according to their abilities. . . . Analyzing their secretions and reactions and so on." Although the Tourist thinks he is a genius whose "destiny is to paint temples in fresco," he turns out to be a "Mediocrity." A Tramp soon announces himself as a beggar, "good for nothing else," and refuses classification because he is convinced of his lack of any distinguishing talent. He is threatened by the Gentleman in charge of the laboratory: "I'll have you arrested and put through the laboratory and classified. That is the law, compulsory for everybody. If you refuse you may be classed as irresponsible. . . . Or you may be classed as dangerous and incorrigible, in which case you'll be liquidated." The tragedy of the Tramp is that he has "tastes but no talents." He explains that he would like to be a Shakespeare, a Raphael, a Mozart or an Einstein but that he can neither write plays, nor paint, nor compose music nor "add two and two. I know a lot and can do nothing." It turns out that the Tramp is really a "genius who thinks he's a nincompoop." We see here the importance of vocational training and classification without which valuable individual potential can neither be realized nor made use of by the community.

EDUCATION OF WOMEN

Marriage in capitalism not only makes a slave of the man but makes the woman his slave, that is, "the slave of a slave which is the worst form of slavery." [98] Since the effect of social pressure is to make marriage compulsory as a woman's profession and since money is of paramount importance, many women either marry or enter into sex relations for money. The result is not only prostitution of the body—whether in or out

[98] Preface to *Getting Married*. See also *The Quintessence of Ibsenism*, p. 45 where Shaw urges every woman to do what Nora did in *A Doll's House*.

of marriage—but of the mind, which is worse since "it is a deeper betrayal of the divine purpose of our powers." [99] With present social institutions, Shaw argues in the Preface to *Getting Married*, emancipation and education of women can never be fully realized.

Shaw's remedy was for a woman to be economically independent. She would thus be enabled to acquire an education which would prepare her for living in a modern society, instead of being "condemned to wait in genteel idleness and uselessness for a husband," [100] or of being enslaved to duty and drudgery in poor households. In the Preface to *Getting Married* Shaw writes: "Women are improved by the escape from home provided by women's colleges; but as very few of them are fortunate enough to enjoy this advantage, most women are so thoroughly home-bred as to be unfit for human society." He felt that even the "corrupt" educational institutions are superior to the home. In 1928 he said that the emancipation of women had been partly realized. Previously, he points out, "The professions were closed to them. The universities were closed to them. The business offices were closed to them." [101] And at present:

Women are now educated as men are: they go to the universities and to the technical colleges if they can afford it; and as Domestic Service is now an educational subject with special colleges, a woman can get trained for such an occupation as that of manageress of a hotel as well as for the practice of law or medicine, or for accountancy and actuarial work. In short, nothing now blocks a woman's way into business or professional life except prejudice, superstition, old-fashioned parents, shyness, snobbery, ignorance of the con-

[99] *Intelligent Woman*, p. 203.
[100] Preface to *Androcles and the Lion*.
[101] *Intelligent Woman*, p. 174.

temporary world, and all the other imbecilities for which there is
no remedy but modern ideas.

He further says that the church is closed to women "to its own
great detriment, as it could easily find picked women, eloquent
in the pulpit and capable in parish management, to replace
the male refuse it has too often to fall back upon." The Preface
to *Good King Charles* contends that it is simply prejudice that
prevents women from being regarded as potential political
leaders.

Several of Shaw's plays reveal that in many of his characterizations of women there lurks an implicit criticism of the kind
of education they have been subjected to. Vivie Warren in
Mrs. Warren's Profession (1893) is a modern young woman
who has been to Newnham College and Cambridge. Eager to
do something constructive, she prepares herself to make a living by specializing in actuarial calculations. "If I thought," she
tells the aesthetic Praed, "that I was going to be a waster, shift-
ing along from one meal to another with no purpose, and no
character . . . I'd open an artery." Her education is in a sense
completed when she learns of her mother's "profession" and of
the sort of life she had lived as a barmaid at Waterloo Station.
Aware now of the world's corruption, and of what the university had not taught her, Vivie tells Crofts, her mother's partner
in an international chain of brothels: "When I think of the society that tolerates you and the laws that protect you. . . ."
But she is soon to learn that the Crofts Scholarship Fund has
been paying for her education. Wildly trying to persuade her
daughter not to leave her, Mrs. Warren tells Vivie that she
was "taught wrong on purpose" at college, and that the "big
people, the clever people, the managing people, all know it."
But Vivie, rejecting offers of money and position, refuses to

be a lady "trotting about the park to advertise my dressmaker and carriage builder." Deaf to the ideals of family duty to which her mother now resorts, Vivie is adamant. "My work is not your work, and my way not your way. We must part." Although the play centers about social problems, it also communicates Shaw's ideas about the educated, independent woman who is aware of false morality and who wants to earn a place in the world by dint of her own efforts.

Well versed in the Bible, art, and acrobatics, Lina in *Misalliance* appears as the allegorical woman of the future. When she steps out of a wrecked airplane which has crashed in John Tarleton's home, all the men—Tarleton and his son Johnny, Lord Summerhays and his son Bentley—fall in love with her. Appalled by the household's mania for love, she says: "It is not healthy. Your women are kept idle and dressed up for no other purpose than to be made love to." She is revolted when Johnny proposes, saying: "He dares to ask me to come and live with him in his rrrrrrabbit hutch, and take my bread from his hand, and ask him for pocket money, and wear soft clothes, and be his woman!" Astounded that Johnny does not think her profession as acrobat a proper one, she characterizes herself as an honest, free, unbought, independent woman, "all that a woman ought to be."

In the thirties he drew in the characters of Aloysia Brollikins in *On the Rocks* and of Begonia Brown in *Geneva* contrasting conceptions of the modern educated woman. Aloysia, a member of the labor delegation visiting Chavender, the Prime Minister, is a self-styled "proletarian, bone and blood"—a fanatical believer in class war. "What we want we shall have to take," she tells the Duke of Domesday. "The good of the community is nothing to you: you care only for surplus value." Accusing

the Duke of having turned the little farms of hardworking
Scotch crofters into deer forests "because you could get more
shooting rents out of them," she adds: "You will not find it
in your school histories; but in the histories of the proletariat
. . . written, not by venal academic triflers you call historians,
but by the prophets of the new order." Hipney, the old socialist, advises Chavender that the "labor movement is rotten with
book learning" and cites Aloysia, who is so proficient in "examinations and scholarships and certificates and gold medals."
Hipney concludes: "Your hearts are not in your education; but
our young people lift themselves out of the gutter with it."

Although, like Aloysia, Begonia Brown has won a London
County Council scholarship and "lots of prizes and certificates," the net result of her academic distinctions is that she
is bigoted, chauvinistic, war-minded, anti-intellectual, in.short
"a complete ignoramus" as the Secretary of the League of Nations puts it. "Always at the top of my class at school," Begonia
admits she was frightened of the "girls that went in for being
clever and having original ideas and all that sort of cranki-
ness. But I beat them easily in examinations." She is the secretary of the International Committee for Intellectual Co-opera-
tion, but Begonia is more interested in betting on dancing
tournaments than in Germany's withdrawing from the League
of Nations. "Theres a book in the office about the League," she
says. "I tried to read it; but it was such dry stuff I went to
sleep over it." With few scruples about waging war, she is for
reminding the foreigners "when they get out of hand" that
"England has never lost a battle." Empire-minded, she proudly
recalls that "when I was at school I was chosen five times to
recite on Empire Day. . . . Say a word against the Empire,
and you have finished with Begonia Brown." Furious that the

British flag has been insulted by the "niggers," she is indifferent to the fact that three convents and two churches have also
been burnt. "Thats nothing," she says contemptuously. "Theyre
only Catholic churches." Eventually she becomes the Camberwell representative in Parliament and is made a Dame of the
British Empire, who "draws the line at Communism and atheism and nationalization of women and doing away with marriage and the family and everybody stealing everybody's property. . . ." Shaw saw Begonia as a symbol of the intellectual
degeneration of women educated in England's schools.

SEX EDUCATION

In his long battle for a realistic drama Shaw argued for a
"realistic treatment" of sex on the stage. In the Preface to
Three Plays by Brieux Shaw praised the French dramatist for
such a treatment of love and sex:

You may exhibit seduction on the stage, but you must not even
mention illegitimate conception and criminal abortion. We may,
and do, parade prostitution to the point of intoxicating every young
person in the theater; yet no young person may hear a word as to
the diseases that follow prostitution.

Shaw considered sex a necessary and healthy instinct and its
nurture and education one of the most important functions of
all art, particularly the art of the theater. To the "stupid people" who argue that the theater is not the place for warning or
instruction, Shaw replies:

they plead that the proper place is out of hearing of the general
public: that is, not in a school, not in a church, not in a newspaper,
not in a public meeting, but in medical text-books which are only
read by medical students. This is the taboo over again. . . . The
commonsense of the matter is that a public danger needs a public
warning, and the more public the place the more effective the
warning.

Shaw championed the right of all human beings to sexual experience "untainted by the Pauline or romantic view of such experience as sinful in itself" [102] and advocated adequate instruction early in life on the subjects of marriage, child bearing, love, and sex. The fact that the schools practice taboo ultimately has disastrous effects on the physical and emotional patterns of adults. In believing that ignorance may be a "safeguard against precocity" and in refusing to have children taught by "qualified unrelated elders," parents who shrink from the task see to it that "our children are taught by other children in guilty secrets and unclean jests." [103] Every person "has the right to know all there is to know about oneself . . . a human right that sweeps away all the pretences of others to tamper with one's consciousness in order to produce what they choose to consider a good character." The Preface to *Getting Married* treats in great detail woman's right to sex experience and to early instruction in the complexities of marriage and sex; and *The Intelligent Woman* suggests she be informed about methods of contraception.[104] Shaw in a letter to Arnold Crossley in 1908, author of *The Compleat Baby Book,* points out with regard to men, that the "only popular guides to the conduct of childbirth are shilling handbooks for married women which no man dreams of as having any bearing on his own education." [105] Citing a woman, who unaided gave birth on a train on which there were a few students, Shaw adds that "there are a dozen ways . . . in which a man might find himself in the same predicament as the students on the Great Western," and concludes that the *Baby Book* "be made a

[102] Preface to *Getting Married.*   [103] Preface to *Misalliance.*
[104] *Intelligent Woman,* p. 410. See also Henderson, *Playboy and Prophet,* p. 684 for a list of speeches, articles and letters by Shaw on the subject of birth control and venereal disease.
[105] *Doctors' Delusions,* p. 352.

school book for all adolescent students." Shaw once suggested
that D. H. Lawrence's *Lady Chatterley's Lover* "should be on
the shelves of every college for budding girls. They should be
forced to read it on pain of being refused a marriage license." [106] He advised that adolescents be taught that there
may be strong sexual attraction between persons incompatible
in tastes and that it should never be made the basis of marriage.[107] Young people should also be informed about venereal
diseases, for when they contract them, they "raise the old cry,
'Why was I not told?'" Shaw thought that human beings could
be taught to poetize rather than vulgarize the sex instinct.
With regard to Joyce's *Ulysses* Shaw said that the Dublin
"medical students, the young bloods about town, were very
like that. Their conversation was dirty; and it defiled their
sexuality, which might just as easily have been held up to
them as poetic and vital." [108] Romantic, religious, and scholas-
tic taboos, Shaw urged, must be eliminated so that everyone
early in life can learn all there is to know about love, sex, and
marriage—the most important things in the lives of most people.

Gloria Clandon in *You Never Can Tell* (1896) is a victim
of an advanced system of education which neglected the areas
of passion and sex. Her mother, author of Twentieth Century
Treatises on creeds, clothing, cooking, parents and children,
and a "veteran of the Old Guard of the Women's Rights movement which had for its Bible John Stuart Mill's treatise on The

---

[106] Quoted in Harris, *Bernard Shaw: An Unauthorized Biography*, p.
238.

[107] *What's What*, p. 176. See also Preface to *Getting Married*: "It
would be better for everyone if young people were taught that what
they call love is an appetite which, like all other appetites, is destroyed
for the moment by its gratification."

[108] Henderson, *Table-Talk of G.B.S.*, p. 133.

Subjection of Women," has tried to educate her children, Dolly and Philip (the twins), and Gloria in a highly scientific manner. Believing in university degrees, professions, and the parliamentary franchise for women, she says: "I have educated Gloria to take up my work where I left it." Despite such advanced training, Gloria as the "Twentieth Century Woman" is not equipped to handle the advances of the philandering Valentine. Perceiving this, Valentine attacks with logical adroitness by pretending to despise his own sentimental and animal excesses. The result is that Gloria, now hopelessly confused, falls in love. Valentine explains to Mrs. Clandon that as a modern man he "educated himself scientifically . . . to circumvent the Women's Rights woman" who also had received "a scientific education: your plan." Valentine concludes that the "Higher Education of Women delivered Gloria into my hands; and it was you who taught her to believe in the Higher Education of Women." Gloria is now transformed into a passionate, womanly woman but is unable to understand what is really happening. "Why didn't you educate me properly?" she pitifully reproaches her mother. "You taught me nothing—nothing." And "blushing unendurably she covers her face with her hands and turns away from her mother," crying "Only shame—shame—shame." What is apparent is that Gloria, overwhelmed with guilt for doing what is natural to her instincts and emotions, has not been taught to understand the complex of sex and love.

In *Misalliance*, John Tarleton, the wealthy underwear manufacturer, is used by Shaw to stimulate the audience into seeing the need for education in sex and sex relations:

I've girls in my employment: girls and young men. . . . I used to go to the parents and tell them not to let their children go out into the world without instruction in the dangers and temptations they were going to be thrown into. . . . What did every one of the mothers say to me? "Oh, sir, how could I speak of such things to my daughter?" The men said I was quite right; but they didn't do it, any more than I'd been able to do it myself to Johnny [his son]. I had to leave books in his way; and I felt just awful when I did it.

Despairing that the family relation "can never be an innocent relation," Tarleton suggests that he would rather instruct Lord Summerhays' son, Bentley, in such matters than his own son.

In *Too True To Be Good* the concept that education is the means of bringing about an understanding of the close relationship between sex relations and evolutionary growth is implicit. Sweetie, Aubrey's accomplice, is dominated entirely by her "lower centers" and wants a new man every fortnight and a jolly good time out of life. Attracted to the Sergeant, she tells him that "what I look to you for, my lad, is a bit of fun," but is dismayed that he seems more interested in the Bible and *Pilgrim's Progress*. The Sergeant explains that "when men and women pick one another up just for a bit of fun they find theyve picked up more than they bargained for, because men and women have a top storey as well as a ground floor and you can't have one without the other." The Sergeant's theory is that "nature may be using me as a sort of bait to draw you to take an interest in things of the mind. Nature may be using your pleasant animal warmth to stimulate my mind." Sweetie's verdict is, "I don't call you a man," at which the Sergeant kisses her, explaining that sexual desire is "a hard fact of human nature . . . one of the facts that religion has to make room for."

Appalled by Sweetie's sex mania, Aubrey tells her: "You will be hanged someday because you have not what people call a richly stored mind. I have tried to educate you." But Sweetie admits she couldn't read the books he gave her because "they were as dull as ditchwater." Aubrey's thesis is that

In all the great poetry and literature of the world the higher centers speak. In all respectable conversation the higher centers speak, even when they are saying nothing or telling lies. But the lower centers are there all the time: a sort of guilty secret with every one of us, though they are dumb. I remember asking my tutor at college whether, if anyone's lower centers began to talk, the shock would not be worse than the one Balaam got when his donkey began talking to him. He only told me half a dozen improper stories to shew how open-minded he was. I never mentioned the subject again until I met Sweetie. Sweetie is Balaam's ass.

Passionately denouncing the domination of the lower centers, Aubrey concludes: "They leave us no place to live, no certainties, no workable morality, no heaven, no hell, no commandments, and no God."

In the "Fifth Fable" of *Farfetched Fables,* set in a Genetic Institute in the distant future, two males (Shamrock and Thistle), a female (Rose), and a hermaphrodite are in an animated discussion about the sex practices and beliefs of the nineteenth century. Having explored "every scrap of nineteenth century writing that remains," Shamrock concludes that "their textbooks on physiology dont mention the reproductive organs nor hint at such a thing as sex." "Being myself a hermaphrodite," adds Hermaphrodite, "I have looked myself up in the nineteenth century books; and I simply wasnt there." Rose declares, "Our business is the first business of any human society: the reproduction of the human race, the most mentionable subject in the world and the most important." An important reason why they considered sex unmentionable, Rose suggests, is that "their methods [vulgar bodily contacts] were so disgusting they had no decent language for them." [109]

[109] See "The Revolutionist's Handbook," *Man and Superman:* "We

HEALTH EDUCATION

Shaw had looked forward to an "extension of school clinics, school meals, and public as distinguished from private and parental care of children." [110] The conclusion of his attack on the medical profession contained a list of urgent measures for securing public health, the last of which champions a public medical service for the schools:

A public medical service, specialized, graded and equipped with laboratories for diagnosis, conducting a full complement of school clinics, hospitals, and nursing homes, to be a compulsory part of the machinery of Public Health in every centre of population, reporting to an independent statistical department under lay control for the collation of results. [111]

The conclusion of the Preface to *The Doctor's Dilemma* advises all beginners in life to secure good health in these ways:

Take the utmost care to get well born and well brought up. . . . Be careful to go to a good school where there is what they call a school clinic, where your nutrition and teeth and eyesight and other matters of importance to you will be attended to. Be particularly careful to have all this done at the expense of the nation, as otherwise it will not be done at all, the chances being about forty to one against your being able to pay for it directly yourself, even if you know how to set about it. Otherwise you will be what most people are at present: an unsound citizen of an unsound nation, without sense enough to be ashamed or unhappy about it. [112]

---

are not taught to think decently [about matters of sex], and consequently we have no language for them except indecent language. We therefore have to declare them unfit for public discussion, because the only terms in which we can conduct the discussion are unfit for public use." These lines were written more than forty years before *Farfetched Fables*.

[110] *Doctors' Delusions*, p. 65.   [111] *Ibid.*, p. 69.

[112] See the satiric sketch about nutrition, "The Fourth Fable" in *Farfetched Fables*.

ATHLETICS

Shaw frequently ridiculed and condemned the practices in English schools of forcing students to drudge away at compulsory games. There was a time, he claimed, citing Gosse's *Life of Swinburne*, when a boy at Eton could be "left to himself sufficiently to enable him to cultivate tastes of his own and . . . commune with Nature in his own way." [113] Ridiculing the recent (1918) books written by those who were proud of their public school education and who boasted of being thrashed "because they tried to botanize, or naturalize, or take country walks, or read" instead of playing games, Shaw charged that such a condition "exhibits the complete capture of the school by the athletic schoolboy and the athletic schoolmaster, the medieval system being restored with the substitution of football and cricket for Latin and Greek." In an article written in 1923, Shaw again denounced compulsory athletics after a boy, as a result of being bullied in this way, committed suicide. He ironically suggested that "parents whose boys are of this unmanly intellectual type send them to institutions for the mentally defective where games are not compulsory." [114] Shaw's conclusion was that English schools merely reflect the contempt with which these "kickees or despised intelligentsia" are regarded outside the schools. In the Preface to *Misalliance* he had suggested that "the sacrifice of mental accomplishments to athletics" in the schools is the result of compulsory education maiming unwilling minds. Preoccupied with denouncing compulsory sports, Shaw does not consider any positive program of athletics for the schools.

[113] Preface to W.E.A. *Year Book* in *Doctors' Delusions.*
[114] *Doctors' Delusions*, p. 345.

MASS MEDIA OF COMMUNICATIONS

The corruption and falsification of the mass media of communications are so enormous, Shaw charged, that the minds of ordinary people, nourished in equally corrupt schools, are unable to understand. Regarding newspapers Shaw wrote:

The corruption of the schools would not matter so much if the Press were free. . . . As it costs at least a quarter of a million to establish a daily newspaper in London, the newspapers are owned by rich men. And they depend on the advertisements of other rich men. Editors and journalists who express opinions in print that are opposed to the interests of the rich are dismissed. . . . The newspapers therefore must continue the work begun by the schools and colleges; so that only the strongest and most independent and original minds can escape from the mass of false doctrine.[115]

Thus, popular lies, which may "easily last a century and a half," [116] are constantly swallowed by a "politically uneducated and systematically hoodwinked electorate." [117] Like Toynbee, Shaw despairs of a society "in which everybody knows how to read and nobody knows what to read, and in which the crudest, darkest, poorest minds are allowed to propagate . . . through the Press." [118]

Not only the newspapers but also novels, periodicals, films, and radio contribute to this obfuscation of the mass mind. "It has never raged so incessantly as in the present century, because never before have such vast masses of untrained readers been let loose on literature by elementary education and cheap books." [119] In 1944, Shaw wrote of the cinema:

[115] *Intelligent Woman*, p. 64. See *Peace Conference Hints*, p. 37.
[116] *What's What*, p. 295.　　　　[117] *Ibid.*, p. 303.
[118] Preface to W.E.A. *Year Book* in *Doctors' Delusions*.
[119] *Pen Portraits and Reviews*, p. 143.

Nietzsche defined nations as people who read the same newspapers.
. . . What he would have said of the invention of the cinema,
which brings the same dramas to action and speech over the whole
inhabited world, and has made Hollywood an international city
aesthetically spreading its doctrine as no established Church has
ever succeeded in doing . . . I shall not guess.[120]

Earlier in the century Shaw had been aware of the screen's
educational potential. Questioned on the subject, Shaw is re-
ported to have said: "The cinematograph begins educating
people when the projection lantern begins clicking and does
not stop until it leaves off. And it is educating you far more
effectively when you think it is only amusing than when it is
avowedly instructing you in the habits of lobsters." [121] The
cinema, he had hoped, would reform the art school "with its
life class studying an absurdly unlifelike naked human being
in a condition of painful . . . paralysis." Regarding athletic
exercises, the cinema could instruct us in "elegance, grace,
beauty. . . ." And from a social view, the cinema would be
able to teach by exhibiting "to masses of poor children the
habits, dress, manners, and surroundings of people who can
afford to live decently." Because of the vast world-wide audiences viewing programs on film and television, it is not hard to
imagine what Shaw would say today about the unlimited educational potential of these media.

Shaw believed that the statesmen and the schools of the future would have to be responsible for a positive utilization of
the mass media. For without a people carefully instructed in
the complex of controversy, which the newspapers are sup-

[120] *What's What*, p. 185. See also *Intelligent Woman*, p. 164.
[121] "Education and the Cinematograph," *The Bioscope* (June 18,
1914). See also "A Relief from the Romantic Film," *Illustrated London
News* (December 3, 1927); Henderson, *Table-Talk of G.B.S.*, pp. 44–46.

posed to deal with, and the art of the cinema, which is to Shaw
the theater magnified, "fantastic codes of honor and dishonor,
of love and hate, praise and blame, patriotism and treason,
manliness and womanliness, and conduct generally, take the
place of observation and reasoning, and make democracy a
fantasy acted by people in a dream." [122] Shaw precursed many
current writers who believe that since the mass media—distinguished by adroit formulas and false fictive archetypes
rather than by true art—are not concerned with life's potentials, society is thus denied a most important form of education.

TESTS AND MEASUREMENTS

Although Shaw believed that the "most elaborate tests of
intellectual capacity we have yet established by law and custom are the university and civil service examinations," [123] the
difficulty is that while they "ensure a body of civil servants
who can at least read, write, and cipher," the questions soon
became known, and the coaching of candidates becomes a
profession by the aid of which "any blockhead who has a good
memory and has been broken-in to school drudgery can be
crammed with a list of readymade answers." In this way, Shaw
argued, such tests exclude "the thinkers whose memories will
not retain things not worth remembering, and who cannot
stomach school books, though their appetites for books which
are works of art or helps to criticism of existing life are in-
satiable." [124] In the Preface to *The Apple Cart* Shaw asserts

[122] *What's What*, p. 185.   [123] *Ibid.*, p. 309.
[124] *Ibid.* See *Pen Portraits and Reviews*, p. 150: "the secret of a liberal
education is to learn what you want to know for the sake of your own
enlightenment, and not let anybody teach you anything whatever for
the purpose of pulling you through an examination, especially one conducted by persons who have been taught in the same way." See also

that such tests tend to strengthen class distinctions, for the civil servants are selected "by an educational test which nobody but an expensively schooled youth can pass, thus making the most powerful . . . part of our government an irresponsible class government."

Shaw classified intelligence tests as "capacity tests instead of the mere memory tests which enable so many teachers and scholars to be certified as proficient when they should have been certified as mentally defective." [125] He confessed that he had never come across an intelligence test "that I could pass. . . . Whether this is a high recommendation of them or a disparagement it is not for me to say." [126]

In general Shaw did not condemn examinations, for "without some cerebrotonics a political machine as complicated as a modern democratic State cannot be kept in order." [127] Any examination system, he thought, could be reduced to absurdity by wrong methods or irrelevant questions. The main difficulty is how to evolve tests which will put the best minds to work. He praised the British *Journal of Psychology* for continuing the work begun by Karl Pearson in *Biometrika* in experiments with tests of vocational aptitudes for children. Opti-

---

Preface to *Farfetched Fables*: "Universities are infested with pedants who have all recorded history at their tongues' ends, but can make no use of it except to disqualify examinees." See also how Shaw satirizes typical examination questions. "Give the family names of Domenichino and Titian; and write an essay not exceeding 32 words on their respective styles and influence on Renaissance art. . . . Give the dates of six of Shakespear's plays, with the acreage occupied by the Globe Theater."
[125] *What's What*, p. 310.
[126] See Pearson, *G.B.S.: A Postscript*, p. 86: "When you get to heaven," Mrs. Pearson once asked Shaw, "which of your activities do you think God will give you most marks for?" "If God starts giving me examination marks for any of my activities, there will be serious trouble between us," Shaw replied.
[127] *What's What*, p. 309.

mistic about the future of this science, Shaw advised modern statesmen and schools to keep acquainted with its progress.

He believed that in the school it was possible "to ascertain by better devised examination papers and conversations the mental range of an examinee." He recommended that the single decisive examination with the possibility of coaching be scrapped, and a series of tests be substituted—such as those taken during a period of apprenticeship under critical observation in the army, navy, and merchant marine. These examinations must test not so much for technical efficiency as for comprehension. Oddly enough, he seems to think that "fifteen minutes conversation should be amply sufficient; but the conversation must not be in abstract terms." In this chapter, "Our Attempts at Anthropometry," in his *What's What* Shaw fails to define explicitly what he means by comprehension; and in the long discussion about economic rent which follows, he seems to befog the problem. He does specify that an examinee must have intellectual freedom. "There must be no dogmatism . . . no dictated answers to the questions nor orthodox tendencies prescribed for the essays and conversations."

Competitive examinations in the schools should be abolished, "as they give the competitors an interest in oneanother's ignorance and failure, and associate success with the notion of doing the other fellow down." [128] If there is competition, Shaw would have it between teams because such opposition stimulates the members to share knowledge and help each other. An article written in 1916 details a series of prizes he was asked to distribute to various competitors in written composition. After listing his corrections and assigning the rewards, Shaw concluded that "though each child had its attention called to its mistakes in a manner which suggested

[128] *Ibid.*, p. 177.

that they had cost it something, yet they all got the same sum (eighteenpence) and therefore were not provoked to envy and hate one another . . . if their prizes had varied in amount." [129]

PHONETICS

While Shaw wrote much [130] and lectured often about phonetics, the most elaborate treatment is to be found in his Preface to Richard Albert Wilson's *The Miraculous Birth of Language* (1948), "a book . . . in which I should like everyone to be examined before being certified as educated or eligible for the franchise or for any scientific, religious, legal, or civil employment." An exposition of his main contentions will readily reveal the implications and burdens for the schools.

In the main Shaw argued that our alphabet "is reduced to absurdity by a foolish orthography based on the notion that the business of spelling is to represent the origin and history of a word instead of its sound and meaning." Why should an intelligent child, Shaw asks, be asked to spell "debt" with a b simply because Julius Caesar spelled the Latin word with a b? Presenting a wealth of illustration, Shaw maintained that phonetic spelling would eliminate difficulties in the language which are confusing to a learner. What is even more important is that a prodigious total of manual labor in literature, journalism, and commercial correspondence could be halved, or at least reduced by discarding useless grammar and spelling phonetically.[131]

---

[129] *Doctors' Delusions*, p. 352.

[130] See The Morning *Post* (October 5, 1922); The Manchester *Guardian* (June 2, 1924); The New York *Times* (January 2, 1927 and January 15, 1928); "The Dying Tongue of Great Elizabeth," *The Saturday Review* (February 11, 1905). For a technical treatment of Shaw's system of phonetics, see Joseph Saxe, *Bernard Shaw's Phonetics*.

[131] See Preface to *Geneva:* England could not "even design an alphabet

By useless grammar he meant those patterns which are vestiges of the "old grammatic inflections that make Latin and its modern dialects so troublesome to learn." [132] Shaw would go so far as to prefer the Chinese Pidgin, "Sorry no can" to "I regret that I shall be unable to comply with your request." He advocated neglecting the irregular verbs in learning a foreign language since a child's "I thinked" is quite intelligible. He approved of the Basic English of the Orthological Society "by which foreigners can express all their wants in England by learning 800 English words. It is thought-out pidgin and gets rid of much of our grammatical superfluities."

Shaw insisted that the English language could not be spelled with five Latin vowels. Eighteen vowels are needed in order "to preserve the language from the continual change which goes on at present because the written word teaches nothing as to the pronunciation, and frequently belies it." "Though" could be spelled with two letters, "should" with three, and "enough" with four, that is, nine letters instead of eighteen, a saving of one hundred percent. So long as we cannot note down "the diphthongal pronunciation until we have a separate single letter for every vowel," vulgarisms in pronunciation as well as eccentric variations will be prevalent. Shaw cites his grandfather's varchoo for vert-yoo, a famous orator's Russ-ya and Pruss-ya, and Annie Besant's rhyme of the article a with pay. "In short we are all over the shop with our vowels because we cannot spell them with our alphabet." Moreover,

---

capable of saving a billionsworth of British time, ink, paper, by spelling English speech sounds unequivocally and economically." See also *What's What,* p. 136: "The economic case for an alphabet capable of spelling my name with two letters . . . is enormously more pressing than . . . adjusting our watches to the two hour difference between midsummer and midwinter daylight."

[132] Preface to Wilson, *Miraculous Birth of Language.*

spelling becomes a "will o' the wisp." [133] Shaw maintained that a new alphabet would eliminate spelling ignorance—particularly for those who do not read and whose word memory is aural—and would make teaching and learning easier. Our present alphabet also makes it impossible to teach children that euphony is important and that "if they make ugly or slovenly sounds when they speak they will never be respected." [134] Shaw was revolted that the worst vulgarism was actually taught in the schools—the habit of prefixing the neutral vowel (the schwa), which phoneticians usually indicate by an e upside down, to all vowels and diphthongs.

The woman who asks for "e kapp e te-ee" is at once classed as, at best, lower middle. When I pass an elementary school and hear the children repeating the alphabet in unison, and chanting unrebuked "Ah-yee, Be-yee, Ce-yee, De-yee" I am restrained from going in and shooting the teacher only by the fact that I do not carry a gun and by my fear of the police.

Shaw argued that our inadequate alphabet leads to affectation in speech. Masses of our population become bilingual, that is, "they have an official speech as part of their company manners which they do not use at home or in conversation with their equals." He believed that neither speech nor writing could be depended on as class indexes. "Oxford graduates and costermongers alike call the sun the san and a rose a rah-ooz." The solution is a new alphabet of 18 new vowels and 24

[133] With regard to Shaw's experiences as chairman of the Spoken English Committee of the British Broadcasting Corporation, see Dr. Daniel Jones, "G.B.S. and Phonetics" in *G.B.S. 90*. See "Problem of a Common Language," *Atlantic* (October, 1950). Shaw attacks Johnson's spelling and charges that the elementary schools fail to teach children "to speak ʾr write English well enough to qualify them for clerical or professional appointments. All our phonetic propaganda is sterilized by the dread that the cost of the change would be colossal."

[134] Preface, Wilson, *Miraculous Birth of Language.*

new consonants, making in all 42 letters. "The rule is to be
One Sound One Letter, with every letter unmistakably different from all the others." To retain the 26 letters of the
existing alphabet and invent only the ones in which it is deficient would result in a spelling "which would not only lead
the first generation of its readers to dismiss the writers as
crudely illiterate, but would present unexpected obscenities
which no decent person could be induced to write." The new
alphabet must be completely different from the old and should
be used, he said, with the present lettering until the better
ousts the worse. Shaw thought this a problem primarily for
artists, statisticians, mathematicians, and psychologists. If
such research proves to be successful, the educational authorities would be obliged to recognize spelling and phonetic
reforms. The seriousness with which Shaw considered his new
alphabet is evident in his will, which empowered his executors
to finance any educational organization willing to undertake
the requisite research. The will also specifies that a phonetic
expert be employed "to transliterate my play *Androcles and
the Lion* into the proposed British Alphabet" [135] and that copies
of the play be published side by side and page for page with
the 26-letter version. Shortly after the will was filed an un-
known person paid the shilling the law requires, and filed a
petition to the effect that the legacy to further a phonetic alphabet would "gravely affect the majesty of the English language
and would have serious repercussions on English literature." [136]

Pygmalion dramatizes the concept that adequate education
in phonetics and speech can help to eliminate the barriers between different levels of society. In the Preface Shaw states
that "for the encouragement of people troubled with accents
that cut them off from all high employment, I may add that

[135] *Last Will and Testament.*
[136] The New York *Times* (December 10, 1950).

the change wrought by Professor Higgins in the flower-girl is neither impossible nor uncommon." The purpose of the play, Shaw explains, is to make "the public aware that there are such people as phoneticians, and that they are among the most important people in England at present." Although the deficiencies of Professor Higgins as a teacher have already been discussed, his elocutionary values are similar to Shaw's when he states "how frightfully interesting it is to take a human being and change her into a quite different human being by creating a new speech for her. It's filling up the deepest gulf that separates class from class and soul from soul." Shaw's belief that such speech training must be undertaken by the schools is evident when he states in the Preface that it "has to be done scientifically, or the last state of the aspirant may be worse than the first. An honest and natural slum dialect is more tolerable than the attempt of a phonetically untaught person to imitate the vulgar dialect of the golf club." In his *Last Will and Testament* he expressed the hope that the "ministry of Education may institute the enquiry and adopt the Proposed British Alphabet to be taught in the schools it controls."

It is evident that Shaw's socialist state would dictate the goals, methods, and curricula in the schools. Technical or required training—the minimum everyone must master to justify his living in a civilized state—would be a prerequisite for higher or liberal education. This, however, would be based upon pleasure, self-discovery, and social orientation, not with a pedantic accumulation of obsolete knowledge. Despite his attempt to reconcile education and liberty, he would impose his own system of compulsion, even to the point of exterminating those deemed undesirables. Nevertheless, Shaw, as was shown, makes many valuable suggestions which could be practicable in a free society.

9   Diverse education for diverse people

Throughout a long life Shaw wrote prolifically about the need to educate society's rulers, about doctors and scientific method, about the injustices heaped on lawbreakers, and about—what is really a specialized area for him—the training of stage performers. Here he is perhaps at his best, speaking from great experience and authority. Shaw's preoccupation with these areas is evidenced in many of the plays.

THE EDUCATION OF LEADERS

In his contribution to *Fabian Essays* Shaw suggested that a "wise electorate would ask for some incorruptible scientific test of capacity, taking capacity in its widest sense to include intellectual integrity and social instinct." Toward the close of World War I Shaw pointed out what has become even more impressive by the invention of nuclear bombs, namely, the danger of "inventing weapons capable of destroying civilization faster than we produce men who can be trusted to use them wisely." [1] Toward the close of World War II Shaw stated that the problem of selecting capable rulers "clearly

[1] "Commonsense About the War," *What I Really Wrote About the War*, p. 84.

involves an educational and a testing system," [2] for the practice of having leaders "partly self-chosen and partly the result of Darwinian natural selection: that is, of pure luck" [3] must be abandoned if genuine democracy is to be realized. Government must become a profession like any other profession. In the Preface to *Farfetched Fables*, which testifies to his lasting concern with this problem, he writes:

We already have in our professional and university examinations virtual panels of persons tested and registered as qualified to exercise ruling functions as Astronomers Royal, Archbishops, Lord Chief Justices, and public schoolmasters. Even police constables are instructed. Yet for the ministers who are supposed to direct and control them we have no guarantee that they can read or write, or could manage a baked potato stall successfully.

Fifteen years earlier in the Preface to *Too True To Be Good* Shaw had called for an improvement in democratic leadership through panels of candidates qualified by training and competitive examination. "Panel A would be for diplomacy and international finance, Panel B for national affairs, Panel C for municipal and county affairs, Panel D for the village councils and so forth." From time to time Shaw urged that democratic governments need cabinets of thinkers as well as cabinets of administrators—all of whom must be properly empanelled.[4]

How, then, would Shaw test potential leaders? He declared when challenged to produce "my anthropometric machine or my endocrine or phrenological tests" [5] that they have not yet been invented, but that the present system of competitive examinations was worse than useless. Although the stated purpose of his *What's What* is to agitate for proper selection of

[2] *What's What*, p. 36.   [3] *Ibid.*, p. 31.
[4] "In Praise of Guy Fawkes," *Where Stands Socialism Today?* p. 183.
[5] Preface to *Too True To Be Good*.

leaders, the book says nothing about specific methods of testing. In the Preface to *Farfetched Fables* one can, however, find a series of Shavian tests. Shaw admits that a scientific method is beyond his powers and that these tests are the "best suggestions I can think of."

Unless a candidate for first class honors in politics can write an essay demonstrating a mastery of the theory of rent and the theory of exchange value, "the top panel must be closed against him." "Had the late President Franklin Roosevelt, a thoroughly schooled gentleman-amateur Socialist, been taught the law of rent, his first attempts at The New Deal would not have failed so often." [6]

Candidates for the top panel would also be given an "esthetic test." Shaw would have them taken into a gallery containing unlabeled reproductions of the famous pictures of the world, and "asked how many of the painters they can name at sight, and whether they have anything to say about them, or are in any way interested in them." An interrogation about music would be given to test a candidate's ability "to sing or whistle or hum or play as many of the leading themes of the symphonies, concertos, string quartets, and opera tunes of Mozart and Beethoven, and the Leitmotifs of Wagner, as they can remember." The object would be "not to test their executive skill but to ascertain their knowledge of the best music and their interest in and enjoyment of it, if any." Taken into a library stocked with the masterpieces of literature, candidates would be asked "which of them they had ever read, and whether they read anything but newspapers and detective

[6] Shaw adds here: "This would plough Adam Smith, Ricardo, Ruskin, and Marx. . . . Stanley Jevons would pass it. . . . When he . . . became a university professor, he taught anything and everything the old examiners expected him to teach, and so he might have failed in a character test."

stories." Shaw justified his aesthetic test on the ground that "leaders should be cultivated aesthetically so as not to be liable to the popular error of confusing recreative art with the debauchery and pornography of its prostitutions." [7] Furthermore, cultivated rulers must understand that "art is as powerful for evil as for good." [8]

A candidate would also have to be well educated in past politics and history, for, as he had earlier stated in the Preface to *The Shewing-Up of Blanco Posnet*, it is disastrous for rulers ignorant of the commonplaces of history "to repeat experiments which have in the past produced national catastrophe." In the *What's What* he suggests that we must not "rush to the conclusion that statesmen must know everything, and build a perfectly scientific policy on a perfectly scientific basis." [9] Thus the assumptions and purposes with which a statesman works are to take precedence over sheer omniscience.

Therefore when facing contemporary situations and acting on them the statesman has not the alternative of omniscience: he must be guided by his knowledge of how human nature reacts to external pressures. He must be apriorist to the extent of being a psychologist and physicist guessing with very imperfect data to go upon. He cannot wait until he has read a thousand books and all the documents in the Record Office.

The last page of *What's What* prescribes that a statesman must at least have read Macaulay's *History of England* and the Communist Manifesto and have "comprehended the change in historical outlook from one to the other."

The future leader must be trained to be religious but "he must discard every element in his religion that is not universal." [10] When Shaw states that a statesman must not look

---

[7] *What's What*, p. 343.   [8] *Ibid.*, p. 186.
[9] *Ibid.*, p. 363.   [10] *Ibid.*, p. 329.

to God to do his work for him and that "he must regard himself as a fallible servant of a fallible God," he means that all future rulers had better practice the religion of Creative Evolution.

With all this there is still no way of telling whether the examinee is possessed of the evolutionary appetite to do good. Citing many examples of past rulers, Shaw concludes that passing tests should merely "ensure registration on panels of the citizens most capable of political work in its various grades, and available for election." [11] He confessed that he knew of no method which could help evaluate a candidate's bent for righteousness. This becomes increasingly difficult since our notions of correct conduct and ethics are continually changing.

In *Caesar and Cleopatra* (1898) we find the ideal of the properly educated leader in Caesar. He is tortured that men are not what they could be and soliloquizes before the Sphinx: "Sphinx, you and I, strangers to the race of men, are no strangers to one another." Cleopatra, in a playful conversation, is revealed as a young, uneducated barbarian filled with savage superstitions and committed to violence, vengeance, and cruelty to those who serve her. Shaw explains in the notes appended to the play that she is unfit to be a ruler of men. Discussing her education, he states that Cleopatra, being a queen, "was therefore not the typical Greek-cultured, educated Egyptian lady of her time. . . . I do not feel bound to believe that she was well educated." It is Caesar, intent on making Cleopatra a more civilized ruler, who educates her in the course of the play by opening her eyes to his essential humanity. Denouncing Lucius Septimus' murder of Pompey, Britannus for giving him the names of all his enemies in Egypt, Cleopatra for ordering the murder of Pothinus, and himself for the

[11] *Ibid.*, p. 324.

murder of Vercingetorix as "a necessary protection to the commonwealth, a duty of statesmanship—follies and fictions ten times bloodier than honest vengeance," Caesar cries: "And so, to the end of history, murder shall breed murder, always in the name of right and honor and peace, until the gods are tired of blood and create a race that can understand." Apparently Cleopatra learns the lessons Caesar prepares for her, for she later admits that Caesar "has no hatred in him. . . . His kindness to me is a wonder: neither mother, father, nor nurse have ever taken so much care for me, or thrown open their thoughts to me so freely." And at the end as Caesar is about to leave for Rome, she recognizes that his way of ruling is "Without punishment. Without revenge. Without judgment." Yet the reader is left wondering about Shaw's meaning when the merciful Caesar approves Ruffio's slaying of Cleopatra's maid, Ftatateeta, which he says was "natural slaying: I feel no horror at it." In short, Ruffio is exonerated because he had not put himself "in the seat of the judge, and with hateful ceremonies and appeals to the gods handed that woman over to some hired executioner to be slain before the people in the name of justice." In his desire to rid his ideal ruler of false ideals and moralities, Shaw seems to accept revenge and murder on grounds equally, if not more, dangerous. The play, on the whole, suggests that rulers must be educated into understanding the concepts, as Caesar put it: "Is peace not an art? is war not an art? is government not an art? is civilization not an art?"

In *Back to Methuselah* (1921) neither Burge nor Lubin, the ex-Prime Ministers who impugn each other's ability to govern as head of the Liberal Party, have been properly educated for the job. Although Lubin excoriates the "dangerously half-educated masses" and boasts that "at the university I was a

classical scholar; and my profession was the law," he is convinced that the production and distribution of wealth cannot
be "controlled by legislation or by any human action" since
there are scientific laws, "ascertained and settled finally by the
highest economic authorities." Accused by Burge of having
neither foresight nor vision, Lubin retorts that "your mind is
not a trained mind: it has not been . . . cultivated by intercourse with educated minds at any of our great seats of learning." But both Burge and Lubin are apparently intellectually
incapable of grasping the significance of the evolutionary concepts propounded by Franklyn and Conrad Barnabas. In the
next play, *The Thing Happens,* Burge and Lubin become a
composite Burge-Lubin whom Confucius, the Chinese Chief
Secretary, classes as a barbarian who lusts after the Negress
Minister of Health and who prefers vulgar sports to contemplation. Contemptuous of Burge-Lubin's inability to govern,
Confucius tells him: "Government is an art of which you are
congenitally incapable. Accordingly, you imported educated
negresses and Chinese to govern you. Since then you have done
very well." In *What's What* Shaw has explained Confucius'
claim to being "held in awe" as follows:

This power is called Awe. It enables a head master to control
masses of schoolboys who could mob him and tear him to pieces.
. . . The statesman has to exploit it because he has to give authority not only to superior persons who naturally inspire it, but to
ordinary Yahoos who can be made to produce an illusion of superiority by unusual robes, retinues and escorts, magnificent liveries
and uniforms.[12]

Shaw's point is that such "artificial Awe producers give authority to persons who are not natural Awe producers." When
Burge-Lubin asks Confucius what he ought to do to improve

---

[12] *What's What,* p. 286.

himself, he is advised "to give yourself up to contemplation;
and great thoughts will come to you." Apparently Confucius
attributes the awe he generates to this habit of contemplation, the eternal preoccupation of the Ancients themselves.

King Magnus in *The Apple Cart* (1929) would pass Shaw's
tests with honors since he is a philosopher, evolutionist, and
humanitarian. Defending himself in his conflict with the Labor
Cabinet in 1962, Magnus deplores the fact that the educated
refuse to

touch this drudgery of government . . . once the centre of attraction for ability, public spirit, and ambition. . . . It is looked down
upon by our men of genius as dirty work. What great actor would
exchange his stage? what great barrister his court? what great
preacher his pulpit? for the squalor of the political arena. . . . The
scientists will have nothing to do with us; for the atmosphere of
politics is not the atmosphere of science. . . . All the talent and
genius of the country is bought up by the flood of unearned money.
. . . Politics . . . has now become the refuge of a few fanciers
of public speaking and party intrigue who find all the avenues to
distinction closed to them either by their lack of practical ability,
their comparative poverty and lack of education.

Recognizing this state of affairs to be the result of an inadequate educational system, Magnus declares: "In spite of my
urgings and remonstrances you have not yet dared to take
command of our schools and put a stop to the inculcation upon
your unfortunate children of superstitions and prejudices that
stand like stone walls across every forward path." Magnus
emerges as a true Shavian ruler as he proclaims his credo:
"I stand for the great abstractions: for conscience and virtue;
for the eternal against the expedient; for the evolutionary appetite against the day's gluttony; for intellectual integrity, for
humanity, for the rescue of industry from commercialism and
of science from professionalism."

THE EDUCATION OF DOCTORS

Professor J. D. Bernal in his essay, "Shaw the Scientist," in *G.B.S. 90* believes that Shaw's Preface to *The Doctor's Dilemma* "shows to the full his capacity for social understanding of the medical profession exceeding anything that has been written of it before or since" and that the Preface to *Back to Methuselah* "is a document which should form part of every biological student's education." While any attempt to prove or disprove this claim would be beyond the scope of this book, an attempt will be made to organize Shaw's suggestions about the sort of education doctors should get.

Shaw saw the medical profession as just another exploiting agency in a capitalist society. He contended that the ordinary doctor could not realize his highest integrity simply because money is to be derived from ill health and because there are few doctors who can resist money. Medical societies, he charged, are saturated with superstition, resistance to change, and unscientific modes of thought. And all this is the result of the training to which doctors are subjected. His main conclusion was that "until the medical profession becomes a body of men trained and paid by the country to keep the country in health it will remain what it is at present: a conspiracy to exploit popular credulity and human suffering." [13]

Although Shaw admitted that the conventionally certified doctor has at least "had a minimum of liberal education . . . some clinical practice, and that he has been coached in the main facts of anatomy and physiology," [14] he was not willing

[13] Preface to *The Doctor's Dilemma*.
[14] "What Is To Be Done With the Doctors?" *The English Review* (December, 1917–March, 1918) in *Doctors' Delusions*, p. 6.

to admit that doctors were trained to understand true scientific method.

The remedy is, not less science and more laissez-faire, but more science and still more. A little science is a dangerous thing, and science in science-tight compartments is worse. Bring to bear on every department the coordinated science of all the other departments, and the doctors will be promptly driven beyond their crudities and follies . . . into as sound positions and as reasonable methods as humanity is capable of.[15]

Since Shaw believed that the "only real safeguard against the tyrannies of sectional science is lay scientific control," he warned that the "self-styled Science of the medical profession should be constantly checked by the political, the mathematical, and, generally, the sociological sciences."

Shaw's attack on vivisection was an attack on a particular scientific method. From the practical point of view he argues that vivisection has failed to bring to light any really new knowledge, and that public belief has been the result of propaganda playing upon ignorance. "One of the devices by which doctors save themselves the trouble of thinking is the convention that a clinical observation does not become scientific until it has been repeated on the body of a rabbit, guinea-pig, frog, cat, or stolen dog." [16] The moral view suggests that even if it were proved that vivisection had actually produced new knowledge it would still be ethically unacceptable. Doctors "absurdly infer," he said in the Preface to *London Music,* "that the pursuit of scientific knowledge: that is, of all knowledge, is exempt from moral obligations, and consequently that they are privileged as scientists to commit the most revolting cruelties when they are engaged in research." He questioned

[15] *Ibid.,* p. 67.   [16] *Ibid.,* p. 35.

whether such experiments on animals are evidences of cruelty for their own sake for "cruelty is one of the primitive pleasures of mankind, and that the detection of its Protean disguises as law, education, medicine, discipline, sport is one of the most difficult of the unending tasks of the legislator." [17]

Since vivisection is "customary as part of the routine of preparing lectures in medical schools," it leads to what Shaw called "routinized cruelty." The most humane of teachers and students eventually become as callous to the cutting-up of animals as if they "were cutting up pieces of paper." Denouncing "such clumsy and lazy ways of teaching," Shaw adds:

> a routine of vivisection . . . soon produces complete indifference to it on the part even of those who are naturally humane. If they pass on from the routine of lecture preparation, not into general practice, but into research work, they carry this acquired indifference with them into the laboratory, where any atrocity is possible, because all atrocities satisfy curiosity. The routine man is in the majority in his profession always.

He concluded that if one accepts the ethics of vivisectionists it is only a step to sanctioning experiments on human subjects. As an evolutionist Shaw saw a substantial unity between men and animals and believed that if this unity is violated in the methods of teaching used in medical schools, the moral roads to knowledge will be destroyed.

Jennifer Dubedat in *The Doctor's Dilemma* (1906) and Androcles in *Androcles and the Lion* (1912) argue for Shaw's ideas about the unity of animal and human souls. Jennifer tells Dr. Ridgeon that she hopes he "may never feel what I felt when I had to put him [Louis, her husband] into the hands of men who defend the torture of animals because they are only brutes." Denouncing those doctors "who get used to

[17] Preface to *The Doctor's Dilemma*.

cruelty and are callous about it," Jennifer adds: "They blind themselves to the souls of animals; and that blinds them to the souls of men and women." When Ferrovius explains to Androcles that he called Spintho a "dog" because he meant that animals "have no souls," Androcles protests that they have. "Just the same as you and me. I really don't think I could consent to go to heaven if I thought there were to be no animals there. Think of what they suffer here."

An earlier play considered the subject of vivisection. A determined experimenter and vivisector, Dr. Paramore in *The Philanderer* (1893) pronounces Colonel Craven's liver ailment incurable, "on the strength of three dogs and an infernal monkey," as the outraged patient puts it. When Paramore learns that "Paramore's disease" has been proved to be non-existent in Europe, he exclaims: "It's the fault of the wickedly sentimental laws of this country. I was not able to make experiments enough—only three dogs and a monkey." Indignant that "a guinea pig's convenience is set above the health and lives of the entire human race," he later contradicts himself when it suits his preconceptions. "I admit," he states, "that the Italian experiments apparently upset my theory. But . . . it is extremely doubtful whether anything can be proved by experiments on animals." Paramore, Shaw's earliest medical portrait, emerges as a professional healer who neither thinks nor practices scientifically.

Shaw had charged in the Preface to *The Doctor's Dilemma* that "doctors are not trained in the use of evidence, nor in biometrics, nor in the psychology of human credulity, nor in the incidence of economic pressure." The two chapters in the more recent *What's What,* "The Medical Man" and "The Collective Statistician," show that even late in life he had not changed his mind. With regard to biometrics Shaw had stated

that too frequently doctors draw disastrous conclusions from
their clinical experience because "they have no conception of
scientific method and believe that the handling of evidence
and statistics needs no expertness." And though Shaw in the
What's What seems to believe that even the expert statisticians
in Karl Pearson's *Biometrika* are "as prejudiced . . . to the
facts they were measuring and the assumptions from which
they started,"[18] he nevertheless recommends that "no figures
[be accepted] from doctors" unless they are checked by a government department of statistics. In the even later Preface to
Farfetched Fables he demanded that "the panel for health
authorities should require a stringent test in statistics." An
antivaccinationist, Shaw maintained that disease can be eliminated by simple sanitation and that the vaccination "ghost
still walks because doctors are ignorant of statistics." To
counteract the popularity of questionable cures, Shaw again
recommends that a Ministry of Statistics be established "with
formidable powers of dealing with lying advertisements of
panaceas, prophylactics, elixirs, immunizers, vaccines, anti-
toxins, vitamins, and professedly hygienic foods and drugs and
drinks of all sort,"[19] and that doctors be trained to understand
not only the need for such a ministry but also the economic
pressures which force them to endorse practices that turn out
to be lucrative. He twitted medical men who are so much the
victims of specialization in their fields that they are never
educated civically and politically, with the result that they not
only charge exorbitant fees but "vote like sheep for the landlords." If Shaw is oblique in suggesting that doctors be edu-

[18] *What's What*, p. 246.
[19] See Bernal, "Shaw the Scientist," S. Winsten, editor, *G.B.S. 90*. "The
path of discovery has not been kind to Shaw: the viruses which were
invisible in his day can now be photographed and the beneficent ones—
the bacteriophages—seen at work attacking their prey."

cated as socialists, he is quite forthright in insisting that they be trained as evolutionists and vegetarians.[20]

Earlier in the century Shaw had attacked the "terrifying assumption" that the registered practitioner is qualified to try his hand at new techniques and administer all the new medicines whether he has studied them or not.[21] Providing many illustrations, he denounced, for example, the use of the X-ray by practitioners who have never really studied it. Convinced that doctors of that day were poorly trained in fundamental skills, Shaw propagandized "for the importance of a test of general surgical knowledge."[22] Even as late as 1944 he made the startling statement that "surgeons receive no specific manual training in the use of their instruments, and have to pick up their craft as best they can in the dissecting room" and that within his memory "obstetric expertness was picked up by medical students in visits to the child-beds of the poor."[23] He posed the problem of how to educate or test a practitioner whose diploma is forty or fifty years out of date—a problem which is with us yet today. In 1917 Shaw suggested that the medical course be extended to five years, that is, "two years less than the traditional apprenticeship of a mason or carpenter,"[24] the financial advantage being with the workers since the "medical student earns nothing not even his board or lodging." This economic factor drives much first-rate profes-

[20] "A Word First," *What's What*. See also "The King and the Doctors," *Doctors' Delusions*. This fictional approach, inspired by the illness of King George V, attacks the social and educational prejudices of the medical profession. When the Prince urges the doctor to use a certain technique in order to save the King's life, the doctor replies that it is impossible because it has not "stood the test of being taught in our medical schools" and because the discoverer was "not only an American, but a Jew."

[21] *Doctors' Delusions*, p. 37.   [22] *Ibid.*, p. 20.
[23] *What's What*, p. 218.   [24] *Doctors' Delusions*, p. 22.

sional material elsewhere, for "any class of educated men thus treated tends to become a brigand class and doctors are no exception to the rule." [25] The result, Shaw said, is that the medical profession has become a special kind of trade union which has arrogated to itself powers denied to other trade unions simply because doctors are supposed to have "miraculous powers, recondite knowledge, and divine wisdom." [26] Shaw attacked the General Medical Council in this way:

All trade union experience shews that the doors of a trade or profession must not be guarded . . . by the members inside. Limitation of output to keep up prices, limitation of apprentices to keep up wages or fees, specialization of qualification to keep out candidates of certain social classes and religious sects, fossilization of the curriculum to keep out new methods, abortion of new discoveries to fit them to obsolete conditions, deliberate persecution of original, independent, or critical individuals, and all the tricks by which moribund institutions and harassed competitive breadwinners struggle for life, are anti-social.[27]

Shaw found the solution to the problem of educating and supervising doctors in socialized medicine. Since there is "nothing more insane in our social system than allowing a doctor's income to depend on the illness of his patients," [28] he wanted a disinterested "State Medical Service" continually subjected to correlation with other sciences. He recommended that the "Government and the Universities send representatives of the public and of disinterested general science to the General Medical Council instead of doctors, leaving the medical corporations to secure a minority representation of that profession." [29]

The varied medical portraits in *The Doctor's Dilemma* illustrate the negative practices of inadequately educated doc-

---

[25] Preface to *The Doctor's Dilemma*.
[26] *Doctors' Delusions*, p. 45.   [27] *Ibid.*, p. 53.
[28] *What's What*, p. 218.   [29] *Doctors' Delusions*, p. 67.

tors. Dr. Bonington, though he claims to revere science and scientific method and denounces the "scandalous advertisements of patent medicines: a huge commercial system of quackery and poison," admits that he uses "all sorts of anti-toxins absolutely indiscriminately, with perfectly satisfactory results." Dr. Walpole is convinced that all patients suffer from blood poisoning which can only be relieved by the removal of the nuciform sac, an operation which has proved so lucrative that he suggests it to everyone, including his professional colleagues. "Cheaply fed and cheaply clothed," Dr. Blenkinsop confesses he has "never opened a book since I was qualified thirty years ago. I used to read medical papers . . . but I can't afford them." It is he who at the end denounces "private practice in medicine . . . and private doctors [who] are ignorant licensed murderers." Dr. Schutzmacher has made himself a lot of money by advertising "Cure Guaranteed" and by prescribing Parrish's Chemical Food, which is nothing but phosphates, to all his patients. Though Dr. Ridgeon is unethical enough to want Dubedat, the consumptive artist, out of the way so he can have his wife, Jennifer, he is at least characterized as an honest man unmotivated by money. Patterned after Sir Almroth Wright whom Shaw admired, Ridgeon attacks the unscientific practice of inoculating indiscriminately without first "testing a patient's opsonin." While Ridgeon, like the elder Sir Patrick Cullen, is profoundly skeptical about the competence of the whole profession, he represents another aspect of medicine that Shaw distrusted—assuming arbitrarily the right to decide which patient is worth saving and which is not. That doctors must be better educated in the complex of ethical conduct is a concept implicit in the play.

The Doctor who treats the hypochondriacal patient in *Too True To Be Good* (1932) is a charlatan. He mistakes measles for influenza, a fact first communicated by the Monster, the measles microbe itself; prescribes an un-Shavian diet of "good fresh meat, a half bottle of champagne at lunch and a glass of port after dinner"; and admits to the Monster that what his patient thought was an opiate "was only an aspirin dissolved in ether." At the insistence of the patient's mother, he agrees to an inoculation and a new prescription because they will set her mind at rest. Claiming that he practices science because "people believe in science," the Doctor admits at the same time that "when there is no microbe I invent one" because patients insist on it. While he admits privately to the Monster that he cannot cure any disease, he cannot see why the patient "should cure herself . . . when she can afford to pay the doctor to cure her. It pays her and it pays me. That's logic, my friend."

The Egyptian Doctor in *The Millionairess* (1935) is a doctor after Shaw's heart. Indifferent to money, he keeps "a clinic for penniless Mahometan refugees." At first he had refused to attend to the wealthy Epifania because, as he tells her, "I have to reserve myself for poor and useful people." Epifania who preaches the "aristocracy of money" fails to understand the Doctor when he says: "There is a good deal to be done in the world besides attending rich imaginary invalids. . . . I make the little money I need by work which I venture to think more important." Dedicated to knowledge and "married to science," he rebukes Epifania for "preying on the poverty of the poor."

THE EDUCATION OF CRIMINALS [30]

Shaw maintained that there are few, if any, repentant criminals in our society for two reasons:

[30] The Humanitarian League, with such active members as John Galsworthy and Sydney Olivier, was concerned with prison reform. Eventually a report was issued as a volume entitled *English Prisons Today* (1922), edited by Stephen Hobhouse and Fenner Brockway. As a mem-

The first is that we are all brought up to believe that we may inflict injuries on anyone against whom we can make out a case of moral inferiority. We have this thrashed into us in our childhood . . . by our parents and teachers. . . . The second is that we are all now brought up to believe . . . that Society can do no wrong. Now not only does Society commit more frightful crimes than any individual, king or commoner: it legalizes its crimes . . . besides torturing anyone who dares expose their true character.[31]

Shaw, challenging the aims of the Prison Commissioners, said that "if you are to punish a man retributively, you must injure him and if you are to reform him, you must improve him." In brief, men can not be improved by injuries, for punishment and reformation are contradictory. Though the reformation of the criminal is theoretically intended by the authorities, "yet the destruction of the prisoner's self respect by systematic humiliation is deliberately ordered and practiced." Deterrence, another aim, is the "crude basis of all our disciplines: home discipline, school discipline, factory discipline, army and navy discipline." At this point he invoked his analysis of capitalist society, which at every turn makes for crime. Of the prison system objectives vengeance is the only one achieved, "one which is nakedly abominable."

It is useless to imprison incorrigibles and monsters because after tormenting them for a fixed period in prison and then releasing them, they resume their operations with a "more savage grudge" against the community. Shaw's solution is to kill them.

---

ber of the committee which investigated prisons, Shaw wrote a long preface. Later when Sidney and Beatrice Webb completed their *Prisons Under Local Government* (1922), Shaw transferred his preface to this book. In 1946 the preface was published in America and titled *The Crime of Imprisonment* with illustrations by William Gropper. It is also included in *Doctors' Delusions*. The many articles in "Crude Criminology" should also be consulted.

[31] "Imprisonment."

His main argument was that imprisonment does not spare the lives of such incorrigibles but wastes them in a cruel way. Further, the lives of those who must supervise such imprisonment are wasted even more than those of the criminals. That the community "has a right to put a price on the right to live in it" is again demonstrated by Shaw. To the question as to who is to decide whether a man is to live or die, he answers: "Such responsibilities must be taken, whether we are fit for them or not, if civilized society is to be organized."

Two classes, called B and C, present special problems. Class B consists of persons defective in the self-control needed for free life in modern society, but who are well behaved under tutelage and discipline devoid of rancor or insult. Class C consists of normal people who have violated the law "during one of those lapses of self-discipline which are as common as colds." These, Shaw warned, should never be imprisoned. They should be required to compensate the state for the injury done —and when possible—the victims. If this is not done, they can be "harassed by frequent compulsory appearances in court to excuse themselves," or be threatened with consignment to the second class as defectives.

It is quite easy to make carelessness and selfishness or petty violence and dishonesty unremunerative and disagreeable, without resorting to imprisonment. In the cases where the offender has fallen into bad habits and bad company, the stupidest course to take is to force him into the worst of all habits and the worst of all company: that is, prison habits and prison company.

It is with offenders of Class B, "too good to be killed or caged, and not good enough for normal liberty, whose treatment bothers us." With regard to the "softer crimes" committed by this group, Shaw advises us to read Butler's *Erewhon* and to learn to "regard crime as pathological, and the criminal

as an invalid, curable or incurable." Concerning the incident
in *Erewhon* where a man is sentenced to prison for having
phthisis, Shaw asks: "Why make the prison so different from
the hospital?" Adequate tutelage and education for this group
can be provided only by a "much greater extension of public
regulation and organization." For those subject to detention
and restraint, Shaw outlines this program of education:

the criminal's right to contact with all the spiritual influences of his
day should be respected, and its exercise encouraged and facilitated.
Conversation, access to books and pictures and music, unfettered
scientific, philosophic, and religious activity, change of scene and
occupation, the free formation of friendships and acquaintances,
marriage and parentage: in short all the normal methods of creation
and recreation must be available for criminals as for other persons,
partly because deprivation of these things is severely punitive, and
partly because it is destructive to the victim, and produces what we
call the criminal type, making a cure impossible. . . . In short, a
criminal should be treated, not as a man who has forfeited all normal rights and liberties by the breaking of a single law, but as one
who, through some specific weakness or weaknesses, is incapable
of exercising some specific liberty or liberties.

To reform a criminal is to educate him in art, science, religion,
philosophy, and decent human relations. This involves a "concept of individual freedom" for the criminal which our society
denies. "The concept of the evolving free man in an evolving
society making all sorts of experiments in conduct . . . is still
unusual, and consequently terrifying." In Shaw's view life in a
prison should be made as much as possible like life outside,
for the primary aim of a prison should be to prepare prisoners
for a normal existence. He concluded that the complex of imprisonment could not be fully understood by those who do not
understand freedom.

Captain Brassbound's Conversion (1899), written twenty

years before "Imprisonment," communicates problems and
methods of rehabilitating criminals. Set in Morocco, the plot
involves Brassbound, known as "Black Paquito," a notorious
smuggler who is convinced that his uncle Sir Howard Hallam,
the judge, once dispossessed Brassbound's illiterate Portu-
guese mother of her estate and drove her to liquor and mad-
ness. His whole life has consequently been dedicated to vengeance. His morbid imagination magnifies the worthless property and transforms his mother into a saintly woman. When
chance places Hallam and his sister-in-law, Lady Cicely
Waynflete in Brassbound's power, and the Captain is about to
realize his passionate desire for vengeance, he discovers that
he cannot go through with it because of the tender personality
and methods of Lady Cicely. She educates not only Brassbound, but his brigands and the fanatical Mohammedan Sheik
as well. Understanding and kind to everyone she meets, Lady
Cicely has an infinite faith in human nature, however degraded,
preferring to believe that men are neither very good nor very
bad and that their good sides respond to encouragement and
consideration rather than to fear and punishment. When Sir
Howard says of the natives that they "have no laws to restrain
them which means . . . that they are habitual thieves and
murderers," Lady Cicely replies indignantly: "You always think
that nothing prevents people killing each other but the fear
of your hanging them for it. . . . If these people weren't here
for some good purpose, they wouldn't have been made." She
believes that people get killed by savages "because instead of
being polite to them and saying Howdyedo? like me, people
aim pistols at them." Convinced that "all men are children in
the nursery," she worries about the health of Brassbound's
outlaws. "Oh," she exclaims, "if I could only shew you my
children from Waynflete Sunday School. . . . I'm sure you

would enjoy having them here, Captain Brassbound; and it would be such an education for your men." She points out to Brassbound, who is furious about Hallam and the state of English justice, that "if you take a man and pay him 5000 pounds a year [as a judge] and praise him for it, and have policemen and courts and laws and juries to drive him into [passing cruel sentences] . . . what can you expect?" And echoing Shaw's essay "Imprisonment," she relates:

We caught a burglar one night at Waynflete when [Hallam] was staying with us; and I insisted on his locking the poor man up, until the police came, in a room with a window opening on the lawn. The man came back next day and said he must return to a life of crime unless I gave him a job in the garden; and I did. It was much more sensible than giving him ten years penal servitude: Howard admitted it. So you see he's not a bit bad really.

This sort of morality eventually persuades Brassbound to forget his vengeance and even to propose to her. To Ellen Terry, Shaw had attempted to explain the role as Lady Cicely:

Listen to me, woman with no religion. . . . Have you found in your own life . . . no warrant for trusting to the good side of people instead of terrorizing the bad side of them. . . . I try to shew you fearing nobody and managing them all as Daniel managed the lions, not by cunning . . . but by simple moral superiority. . . . The wretched Hooligan who gives the final touch by turning from the navy, the bench, and all the powers and principalities to Ellen, in his extremity . . . is dull to you.[32]

The "wretched Hooligan" is a reference to Drinkwater, one of Brassbound's gang, about whose health Lady Cicely is concerned. The stage directions describe him as a "specimen of the abortion produced by nature in a city slum." Apparently the only benefit he derived from his "Board School Education"

[32] *Ellen Terry and Bernard Shaw: A Correspondence,* p. 248.

is a passionate love for the cheapest fiction; and when he learns that his precious library of dirty books, "value each wawn penny, and entitled Sweeny Todd, The Demon Barber of London, The Skeleton Horseman," is to be burnt, he frantically appeals to Lady Cicely, the only one who had ever shown him kindness: "Down't let em burn em, lidy. They dassen't if you horder em not to. Yer dunno wot them books is to me. They took me aht of the sawdid reeyellities of the Waterloo Rowd. They formed maw mawnd: they shaowed me sathink awgher than the squalor of a coster's lawf." This plea reflects the tragedy of a miseducated soul fed on pulp fiction and consequently confirmed in false ethics and morality to the detriment of a society which ignores the potential rehabilitation of criminals.

The later *Major Barbara* (1905) pursues this concept further. Barbara's methods differ from those of Lady Cicely, who is more of a sentimental humanitarian. Barbara practices what Shaw preaches in the Preface, namely, that "we shall never have real moral responsibility until everyone knows that his deeds are irrevocable, and that his life depends on his usefulness." When the brutal ruffian, Bill Walker, beats Jenny, his girl, and an old woman named Rummy, Barbara, believing there are no absolute scoundrels in the world, works on Bill's conscience. Thoroughly ashamed, Bill wants to expiate his crime by letting Todger Fairmile, the wrestler, bash his face, and by offering a token payment to Jenny. But Barbara makes it clear that Bill cannot buy his salvation. He must change himself or continue to be troubled by his conscience. The fallacy of redemption and the futility of punishment are thus dramatized. Shaw states in the Preface that "every practicable man (and woman) is a potential scoundrel and a potential good citizen" and that such a character as Bill Walker can be educated to be good and useful for "it is quite useless to declare that all men are born free if you deny that they are born good." Instead of trying to educate Bill by means of futile punishments, Barbara "stands up to Bill Walker . . . with the result that the ruffian who cannot get hated, has to hate himself."

THE EDUCATION OF ACTORS

In his attack on romance as the "great heresy to be rooted out from art and life," [33] Shaw denounced not only the theater and the audience, but also the actors. Most of them are the victims of romance in that "their demonstrations of emotion have made a second nature of stage custom which is often very much out of date as a representation of contemporary life." As a dramatist Shaw claimed that he had taxed the performer's intelligence severely by demanding not only "nuances of execution quite beyond the average skill" but intellectual and artistic understanding of the meanings of the play. To enable stage players to meet such requirements, Shaw recommended that they must undergo long and arduous training in professional schools.

Shaw's dramatic criticism and his correspondence with famous actresses reveal to a great extent what he believed about such schooling. Once he wrote to Florence Farr: "Someday I shall put in very strongly for the need of really scientific phonetic training for actors, and denounce all that Dramatic School stuff." [34] In another letter he urged her if she were "to make an original and lasting place as a teacher [of actors]" [35] to go to Oxford and study the science of pronunciation and phonetics with Henry Sweet. Elsewhere he sug-

[33] Preface to *Plays: Pleasant and Unpleasant*, II.
[34] *Florence Farr, Bernard Shaw, W. B. Yeats*, p. 23.
[35] *Ibid.*, p. 37.

gested that "the old actor who professes to teach acting and knows nothing of phonetic speech training is to be avoided like the plague." [36]

But for practical teaching the old rule remains: take care of the consonants and the vowels will take care of themselves. You want to get first an athletic articulation. With that you can give effect to the real, which is your sense of the meaning of the words, your emotional and intellectual conviction.[37]

To Ellen Terry he would frequently point out lapses in actors' articulation, emphasizing the need for players to practice their alphabets in the same way that a great pianist practices his scales.[38] Lillah McCarthy relates how Shaw often criticized her speech, once noting that in a performance of *Oedipus* she had said "I near" for "eye and ear." [39] And to Mrs. Patrick Campbell he wrote:

The first thing you have to knock into a stage novice is staccato alphabet so staccatissimo that every consonant will put out a candle at the back of the gallery. Not until her tongue and lips are like a pianist's fingers should she begin to dare think of speaking to an audience. . . . If your pupils want to be trained for the phonofilm or Movietone they must [learn] . . . a delicacy of touch and a subtlety of nuance.[40]

Discussing the character and art of Beerbohm Tree, Shaw stressed the "general need in England for a school of physical training for the arts of public life as distinguished from sports." [41] And he adds:

[36] *Sixteen Self Sketches*, p. 105.
[37] *Florence Farr, Bernard Shaw, W. B. Yeats*, p. 23.
[38] *Ellen Terry and Bernard Shaw: A Correspondence*, p. 271.
[39] *Myself and My Friends*, p. 299.
[40] *Bernard Shaw and Mrs. Patrick Campbell: Their Correspondence*, p. 305. See also *Ladies Home Journal* 43 (February, 1926), for a letter from Shaw to John Barrymore, in which he states that "an actor must do nine-tenths of his acting with his voice."
[41] *Pen Portraits and Reviews*, p. 288.

An author who understands acting and writes for the actor as a composer writes for an instrument, giving it the material suitable to its range, tone, character, agility and mechanism, necessarily assumes a certain technical accomplishment common to all actors; and this requires the existence of a school of acting.

Under the existing system, Shaw observed, an actor—instead of laying the foundation of a general technique of speech and action—is forced, by the absence of any school in which he can acquire such a technique, to develop his own personality and acquire a method of exploiting that personality which is not applicable to any other purpose. The result is "friction at rehearsals if the author produces his own play, as all authors should." [42] And of those rehearsals of *Pygmalion* which caused such friction, Shaw says of Tree: "What did he care for Higgins or Hamlet? His real objective was his amazing self." [43]

What Shaw called general artistic culture is essential to the making of a great actor. Of Henry Irving Shaw wrote: "the environment and tradition which an actor can obtain in Vienna cannot be obtained in England, and he had to do his best to supply them out of his own romantic imagination, without much schooling and virtually without any general artistic culture." [44] In a letter to Forbes-Robertson about the famous actor's book of memoirs, *The Stage in My Time,* Shaw suggested that he send a copy to the Royal Academy of Dramatic Arts in order

to show the students that to reach the highest rank it is not necessary to be an egotist or a monster, and that though good-looking

[42] *Ibid.,* p. 291.

[43] *Ibid.,* p. 293. See *The Art of Rehearsal* where Shaw advises directors in methods of coaching and teaching actors. "If you get angry and complain that you have repeatedly called attention, etc., like a schoolmaster, you will destroy the whole atmosphere in which art breathes." See also "Rules for Directors," *Theatre Arts* 33 (August, 1949).

[44] *Pen Portraits and Reviews,* p. 164.

spooks can do very well on the stage as long as there are authors and producers to fit their poor hollow bodies with souls, still, the man with positive character and artistic culture . . . is the only man who can become finally a classic actor.[45]

In his dramatic reviews Shaw stressed that "the awakening and culture of the artistic conscience is a real service which a teacher can render an actor." [46]

Shaw complained that the art of acting rhetorical and poetic drama had become a lost art in fashionable London theaters and that actors had neither the facilities to be taught this art nor the opportunity to practice it. Critical of the cup-and-saucer type of performer who knew nothing of any sort of acting except that of the drawing room and who "considered a speech of more than twenty words impossibly long," [47] Shaw suggests that most actors took the utmost care to avoid acting, that is, "letting themselves go if the need arose, as in the broadly comic part of Burgess in Candida." Citing the actor who, during rehearsal, had said in subdued tones, "Mr. Shaw . . . in the intellectual drama I never clown," Shaw adds:

I was continually struggling with the conscientious efforts of our players to underdo their parts lest they should be considered stagey. Much as if Titian had worked in black and grey lest he should be considered painty. It took a European war to cure them of wanting to be ladies and gentlemen first and actresses and actors after.

Shaw believed that only persons endowed with extraordinary personalities ought to have pretensions to the stage. "Unless an actress can be at least ten times as interesting as a real

[45] Quoted in Pearson, *A Full Length Portrait*, p. 346.

[46] *Dramatic Opinions*, I, 207. See *Ibid.*, II, 317, where Shaw says of Forbes-Robertson that he "can present a dramatic hero as a man whose passions are those which have produced the philosophy, the poetry, the art . . . of the world."

[47] "An Aside," McCarthy, *Myself and My Friends*.

lady, why should she leave the drawing room and go on the stage?"[48] Speaking of Lillah McCarthy Shaw emphasized: "It is an actress's profession to be extraordinary; but Lillah was extraordinary even among actresses. The first natural qualification of an actress who is not a mere puppet . . . is imagination."[49] While imagination cannot be taught, Shaw insisted that a performer be guided by an artistic sense "cultivated to such a degree of sensitiveness that a coarse or prosaic tone or an awkward gesture jars instantly."[50] The actor or actress must be an artist who has mastered an unusual range of physical and vocal expression, always compatible with the intellectual and artistic intent of the author. The school for players Shaw has in mind would at least inculcate such ideals.

Shaw also demands of a performer that he or she be a person of principle stimulated by a sense of dedication to the world. Praising Mary Anderson who was "essentially a woman of principle which the actress essentially is not,"[51] Shaw attacks that "lawless and fearless following of the affectionate impulses which is the characteristic morality of the artist, especially the woman artist of the stage." Principle means also a profound understanding on the part of an actor of the vulgar tastes of the public and the commercialism of managers. An actor of principle would regard the theater as a cathedral where great emotions and great ideas are communicated.

His active interest in the Royal Academy of Dramatic Arts demonstrates how Shaw tried to promote these ideals. Sir Kenneth Barnes in his essay "G.B.S. and the Royal Academy of Dramatic Arts," a contribution to the volume *G.B.S. 90*, detailed Shaw's influence on this school for actors. When he

[48] *Dramatic Opinions*, II, 51.
[49] "An Aside," McCarthy, *Myself and My Friends*.
[50] *Dramatic Opinions*, I, 207.   [51] *Ibid.*, I, 375.

was elected to the council upon the death of Sir William Gilbert in 1911, Shaw wanted to make the school a public institution "in which speech, deportment, and acting could be taught, and for which, ultimately Government recognition could be sought." At one meeting, Barnes relates, Shaw declared that it was the school's duty to give the students as liberal an education as possible in subjects required for an Art's degree at a university. "His influence," Barnes writes, "was a bracing one and emphasized the need for an institution in London which could form a link between the discordant worlds of Education and the Theatre." In 1921 this aim was realized when Royal Patronage was conferred on the institution. Shaw was pleased when London County Council Scholarships for Dramatic Art were obtained and when a Diploma in Dramatic Art was recognized by the University of London. Shaw was also instrumental in putting the Academy on the same footing with the public as the Royal College of Music. Since music was recognized by law as a fine art by an Act passed in 1843 and acting was not, the Academy was not tax exempt. Shaw propagandized for the same tax exemption that the College of Music enjoyed, and in 1930 acting was legally recognized as a fine art. Shaw contributed five thousand pounds toward the erection of a new building in Gower Street.

In 1941 Shaw suggested that the students who had earned a diploma be given a little book embodying the advice of various members of the Council. The most valuable part of the book which Shaw named *The R.A.D.A. Graduate's Keepsake and Counsellor*, states Barnes, was the introduction written by Shaw, although he refused to have his name attached to it. In the opening paragraphs quoted by Barnes, Shaw advises the new graduate that "his personal reputation and professional achievements are henceforth bound up with the credit, not only of the Academy, but with that of the standing of theatrical art in the civilized world." There is also the reminder that "a successful player has no private life." Blanche Patch, Shaw's secretary for thirty years, has said that all young persons determined to go on the stage were always directed by Shaw to the Academy.[52] Many famous stars have attended, including John Gielgud, Cedric Hardwicke, Celia Johnson, Charles Laughton, Vivien Leigh, Margaret Lockwood, and Robert Morley.

[52] *Thirty Years with G.B.S.*, p. 66.

10 *The meaning of life*

In GENERAL it can be said that the ends and purposes of education, like the ends and purposes of life itself, cannot be known except through understanding the nature of the individual, the meaning of life, and the way that is good for man to live in this world. Shaw's ultimate desire was to persuade man to build a social organization by which all men could attain their highest potential. In this sense a realization of the individual's possibilities meant not only a contribution to the common welfare in any one generation to Shaw, but also furthering the Life Force, which constantly strives to evolve the perfect human being. C. E. M. Joad, who has contributed a valuable analysis of Shaw's philosophy, states:

If we are instruments created by Life's instinctive purpose, our raison d'être will be found in the fulfilment of Life's intentions in regard to us; not then in the pursuit of our own purposes. The furtherance of Life's purpose will consist in the being used up to the last ounce of one's energy and capacity in work that seems to one to be worth while for its own sake. It is by the maximum expenditure of effort in the ardours and endurances of living and thinking that one will develop and improve one's initial endowment of faculty and accomplishment, thus returning them at death with interest—an interest which is to be measured by the degree of the realized improvement upon the initially given potentiality—to the general stream of life of which we are the individualized expressions, with the result that when Life expresses itself in the next generation of living organisms it will do so at a slightly higher level than it did before, because of the enrichments of acquisitions and accomplishment that we have brought to it.[1]

This is a most adequate interpretation of what Shaw may have meant when he stated in the Preface to *Misalliance* that "there is only one belief that can rob death of its sting and the grave of its victory . . . for without death we cannot be born again."

Effort and endeavor are the means to successful life, since happiness is to be found in the furtherance of the purpose for which we were created. "The secret of being miserable is to have leisure to bother about whether you are happy or not." In *The Sanity of Art* Shaw warned that happiness cannot be realized by plunging "recklessly into the insupportable tedium of what is called a life of pleasure." The error into which Schopenhauer fell, Shaw maintained, consisted in making happiness the test of the value of life. In the "Epistle Dedicatory" to *Man and Superman* there is Shaw's well-known "true-joy-of-life" passage:

This is the true joy of life, the being used for a purpose recognized by yourself as a mighty one; the being thoroughly worn out before you are thrown on the scrap heap; the being a force of Nature instead of a feverish selfish little clod of ailments and grievances that the world will not devote itself to making you happy. And also the real tragedy in life is the being used by personally minded men for purposes you recognize to be base.

So concerned was Shaw about the place of happiness in one's values that he recommended putting "the happiness of children rather carefully in its place, which is really not a front

[1] "Shaw's Philosophy," S. Winsten, editor, *G.B.S. 90.*

place.' - in effect, Shaw's socialism and evolution provide a new basis for the traditional philosopher's criticism of the life of pleasure seeking.

Shaw rejected the ideals of pleasure and happiness because they are primarily pursuits of one's own concerns or perversions of life's real functions—the individual's hopes for society, for the world, and even for the eventual destiny of man and of the universe.

The man who believes that there is a purpose in the universe, and identifies his own purpose with it, and makes the achievement of that purpose an act, not of self sacrifice for himself, but of self-realization: that is the effective man and the happy man, whether he calls the purpose the will of God, or socialism, or the religion of humanity.[3]

Shaw once defined a religious person as one who conceives himself "to be the instrument of some purpose in the universe which is a high purpose, and is the motive power of evolution, that is, of a continual ascent in organization and power of life, and extension of life." [4] Cited previously were Shaw's frequent uses of the same words in opposite senses, such as "science" and "democracy." In a speech delivered before the National Liberal Club in 1913, Shaw does the same with the word "gentleman," redefining it and clearly indicating the obligations of education in implementing the ideal set forth.[5]

What is the ideal of a gentleman? The gentleman makes a certain claim on his country to begin with. He makes a claim for a hand-

[2] Preface to *Misalliance*.

[3] Quoted by Henderson, *George Bernard Shaw: His Life and Works,* p. 487.

[4] "Modern Religion," *The Christian Commonwealth,* Supplement No. 69 (April 3, 1912).

[5] See "The Revolutionist's Handbook," *Man and Superman:* "He who believes in education, criminal law, and sport, needs only property to make him a perfect modern gentleman."

some and dignified existence and subsistence; and he makes that as a primary thing not to be dependent on his work in any way; not to be doled out according to the thing he has done or according to the talents he has displayed. He says, in effect: "I want to be a cultured human being; I want to live in the fullest sense; I require a generous subsistence for that; and I expect my country to organize itself in such a way as to secure me that." Also the real gentleman says—and here is where the real gentleman parts company with the sham gentleman, of whom we have so many: "In return for that I am willing to give my country the best service of which I am capable. . . . My ideal shall be also that, no matter how much I have demanded from my country, or how much my country has given me, I hope . . . to give to my country in return more than it has given me; so that when I die my country shall be the richer for my life. . . ." The real constructive scheme you want is the practical inculcation into everybody that what the country needs, and should seek through its social education, its social sense, and religious feeling, is to create gentlemen; and when you create them, all other things shall be added unto you.[6]

The Devil's Disciple (1897) and *The Shewing-Up of Blanco Posnet* (1909) communicate themes pertinent to these ideals. Dick Dudgeon, reacting against a religion that conceives goodness simply as self-denial, has proclaimed himself a disciple of Satan. In 1777 when the British troops arrive to execute a rebel as an example to the populace, Dick is mistaken for the Minister Anderson, a leader in the fight for independence, and is arrested, unresisting. Judith, the minister's wife, who is hor-

---

[6] Fuchs, editor, *The Socialism of Shaw*, p. 83. See Henderson, *His Life and Works*, p. 512 where Shaw is quoted: "I am of the opinion that my life belongs to the whole community, and as long as I live it is my privilege to do for it whatsoever I can. . . . Life . . . is a sort of splendid torch, which I have got hold of for the moment; and I want to make it burn as brightly as possible before handing it on to future generations." See also Preface to *Androcles and the Lion:* Jesus taught "that we should all be gentlemen and take care of our country . . . instead of the commercialized cads we are, doing everything and anything for money, and selling our souls and bodies."

rified at Dick's diabolonianism, sees in this sacrificial act no other motive than that he is in love with her. Dick gives up his life, as Shaw explains in the Preface; not because he loves Judith or because he is trying to impress her with his courage, but rather simply from no motive at all. Dick's own version is:

> I had no motive and no interest: all I can tell you is that when it came to the point whether I would take my neck out of the noose and put another man's into it, I could not do it. I don't know why not . . . but I could not and I cannot. I have been brought up standing by the law of my own nature; and I may not go against it, gallows or no gallows.

Dick, Shaw states in the Preface, is a "Puritan of Puritans . . . brought up in a household where the Puritan religion has died, and become, in its corruption, an excuse for his mother's master passion of hatred in all its phases of cruelty and envy." Comparing Dick with other great Diabolonians like Prometheus, Siegfried, Bunyan, and Blake, Shaw explains that "pity instead of hatred" is Dick's master passion. "He thus becomes, like all genuinely religious men, a reprobate and an outcast." What Shaw dramatizes in the play is the ideal that we are all members of one another but we have not been educated to understand this; that since society with its accent on selfish motives brings out the devil in us, people have become quite unable to understand a deed without a selfish motive.[7]

The character of "Gentlemanly Johnny" Burgoyne can be misunderstood without a knowledge of Shaw's definition of the two types of gentlemen. Urbane and humane, Burgoyne shows every consideration to the prisoner on the gallows, even

---

[7] See *The Quintessence of Ibsenism*, p. 155 where Shaw praises Ibsen for stating in *Little Eyolf* that "we are members of one another." Shaw concludes that man "can have no life except a share in the life of the community."

to playing Handel. Burgoyne is "visibly shaken" when Judith cries out: "Is it nothing to you what wicked thing you do if only you do it like a gentleman?" In a letter to Ellen Terry in 1897 Shaw tried to explain his intention in creating Burgoyne:

> Burgoyne is a gentleman; and that is the whole meaning of that part of the play. It is not enough, for the instruction of this generation, that Richard should be superior to religion and morality as typified by his mother and his home, or to love as typified by Judith. He must also be superior to gentility: that is, to the whole idea of modern society.[8]

Burgoyne, although he is for "softening and easing the trial by reciprocal politeness" is the wrong kind of gentleman because of the "villainy of his gallows, the unworthiness of his cause, and the murderousness of his profession." The true gentleman will try, like Dick, to leave the world better than he found it.

Like Dick, Blanco Posnet is driven to doing good deeds by something greater than himself. Accused of horse-stealing, Blanco had really run off with his brother's horse in payment for a debt. At the trial it is revealed that he had given the horse to a woman with a sick child. Suddenly appearing in court, the woman testifies:

> The man looked a bad man. He cursed me; and he cursed the child: God forgive him! But something came over him. I put the child in his arms; and it got its little fingers down his neck and called him Daddy and tried to kiss him. He said it was a little Judas kid, and that it was betraying him with a kiss. And then he gave me the horse, and went away crying and laughing and singing dreadful dirty wicked words to hymn tunes.

[8] *Ellen Terry and Bernard Shaw*, p. 124.

At this, Feemy Evans, the town prostitute who had testified against Blanco, now confesses she had lied. Set free, Blanco mounts a table and tells the audience:

We're all frauds. There's none of us real good and none of us real bad. . . . Why did the child die? He can't have wanted to kill the child. . . . Why should He go hard on the innocent kid and go soft on a rotten thing like me? . . . Why did the Sheriff go soft? Why did Feemy go soft? What's this game that upsets our game? For seems to me there's two games being played. Our game is a rotten game that makes me feel I'm dirt. . . . T'other game may be a silly game; but it ain't rotten. . . . When Feemy played it the paint nearly dropped off her face. When I played it I cursed myself for a fool; but I lost the rotten feeling.

When his brother, the sanctimonious Elder Daniels, tells him that "it was the Lord speaking to your soul," Blanco, denying this conventional God, becomes a spokesman for Creative Evolution: "You bet He didn't make us for nothing; and He wouldn't have made us at all if He could have done His work without us. . . . He made me because He had a job for me. He let me run loose til the job was ready." Both *The Devil's Disciple* and this play are dramatic interpretations of Shaw's religious creed which affirms that men, living and working together and sharing experiences, must realize their own potential perfection by doing good deeds. If the assumption that Shaw's plays were designed to educate audiences into thinking and acting in new ways is correct, then the themes of these plays expound ideals of conduct which his formal programs of education must seek to achieve.

Father Keegan in *John Bull's Other Island* (1904) visions mystically the ideals which ought to govern men's lives. Like Juan in *Man and Superman* he aspires to heaven, rejecting utterly the hell of this world which is clearly a place of torment and penance, a place where the fool flourishes and the good and wise are hated and persecuted . . . a place where children are scourged and enslaved in the name of parental duty and education . . . where the hardest toil is a refuge from the horror and tedium of pleasure, and where charity and good works are done only for hire to ransom the souls of the spoiler and the sybarite.

Shaw describes him as "a man with the face of a young saint . . . looking over the hills as if by mere intensity of gaze he could pierce the glories of the sunset and see into the streets of heaven." He tells Nora: "After a year of Oxford I had to walk to Jerusalem to walk the Oxford feeling off me." Disillusioned not only with education but also with his fellow humans such as Broadbent and Doyle who have worked out a scheme for a land syndicate designed to expropriate the farmers, Keegan perceives to the gap between what men are and what they ought to be. When Larry Doyle bitterly denounces this "dreaming, dreaming, dreaming," Keegan replies with bitter dignity: "Every dream is a prophecy." To Broadbent's facetious question, "What is [Heaven] like in your dreams?" Keegan replies:

In my dreams it is a country where the State is the Church and the Church the people: three in one and one in three. It is a commonwealth in which work is play and play is life: three in one and one in three. It is a temple in which the priest is the worshipper and the worshipper the worshipped: three in one and one in three. It is a Godhead in which all life is human and all humanity divine: three in one and one in three. It is, in short, the dream of a madman.

These dreams are antithetical to the practical and cynical aims of Broadbent and Doyle. "Mr. Broadbent," says Keegan, "spends his life inefficiently admiring the thoughts of great men [Ruskin, Shelley] and efficiently serving the cupidity of base money hunters." What comes clear in the conflict between these opposing concepts of life is that the illusions of Broadbent and Doyle are the objectives of most people in a world where stupidity, ignorance, and greed pay financial dividends. For Shaw, such illusions are not the components of the good life. While Broadbent promises to "found public institutions, a library, a Polytechnic (undenominational, of course), a gymnasium, perhaps an art school," Keegan remarks: "He wastes all his virtues—his efficiency, as you call it—in doing the will of his greedy masters instead of doing the will of Heaven that is in himself." Admitting Broadbent's sincerity, Keegan charges that it is a case of "the right side of your brain [not knowing] what the left side doeth." And he adds: "I learnt at Oxford that this is the secret of the Englishman's strange power of making the best of both worlds." Though Larry Doyle is also an idealist (the wrong kind) and is aware of the baseness and vulgarity of Broadbent's financial and political schemes, he supports him because he fears the Never-Never Land of dreams and visions. Implicit in this three-cornered conflict is Shaw's intention of showing the tragedy of the falsely educated in a world which lacks the will to educate man into understanding and utilizing visions of perfection.

This concept is extended in *Major Barbara* (1905). Both Adolphus Cusins, the professor of Greek, who is a symbol of intellect and culture, and Barbara, who would save men's souls, abhor the gospel of Andrew Undershaft, the munitions manufacturer. Why then do they agree to become the partners of Undershaft at the end of the play? On this point there is little agreement among Shaw's critics. Edmund Fuller thinks the play plays "into the hands of the financial oligarchs," [9] though admitting that it is a multiple-minded play which throws all special pleaders into confusion. Alick West, hewing to the

---

[9] *George Bernard Shaw*, p. 50.

Marxian line, sees Shaw's complete capitulation to the Prince of Darkness, Undershaft, and capitalism.[10] William Irvine believes that "the play concludes with an apotheosis of the munitions manufacturer, whom Shaw designates as the hero." [11] Eric Bentley sees Cusins as the hero who synthesizes "the idealism of Barbara and the realism of Undershaft." [12] And J. S. Collis insists that Undershaft, not Cusins, is Shaw's mouthpiece.[13] While Undershaft airs many of Shaw's ideas about poverty, society, morals, and education, it is suggested here that he is not, as the close of the play reveals, the symbol that should guide men's conduct in this life.

Both Barbara and Cusins accept Undershaft's ideas about poverty, and on a visit to his munitions plant are further convinced when they find a beautiful model town with schools and libraries, churches, and recreation rooms. There is even a Labor Church which is inscribed with William Morris' words: "No man is good enough to be another man's master." Barbara yields because she "wants to make power for the world, but it must be a spiritual power." And Cusins, agreeing with Barbara, says:

I think all power is spiritual: these cannons will not go off by themselves. I have tried to make spiritual power by teaching Greek. But the world can never be really touched by a dead language and a dead civilization. The people must have power; and the people cannot have Greek. Now the power that is made here can be wielded by all men.

That is to say, he must, to spread spiritual power, actually enter the portals of the enemy and try to convert destructive force to constructive force. Cusins' intention is revealed in this speech:

[10] *George Bernard Shaw*, pp. 127–41.
[11] *The Universe of G.B.S.*, p. 260.   [12] *Bernard Shaw*, p. 166.
[13] *Shaw*, p. 72.

You cannot have power for good without having power for evil,
too. . . . The power which only tears men's bodies has never been
so horribly abused as the intellectual power, the imaginative power,
the poetic, religious power that can enslave men's souls. As a teacher
of Greek I gave the intellectual man weapons against the common
man. I now want to give the common man weapons against the
intellectual man. I want to arm them against the lawyer, the doctor,
the priest, the literary man, the professor, the artist, and the poli-
tician, who, once in authority, are the most dangerous, disastrous,
and tyrannical of all the fools, rascals, and impostors. I want a
democratic power strong enough to force the intellectual oligarchy
to use its genius for the general good or else perish.

Cusins means that he will try to reeducate men in the ideals
of intellectual growth geared to Shavian values so as to enable
them to resist the evils of an intellectual oligarchy geared to
false moralities and concentrated power for selfish ends. This
is now his aim, not in a theoretical world of Greek teaching, but
in a realistic world of action. Confronted with Undershaft's
"either the professors of Greek take to making gunpowder, or
else the makers of gunpowder become professors of Greek,"
Cusins chooses the former, telling Barbara: "Dare I make war
on war? I dare. I must. I will." But how he is to promote these
goals by taking over the munitions plant, and what he means
by the "general good" are not sufficiently clarified within the
framework of the play. Barbara, also determined to a more
practical philosophy of action, tells Cusins: "If I were middle
class I should turn my back on my father's business; and we
should both live in an artistic drawing-room, with you reading
the reviews in one corner, and I in the other at the piano, playing Schumann: both very superior persons, and neither of us
a bit of use." Repudiating "the paradise of enthusiasm and
prayer and soul saving" of the Salvation Army, as Cusins his
teaching of Greek, Barbara rejects the bribe of an orthodox

heaven, accepts a "way of life through the factory of death," and becomes Shaw's trumpet for Creative Evolution. More literate than the fumbling Blanco Posnet, she declares: "I have got rid of the bribe of heaven. Let God's work be done for its own sake: the work he had to create us to do because it cannot be done except by living men and women. When I die, let him be in my debt, not I in his."

Major Barbara parallels *John Bull's Other Island* but also goes beyond it. Whereas Keegan has visions of heaven on earth and is, in Larry Doyle's words "dreaming, dreaming," Cusins and Barbara reject an unreal world of visions of perfections which falls short of action; and whereas Keegan refuses to unite with Broadbent and Doyle to implement his dreams, Cusins and Barbara do unite with the world of Bodger, the liquor magnate, and of Undershaft for the purpose of imposing on them superior ideals of living. Shaw may have intended communicating such a contrast since both plays appear in the same volume.

Shaw's ideal individual is one who is dedicated to the welfare of the community, the nation, and the world. He becomes a more highly developed self as he interacts with other human beings for the purpose of bringing into being a better society, for no human achieves excellence by living for himself alone. Shaw's ideal gentleman is well aware that a man can grow only as society grows, for even as a child he has been educated to understand this. Only as society itself comes to value this ideal of service will it seek the means—"through its social education, its social sense, and religious feeling"—to reach such a goal. Shaw's contention was that we do not really want such ideals despite our protestations that we do. Socialism as a way of social organization was to Shaw the only solution in helping to bridge the gap between theory and practice, a dichotomy which was to him the inevitable result of capitalism. What Shaw said throughout his life in one form or another was that social progress and evolution demand intelligent action, motivated by an understanding of the will and the purpose of the universe, toward the kind of society that will encourage human excellence and growth. That it is the obligation of the state, stimulated by leaders educated for the job, to provide this motivating force by means of its educational facilities is fundamental in Shaw's thinking about education. But a power-saturated state could very well bring about retrogression, not growth, of the individual and of society.

11 *Shaw and education in a democracy*

C_{AN} Shaw's ideas about education be used advantageously in a democratic society? The answer to such a question obviously requires commitment to certain criteria determinant of a free society and its education and a comparison with those established by Shaw. Such a discussion at this point could aid in uncovering the democratic and totalitarian strands in Shaw's thinking. It should be pointed out that in the last generation countless volumes have attempted to define the nature and function of education in democracy and that it would be beyond the scope of this book to encompass the many varieties of interpretations. Nevertheless, there will be isolated in the discussion a few characteristics which are largely common to all of them.

While the aims of Shavian education would appear to have much in common with those of democratic education—which also essentially respect the intellectual and spiritual potential of human personality and which are concerned with the definition of the good society—Shaw's concept of the state as the dominant force in education would conflict with that of a free

society. The assumption of complete power over the schools
by a government intent on desirable ends requires critical
examination.

In a democracy it is wise to resist any rigid centralization of
control of education because a decentralized administration
is effective in guaranteeing freedom of thought and discussion,
and in protecting the schools against propaganda of any
groups—nationalistic, militaristic, ecclesiastic, economic, or
racial—temporarily in control of the government. If the schools
are subject to partisan control, there is no assurance that a fair
consideration of common problems will be presented to the
young as an important part of their education. Schools must
not become the agencies through which propaganda advocated by any section of society is spread. The method of control—always a crucial problem—should be in harmony with the
fundamental values and principles of the state and the entire
educational undertaking. Yet it must also be recognized that
freedom is not necessarily endangered by every government
regulation of business, of public welfare, or of education, for
it may well be saved by it. A society with the ethical and
libertarian resources that sustain freedom can venture to give
to the government the control of activities which were previously decentralized. Cooperative planning and control of education are not inconsistent with freedom, but delicate adjustments among the agencies of government, the profession of
teaching, and the people must be effected. The basic democratic principle established by Locke and Jefferson that government should be regarded as the servant, not the master, of
the community is significant in the control and administration
of public education. The function of education in a democracy
has been considered so important that it has been put generally under a separate authority. If a government were to

override such an authority in an attempt to impose its own educational aims and political purposes, it would meet with strong resistance from many areas, since governmental power is frequently checked by basic legal and institutional arrangements and by moral and political traditions.

A fair interpretation of Shaw's scheme for the relation of the state to education is that it is a justification, not of democracy, but of benevolent dictatorship. The difficulty, however, is that no one would ever know how long such a state would remain benevolent. What is more pertinent is that, even assuming perpetual benevolence, such a society could threaten individual freedom in many ways. In Shaw's state, educational institutions would promote a special brand of culture and morality (derived from socialism and Creative Evolution) which could lead, in view of the rigid centralization of authority, to a conformity contrary to individual freedom. Even Shaw's highly educated leaders could misinterpret or prostitute their mission—a point he conceded. If it is also true that such a situation could develop in a democratic society, it should be recognized that in Shaw's socialist state, with its highly centralized control of education, such a possibility could occur more easily. Those in power at the moment could impose upon all individuals formulas of conduct and thought. Indoctrination and propaganda could replace an honest presentation of all possible intellectual alternatives or solutions to problems. These are possibilities. The fact that Shaw's leaders, considering themselves the pioneers of a new society concerned with the general welfare, might act with the purest of motives and in the name of evolutionary progress would not affect the consequences. Remember that in Shaw's scheme the state would be compelled "to enslave everyone ruthlessly in order to secure for everyone the utmost possible freedom." Democratic education stresses the importance of keeping intelligence free for the continuous, cooperative remaking of beliefs; authoritarian education, the too frequent result of concentrated control, tends to subordinate intellectual freedom to the immediate needs of the state. The elimination of such a possible consequence demands the rejection of an all-powerful state, and the general acceptance in theory and practice of a government with limits on the power and jurisdiction over the educational facilities.

A totalitarian atmosphere could easily permeate the Shavian school. Shaw's basic distrust of democratic processes attenuates considerably his premise that "socialism is merely individualism rationalized, organized, clothed in its right mind." He never solved the problem of how people are to live simultaneously in liberty and under extensive regulation. Since his socialist state cannot function without a creed and a set of commandments, it will not refrain "from proselytizing its children accordingly and persecuting heresy." In *The Intelligent Woman* Shaw is forthright in stating that "if teachers are caught inculcating that attitude [contrary to what the state dictates] they will be sacked." While he champions "an abandonment of punishment and its cruelties together with a sufficient school inculcation of social responsibility," he at the same time wants those who are not civilized members contributing to the community to be "painlessly extinguished." If Shaw meant that a program of instruction in the schools must be grounded in a principle of pedagogical authority sanctioned by the people and consistent with the principles of freedom and of democratic processes, he vitiates such a concept with emphasis on the severest kind of state discipline. In his attempt to establish coherence and unity in life and education, he unfortunately put his faith in this sort of totalitarian duress. It is quite reasonable to assume that in Shaw's state the processes employed by any existing government would be similarly inculcated in the schools.

Shaw's program of education in controversy could easily be nullified by his statist ideology. Although he argued that learning cannot take place unless the opinions and convictions of students are jolted, and that intellectual heresy must be privileged in the cause of evolutionary progress, he failed to consider sufficiently that his powerful educational authority might easily narrow the limits of toleration, dogmatize rigid concepts to be taught in the schools, and suppress the "teacher of new truths." In *Back to Methuselah*, it will be recalled, Zoo, in describing her education to the Elderly Gentleman, says that the "tertiaries," the leaders of the advanced society of the future, "encouraged me to rebel . . . and they refuse all other power; and the consequence is that there are no limits to their power except the limits they set themselves." Though apparently approving, in this dramatic context, of self-imposed restrictions of power on the part of his rulers, Shaw assumes that such statist benevolence will always result under the aegis of wise leaders. While he is well aware that power can easily corrupt, Shaw admits in the *Political What's What* that he prefers to take a chance with profoundly educated leaders rather than trust to current democratic processes. In effect, if governments must determine "what and when to persecute and what and when to tolerate," it is reasonable to assume that a too powerful state can easily decide in favor of persecution rather than toleration.

It is also reasonable to assume that in Shaw's state, education could not influence the reformation of social policy or the redirection of social change—processes desirable in a free milieu. If the control of the schools and their content of instruction derive from a central agency, the whole process of education could merely be designed to strengthen the hold of a dominant group. One of the distinctive characteristics of democratic education is that it is not only an expression and a criticism of the society that sustains it, but also a challenge to all forms of absolutism. Education can and should do much to influence social, moral, and intellectual discovery by stimulating critical attitudes of thought in the young. Since he declares categorically in the Preface to *On the Rocks* that the "community must . . . have its mind made up for it by its official thinkers, as to what its children are to be taught and to believe and how they should be trained to behave," education in Shaw's state could readily become the handmaiden of an official ideology—the very thing he attacked in capitalistic democracy!

It has been noted that Shaw's treatment of the ends-means continuum is inadequate. The processes of authoritarianism or of totalitarianism—whatever good intentions are involved—cannot be employed to achieve the purposes of democracy. If it is assumed that ends and means are interdependent, it is reasonable to conclude that totalitarian means will ultimately defeat the most desirable ends. If a nation wants democracy in its schools, it must first practice it. The spirit that permeates, regardless of ultimate aims, is the spirit that will endure. Since the school is a means to certain ends, it is important that democratic means are employed to attain them. All institutions in a free society belong to the area of means, and are to be judged in terms of the way they work to free human potential. An important purpose in the projection of goals—social or educational—is the isolation of the appropriate means by which difficulties may be overcome. In Shaw's school the means could negate the very ideals he sought. While he propagandized eloquently against cruelty and autocracy in English schools, he failed to foresee that a similar state of affairs—if different in kind and degree—could be ruthlessly imposed on the young of the powerful state he endorsed.

One ought not to conclude that Shaw's concept of the state nullifies any value his corollary ideas may have for democratic education. Many of his suggestions can add potency to learning in a free society. Shaw's attack at the turn of the century on the dogma of a fixed and unvarying human nature—now amply sustained by the accumulated results of anthropological, sociological, and psychological investigation—may have given impetus to newer concepts of growth in education. Since human beings are precious experiments of the Life Force, they must be cultivated very carefully and expensively and freed of the incubus of superfluous economic cares which ultimately prevent intellectual and aesthetic realization. Economic security would not automatically produce ideal human beings; but without it a people could not long continue to be culturally and politically free. Mediocrity and degeneration result, Shaw charged, because society is so corrupted by mercenary ideals that it is not concerned with man as he could be. A well-integrated state geared to create a richer social and cultural environment will breed richer individuals, whose growth of spirit and mind constitutes the true criterion of moral and social progress. This becomes impossible, he claimed, since the social, moral, and economic conflicts obstruct at the start attempts to create "The Just Man Made Perfect." What is suggested here is that a state must try to resolve such conflicts within the democratic framework in order to facilitate the process of growth. Like the pragmatists in America, Shaw understood that growth is not an automatic process of unfolding from within, but that it can be brought about only as society and its schools explore exhaustively the resources and problems of the culture in which the child lives.

Despite totalitarian overtones, Shaw insisted on the need for democratizing the school and for reconciling education with liberty. Since children must be educated into "manhood and freedom," he demanded liberty for the child, the right to live in "a child world of which it can be a little citizen." Here again he agrees with the pragmatists who believe that the growth of the child is the supreme moral aim of education. The development of the young, however, must be viewed not only from their perspective, but also from the perspective of the values, problems, and the social world in which they are nurtured. Shaw was opposed to those traditionalists who wanted to curb child development by subordinating it to inherited and established institutional patterns. (There are reformers today who unwittingly curb growth by turning the school into an agency for imposition of their dogmatic programs for social reconstruction.) Beyond the required training, Shaw would place learning on the voluntary footing of sport, letting the child find out for himself (with the aid of guidance facilities) what he wants to do for higher cultivation. By this Shaw did not mean that the child in his teens is to be the sole architect of his own program of education, for he would have already been exposed to a system of technical or required training. Shaw's insistence that the school must understand the child's need for liberty and for humane incentives in learning foreshadowed concepts of modern progressive education.

Shaw repudiated traditional concepts that regard the individual as passive and learning as a "pouring in" process regardless of the interests of the student. Learning must be uncoerced and compatible with a sense of emotional and intel-

lectual liberty. Condemning what he called "the fundamental
vice of imposing as education a system of imprisonment and
breaking-in," Shaw emphasized the active, experiential, and
creative aspects of study. He would seem to be in agreement
with the philosophy of experimentalism, which holds that the
individual is a dynamic whole, that learning takes place when
the needs and interests of the student provide the driving
power, and that the essence of education is the reconstruction
of experience through the method of reflective, critical thought
which everyone, in varying degree, can be taught to acquire.

That profound experiences in art and intellectual controversy accelerate learning processes is a Shavian concept which
could be utilized to great advantage in a free state. His program of education in controversy which demands a fair hearing of all manner of doctrines—particularly unpopular ones—
is designed to teach people to acquire and use the skills and
habits involved in constructive thought. Such a program is
consistent with democratic education, which fails, in so far as
it denies opportunity for the presentation of any fact, idea,
proposal, criticism, or hypothesis. This denial predicates indoctrination rather than honest teaching. The primary intellectual necessity for modern living is an awareness of what
the biggest issues are and how they can be settled. If modern
teachers refuse to consider controversial issues in an effective
way, they are thereby leading either to uncritical acceptance
or to uncritical rejection of new proposals. One of the distinguishing characteristics of democratic learning is that it places
emphasis on the right of the young to know about controversial issues in contemporary life and that it makes the improvement of ways of living and of thinking a conscious principle.
For Shaw, training in the skills of controversy and thought
could help people to understand the teacher of new truths, the

genius who contributes to evolutionary progress. It is suggested that a cardinal function of education in controversy is to provide a framework and methodology for the cooperative deliberation and adjustment of conflicting ideas, interests, and purposes in a democratic society.

Few, if any, teachers would reject Shaw's ideas about aesthetic education. It will be recalled that for Shaw the cultivation of aesthetic tastes in the learner dominates the educative process, for art is "an instrument of culture, a method of schooling, a form of science, an indispensable adjunct of religion." Only the cultivation of the individual's sensitivity to art, he claimed, can eliminate mass ignorance and prejudice, and make possible a high degree of civilization.

Although educators since Plato have through the centuries appreciated the significance of the aesthetic side of human personality, a signal defect in much of modern education is the failure to communicate the truth that music, painting, sculpture, the dance, the drama, and others of the arts are authentic statements of experience which can broaden and deepen the perceptions and sympathies, and provide imaginative insight into the emotions, drives, and aspirations of one's fellowman. Properly cultivated, man's aesthetic nature can be a fertile source of growth, of creative imagination, of religious experience, of love and friendship, of humility and integrity. Art is a device for making sense of the chaos of experience, a method of self-discovery and self-expression, a means of stimulating thought. Unfortunately, such ends are frequently defeated because of what Shaw called the academic methodology, with its emphasis upon fact finding and logical investigations. That in the pursuit of art "it is feeling that sets a man thinking and not thought that sets him feeling" defines a process which could be of considerable value to teachers of the arts. Written during the nineties, these words testify to Shaw's early insight regarding the relation of the life of feeling to the life of intelligence. As an evolutionary thinker he was well aware that there are important elements in our culture that tend to oppose the two, and that the evolutionary explanation demonstrates that the world of man's feelings actually provides the source through which the life of the intellect develops. Over sixty years ago Shaw heralded a truth just beginning to be recognized—namely, that in order to cultivate the intelligence of the young it is not necessary to throttle emotion in the aesthetic approach to their experience. It would be well for teachers to understand that art has a perennial, broadly inclusive function in cultural evolution, and that it helps man to evolve new forms of thought, behavior, and expression. To a great extent in the near future education will depend on how systematically and directly aesthetic programs in the schools are reoriented to develop human personality.

Aware that the vulgarity of mass communications takes precedence over art in molding the mass mind, Shaw condemned their negative influences. Like many modern educators, he despaired half a century ago that bad schools, coupled with a superstructure of communications based on pecuniary profit, made it possible for only "the strongest and most independent and original minds to escape from the mass of false doctrine." Alert to the educational possibilities of film and play, he demanded that these be artistically produced, for "bad theaters are as mischievous as bad schools." That Shaw posed a problem basic to education would today be denied by few educators. Despite countless articles, books, teacher conventions and committees, the schools are not coming to grips with helping students properly evaluate the output of mass communications. Democratic education must seek to train people to understand the psychology of mass exploitation if free individuals are sought. But this may not be enough. If it is assumed that schools in a free society should initiate processes of moral and cultural rediscovery, then they can contribute much to eliminate such vulgarity and exploitation not merely by instruction of the student body, but also by appropriate propaganda in the larger social and commercial world.

Shaw advocated many other ideas which are consistent with the principles of education in a democracy. He urged an objective study of all-prevailing creeds in the schools in order to eliminate bigoted attitudes which might be nurtured by the church or the home. It is suggested here that schools can objectively teach religion without advocating any one religious belief, for a knowledge of creeds, other than one's own, is essential to a full understanding of democratic culture, literature, art, history, and current affairs. Associating secondary education with what he called self or adult development, Shaw propagandized early in the century for this now ever-expanding movement in modern schooling. In the field of higher learning, he recommended what is still only partly realized today, namely, state-supported community colleges all over the country, easily accessible to anyone. Although violent diatribes against teachers abound in Shaw's writings, he was an early champion of better teacher training. He admired and respected genuine teachers, and pleaded for their improved status in the community. In the area of vocational education, Shaw believed—what is also now largely accepted—a modern democratic state must find a "remunerative use for every citizen," for failure to provide a person with an occupational niche suited to his talents and capacities is to deprive him of one of the most important means of self-realization and of serving society. Like Dewey, Shaw wanted to eliminate the prejudice that distinguishes between clean and dirty work and between culture and labor, or between the so-called practical and the so-called impractical. He condemned mere concentration on vocational and utilitarian studies to the exclusion of the intellectual, aesthetic, and the cultural, since he believed that a human being is a dynamic complex of varied potentials, not an "efficient robot." His *Intelligent Woman* argued for a more democratic system grounded in the principle of the moral value of all socially useful work. On the subject of sex education, Shaw advocated adequate instruction early in life about marriage and child bearing. Such training for the young should contribute to a more healthy awareness of the beauty of sex and its concomitants; this is a principle of health education which must now be seriously considered. While there are authoritarian ideas in Shaw's program for the education of leaders, he does pose this vital problem for a democracy: that the success of a free state depends entirely upon the ability of the people to choose the right kind of representatives or leaders. One of the main functions of all learning should be to qualify the student, adequately oriented in community, national, and international problems, to choose from candidates for leadership those who will improve his country. In order "to qualify [the immature] for their part as responsible citizens of a free state," the schools, he insisted, must eliminate the gap between the world of books or culture and the experiences of life itself, for the young must emerge with a rational understanding of the problems of life, particularly social life. About all of these matters Shaw has written with penetration and wit, and has presented facets of these problems not usually found in books about education.

That Shaw's doctrine of Creative Evolution largely determines the meaning of life for him should now be clear. Concepts of unlimited growth are focal points in his thinking about education, and his goal, if there is one, is molding a being whose highest aspiration is to create something higher than himself, "a being that cannot be improved upon." Maintaining that man can be educated into cultivating the mystic will to grow, Shaw urged us to create schools whose prime purpose would be to communicate this passion for growth. Education, in Juan's words in *Man and Superman*, will thus discover "the means of fulfilling that will, and in action to do that will by the so-discovered means."

The educative process, for Shaw, predicates the creation of people dedicated to their own betterment and to that of civilization, present and future. The cultivated man is one who "believes that there is a purpose in the universe and identifies his own purpose with it," and who consequently will try to leave the world better than he found it. That there is no room for isolationism in any successful life, personal or otherwise, and that no man can live to himself alone expecting to benefit from social progress without contributing to it were fundamental convictions. Shaw viewed man not as a disinterested member of a predetermined social system, but rather as participant and contributor in community affairs, striving to improve ways of thinking and living, thereby defining the true meaning of existence. If the best society is one in which all cooperate for the common good, then teaching and learning must, Shaw was convinced, be invested with public service and need to inspire the young with social as well as evolutionary aims. If democracy means mass participation and self-government and depends on individuals who are free, rational, informed, responsible, and capable of unselfish devotion to the common welfare, then Shaw's ideas in this area, divested of totalitarian modes, can be implemented toward a more potent democracy which may thus be capable of meeting the powerful challenge of fascism and communism in the crucial years ahead.

Shaw's theory of Creative Evolution, stripped of its pretensions as a universal religion, can be of importance to educators in a free society. Among all the myriad forms of matter and of life on earth, man is unique. Embodying the highest form of organization of matter and energy that has ever appeared, man depends on learning and on the inheritance of knowledge for his survival and growth. Man is unique in that he has plans, purposes, and goals which require the need for criteria of choice. The need for ethical values is within man whose future may largely be determined by the choices he makes. If man is to build a civilization of surviving beauty and grandeur, he must be educated to make choices and to see that they are realized in free association with others. Man is also unique in that for the first time in the history of living things, he has increasing power to influence his own future evolution.

As an evolutionist, Shaw realized that the change from the purposeless adjustments of the living creature into the consciously purposeful activities of the human being was a momentous one, and that this evolutionary development marked the genesis of mind. This meant for Shaw that we live in a world which is constantly changing and developing in unpredictable ways, and consequently a world in which human effort, guided by thought, can shape the nature of eventual results. His ideas about growth of the individual predicate, not mind as an inborn essence that develops according to its own fixed laws, but mind as a potential essence that evolves through the life experiences of a particular culture. Mind grows, he believed, only as the character of the surroundings grows. The process of such mind-growth, he held, could be accelerated by educating the individual in a cultural, interde-

pendent society which is dynamically aware of the need to
stimulate the individual will to grow. But the difficulty was,
he argued, that good schools, genuine teachers, and a cultural
environment can be realized only "as part of a social synthesis
which involves the reconstruction of many other institutions
besides our schools." For a democracy the solution to such a
problem lies partly in the cooperative organization or reorganization of its institutions; the guidance of human and social
evolution can perhaps be effected most successfully within its
framework, which permits free exploration of what can liber-
ate mind-potential in human beings.

Such organization demands intelligent purpose and discrim-
inating choice. Man can choose to develop his highest capacities, or he can choose otherwise. If, as Shaw cautioned, evolution can go backward as well as forward, man must supply
the right direction for himself. This means that democracy and
its schools are confronted with the supremely crucial task of
determining what are the growth-ends to be sought and how
they are to be used. Such goals, if high individuality is valued,
must not emanate from authoritarian leaders or groups, but
rather from an uncoerced community of consent which primarily depends on personal responsibility. Such cooperative
formulations of values can never be realized unless the state
and its educational institutions are vitally concerned with
creating mature persons—Shaw's "passion beings"—capable of
understanding that intellect is a passion and capable of willing
growth. Shaw was perhaps correct in his contention that the
mystic will to grow—for the will is all-important—seems lacking in our society. Interpreted in terms of the democratic ideal,
Shaw's doctrine of Creative Evolution presents a profound
challenge to the philosophy of education.

Bibliography

SHAW'S WORKS

Note: Most of the volumes listed as originally published by Brentano's are now copyrighted and published by Dodd, Mead & Company.

DRAMATIC

Androcles and the Lion, Overruled, Pygmalion. New York: Dodd, Mead & Company, 1930.

The Apple Cart. New York: Brentano's, 1931.

Back to Methuselah: A Metabiological Pentateuch. Rev. ed. with a Postscript. London: Oxford University Press, 1947.

Buoyant Billions, Farfetched Fables, Shakes Versus Shav. New York: Dodd, Mead & Company, 1951.

The Doctor's Dilemma, Getting Married, and *The Shewing-Up of Blanco Posnet.* New York: Brentano's, 1931.

Geneva, Cymbeline Refinished, Good King Charles. New York: Dodd, Mead & Company, 1947.

Heartbreak House, Great Catherine, and *Playlets of the War.* New York: Brentano's, 1919.

John Bull's Other Island and *Major Barbara.* New York: Brentano's, 1926.

Man and Superman: A Comedy and a Philosophy. New York: Brentano's, 1914.

Misalliance, The Dark Lady of the Sonnets, and *Fanny's First Play: With a Treatise on Parents and Children.* New York: Brentano's, 1914.

Plays: Pleasant and Unpleasant. 2 vols. New York: Brentano's, 1905. Vol. I, *Widowers' Houses, The Philanderer, Mrs. Warren's Profession;* Vol. II, *Arms and the Man, Candida, The Man of Destiny, You Never Can Tell.*

Saint Joan. New York: Brentano's, 1924.

The Simpleton of the Unexpected Isles, The Six of Calais, The Millionairess. New York: Dodd, Mead & Company, 1936.

Three Plays for Puritans (The Devil's Disciple, Caesar and Cleopatra, Captain Brassbound's Conversion). New York: Brentano's, 1912.

Too True To Be Good, Village Wooing, and *On the Rocks.* New York: Dodd, Mead & Company, 1934.

NONDRAMATIC

The Adventures of the Black Girl in Her Search for God. New York: Dodd, Mead & Company, 1933.

The Art of Rehearsal. New York: S. French, 1928.

"Artstruck Englishman," *New Republic* 10 (February 17, 1917), 78–79.

"Art Workers and the State," *Atlantic* 180 (November, 1947), 123–24.

"An Aside," in Lillah McCarthy, *Myself and My Friends.* London: T. Butterworth, Ltd., 1933.

The Author's Apology from Mrs. Warren's Profession. New York: Brentano's, 1905.

Bernard Shaw and Mrs. Patrick Campbell: Their Correspondence, Alan Dent, editor. New York: Alfred A. Knopf, 1952.

Doctors' Delusions, Crude Criminology, Sham Education. London: Constable & Co., Ltd., 1950.

Dramatic Opinions and Essays, 2 vols. New York: Brentano's, 1907.

"Education and the Cinematograph," *The Bioscope* 401, XXIII (June 18, 1914).

Ellen Terry and Bernard Shaw: A Correspondence, Christopher St. John, editor. New York: G. B. Putnam's Sons, 1931.

An Essay on Going to Church. Boston: John W. Luce & Co., 1905.

Everybody's Political What's What? London: Constable & Co., Ltd., 1944.

(Editor) *Fabian Essays in Socialism.* London: George Allen & Unwin, Ltd., 1931.

Florence Farr, Bernard Shaw, W. B. Yeats: Letters, Clifford Bax, editor. New York: Dodd, Mead & Company, 1942.

"If I Were a Priest," *Atlantic* 185 (May, 1950), pp. 70–72.

"In Praise of Guy Fawkes," in *Where Stands Socialism Today?* London: Rich and Cowan, Ltd., 1933.

The Intelligent Woman's Guide to Socialism and Capitalism. New York: Brentano's, 1928.

Last Will and Testament. Flint, Michigan: Apple Tree Press, 1954.

"A Letter to John Barrymore," *Ladies Home Journal* 43 (February, 1926), 17.

"Limits to Education," *Survey* 48 (May 6, 1922), 219. (A digest of a lecture)

London Music in 1888–1889 As Heard by Corno di Bassetto. New York: Dodd, Mead & Company, 1937.

"Modern Religion," *The Christian Commonwealth,* Supplement No. 69, XXVII (April 3, 1912).

Music in London 1890–1894, 3 vols. London: Constable & Co., Ltd., 1932.

Our Theatres in the Nineties, 3 vols. London: Constable & Co., Ltd., 1932.

Peace Conference Hints. London: Constable & Co., Ltd., 1919.

Pen Portraits and Reviews. London: Constable & Co., Ltd., 1931.

The Perfect Wagnerite. New York: Brentano's, 1929.

Preface, Charles Dickens, *Great Expectations.* Edinburgh: R. & R. Clark, Ltd., 1937.

Preface, *Immaturity.* London: Constable & Co., Ltd., 1931.

Preface, *The Irrational Knot.* New York: Brentano's, 1931.

Preface, *Killing for Sport: Essays by Various Writers,* Henry S. Salt, editor. London: George Bell & Sons, Ltd., 1915.

Preface, Richard Albert Wilson, *The Miraculous Birth of Language.* New York: Philosophical Library, 1948.

Preface, *Three Plays by Brieux.* New York: Brentano's, 1913.

"Problem of a Common Language," *Atlantic* 186 (October, 1950), 61–62.

The Quintessence of Ibsenism: Now Completed to the Death of Ibsen. New York: Brentano's, 1913.

"A Relief from the Romantic Film," *The Illustrated London News* 171 (December 3, 1927), p. 1004.

"The Religion of the British Empire," *The Christian Commonwealth* (November 29, 1906).

"The Religion of the Pianoforte," *The Fortnightly Review* 61 (February, 1894), 255–66.

"Rules for Directors," *Theatre Arts* 33 (August, 1949), pp. 6–11.

The Sanity of Art. London: New Age Press, 1908.

Sixteen Self Sketches. New York: Dodd, Mead & Company, 1949.

The Socialism of Shaw, James Fuchs, editor. New York: The Vanguard Press, 1926.

"Some Impressions," in Sydney Olivier, *Letters and Selected Writings,* Margaret Olivier, editor. London: George Allen & Unwin, Ltd., 1948.

What I Really Wrote about the War. London: Constable & Co., Ltd., 1931.

William Morris As I Knew Him. New York: Dodd, Mead & Company, 1936.

ABOUT SHAW

Barzun, Jacques, "From Shaw to Rousseau," *The Energies of Art.* New York: Harper & Brothers, 1956.

Bentley, Eric, *Bernard Shaw: A Reconsideration.* Norfolk, Connecticut: New Directions, 1947.

Collis, J. S., *Shaw.* New York: Alfred A. Knopf, 1925.

Duffin, Henry C., *The Quintessence of Bernard Shaw.* London: George Allen & Unwin, Ltd., 1939.

Ervine, St. John, *Bernard Shaw: His Life, Work and Friends.* New York: William Morrow & Company, 1956.

Fuller, Edmund, *George Bernard Shaw: Critic of Western Morale.* New York: Charles Scribner's Sons, 1950.

Harris, Frank, *Bernard Shaw: An Unauthorized Biography Based on First Hand Information.* New York: Simon & Schuster, 1931.

Henderson, Archibald, *George Bernard Shaw: His Life and Works.* Cincinnati: Stewart & Kidd, 1911.

———— *Table-Talk of G.B.S.* New York: Harper & Brothers, 1925.

———— *Bernard Shaw: Playboy and Prophet.* D. Appleton & Company, 1932.

———— *George Bernard Shaw: Man of the Century.* Appleton-Century-Crofts, Inc., 1956.

Irvine, William, *The Universe of G.B.S.* New York: Whittlesey House, 1949.

Joad, C. E. M., *Shaw.* London: Victor Gollancz, Ltd., 1949.

Krutch, Joseph Wood, "An Open Letter to George Bernard Shaw," *The Saturday Review* XXXIX (July 21, 1956), 12–13.

Laski, Harold J., "Four Literary Portraits," *Living Age* 339 (November, 1930), 289–92.

Patch, Blanche, *Thirty Years with G.B.S.* London: Victor Gollancz, Ltd., 1951.

Pearson, Hesketh, *G.B.S.: A Full Length Portrait.* New York: Harper & Brothers, 1942.

———— *G.B.S.: A Postscript.* New York: Harper & Brothers, 1950.

Pettet, Edwin Burr, *Shavian Socialism and the Shavian Life Force.* New York University: an unpublished doctoral dissertation, 1951.

Rattray, R. F., *Bernard Shaw: A Chronicle.* New York: Roy Publishers, 1951.

Reynolds, A. L., "Bernard Shaw on Art in the Schools," *Journal of Education* 78 (December, 1913), 598–99.

Rook, Clarence, "George Bernard Shaw," The Chap-Book V, 12 (November, 1896), 539.

Saxe, Joseph, *Bernard Shaw's Phonetics.* London: George Allen & Unwin, Ltd., 1936.

Scott, Dixon, "The Innocence of Bernard Shaw," in *Men of Letters.* London: Hodder & Stroughton, 1917.

West, Alick, *George Bernard Shaw: A Good Man Fallen Among Fabians.* New York: International Publishers, 1950.

Winsten, S., editor, *G.B.S. 90.* New York: Dodd, Mead & Company, 1946.

MORE GENERAL WORKS

Allen, B. M., *Sir Robert Morant*. London: Macmillan & Company, Ltd., 1934.

Barnard, H. C., *A Short History of English Education from 1760–1944*. London: University of London Press, Ltd., 1947.

Bergson, Henri, *Creative Evolution*. New York: Henry Holt & Company, 1911.

Brogan, D. W., *The English People*. New York: Alfred A. Knopf, 1943.

Bury, J. B., *The Idea of Progress*. New York: The Macmillan Company, 1932.

Childs, John L., *Education and Morals*. New York: Appleton-Century-Crofts, 1950.

Clarke, Fred, *Education and Social Change*. London: Sheldon Press, 1940.

Cole, G. D. H., and Raymond Postgate, *The British Common People 1746–1938*. New York: Alfred A. Knopf, 1939.

Curtis, S. J., *History of Education in Great Britain*. London: University Tutorial Press, Ltd., 1953.

Dewey, John, *Democracy and Education*. New York: The Macmillan Company, 1916.

Einstein, Albert, *The World As I See It*. New York: Philosophical Library, 1949.

Ensor, R. C. K., *England 1870–1914*. Oxford: The Clarendon Press, 1936.

Gregg, Pauline, *A Social and Economic History of Britain 1760–1950*. London: George G. Harrap & Co., Ltd., 1952.

Hamilton, Henry, *England, A History of the Homeland*, Lancelot Hogben, editor. New York: W. W. Norton & Company, 1948.

Harris, Frank, *Oscar Wilde, His Life and Confessions*. Garden City, New York: Garden City Publishing Co., 1930.

Hearnshaw, F. J. C., editor, *Edwardian England 1901–1910*. London: Ernest Benn, Ltd., 1933.

Huxley, Julian, *Evolution: The Modern Synthesis*. New York: Harper & Brothers, 1942.

Lippincott, Benjamin Evans, *Victorian Critics of Democracy*. Minneapolis: The University of Minnesota Press, 1934.

Mead, George Herbert, *Movements of Thought in the Nineteenth Century*, edited by Merrit H. Moore. Chicago: University of Chicago Press, 1936.

Mill, John Stuart, *On Liberty*. London: George Routledge & Sons, Ltd., 1859.

Pease, Edward R., *The History of the Fabian Society*. London: A. C. Fifield, 1916.

Russell, Bertrand, *A History of Western Philosophy*. New York: Simon & Schuster, 1945.

Schilling, Bernard N., *Human Dignity and the Great Victorians*. New York: Columbia University Press, 1946.

Somervell, D. C., *English Thought in the Nineteenth Century*. London: Methuen & Co., Ltd., 1936.

Toynbee, Arnold J., *A Study of History*. (Abridgment of vols. I–VI by D. C. Somervell.) New York: Oxford University Press, 1947.

Trevelyan, G. M., *British History in the Nineteenth Century*. New York: Longmans, Green & Co., 1922.

———— *English Social History*. New York: Longmans, Green & Co., 1942.

Wingfield-Stratford, Esme, *The Victorian Sunset*. New York: Willam Morrow & Company, 1932.

Index